The Legal Framework and Social Consequences of Free Movement of Persons in the European Union

Studies in law

A series of publications issued
by the Centre of European Law,
King's College London

Volume 3

The aim of this series is to publish studies in the broad area of European Community Law and Comparative European Law. Each publication will provide an important and original contribution to the development of legal scholarship in its field and will be of interest to the legal practitioner, academic, government and Community official.

The titles published in this series are listed at the end of this volume.

CENTRE OF EUROPEAN LAW
KING'S COLLEGE LONDON

The Legal Framework and Social Consequences of Free Movement of Persons in the European Union

Edited by
Elspeth Guild

On behalf of the Immigration Law Practitioners' Association

KLUWER LAW INTERNATIONAL
THE HAGUE/BOSTON/LONDON

Published by Kluwer Law International
P.O. Box 85889
2508 CN The Hague, The Netherlands

Sold and distributed in North, Central and South by
Kluwer Law International
675 Massachusetts Avenue
Cambridge, MA 02139, USA

Sold and distributed in all other countries by
Kluwer Law International
P.O. Box 322
3300 AH Dordrecht, The Netherlands

A C.I.P. Catalogue record for this book is available from the Library of Congress

Printed on acid-free paper

Cover design: Alfred Birnie bNO

ISBN 90-411-1073-9

Kluwer Law International incorporates the publishing programmes of Graham & Trotman Ltd, Kluwer Law and Taxation Publishers and Martinus Nijhoff Publishers

Printed by Antony Rowe Limited

CONTENTS

Part I:

The European Community: Thirty Years of Free Movement of Persons

Introduction

Advocate General F G Jacobs

This book marks thirty years of progress in realising the free movement of persons in the European Union. The book has its origin in a conference held at King's College London; the conference was jointly organised by the Immigration Law Practitioners' Association and the Centre of European Law at King's, and was sponsored by the European Commission.

The book, like the conference, is in two parts.

The first part is entitled The European Community: Thirty Years of Free Movement of Persons; the second part is entitled Third Country Nationals in the European Union: Coming to Terms with Partial Rights. This division reflects the divide between nationals of Member States – now also, by virtue of the Maastricht Treaty, citizens of the European Union – and the 13 million third country nationals who are long-term residents in the territory of the Union but who are excluded from many of the benefits of citizens of the Union.

European Community law creates rights which are directly enforceable in the national courts, and which prevail over any conflicting national provisions. In the field of free movement, it creates rights in an area, that of immigration control, traditionally marked by the high degree of discretion reserved to the national authorities. It draws not only on the free movement provisions themselves, by also on the general principle prohibiting discrimination which requires Community nationals to be treated equally with nationals of the host State.

Discrimination between nationals of Member States is prohibited by Article 6 of the Treaty. Article 6 states:

> "Within the scope of application of this Treaty, and without prejudice to any special provisions contained therein, any discrimination on grounds of nationality shall be prohibited."

The right to equal treatment irrespective of nationality has been described as the most important right provided for by substantive Community law. Indeed it has even been suggested that the entire EC Treaty is simply the principle of equal treatment for nationals "writ large". Although that is obviously a great exaggeration, it is certainly no exaggeration to emphasise the over-arching significance of the principle.

The prohibition of discrimination on grounds of nationality is also of great symbolic importance, inasmuch as it demonstrates that the Community is not just a commercial arrangement between the governments of the Member States but is a common enterprise in which all the citizens of Europe are able to participate as individuals. The nationals of each Member State are entitled to live, work and do business in other Member States on the same terms as the local population. They must not simply be tolerated as aliens, but welcomed by the authorities of the host State as Community nationals who are entitled, within the scope of application of the Treaty, to all the privileges and advantages enjoyed by the nationals of the host State. No other aspect of Community law touches the individual more directly or does more to foster that sense of common identity and shared destiny without which the ever closer union among the peoples of Europe, proclaimed by the preamble to the Treaty, would be an empty slogan.

The general principle laid down in Article 6 is implemented in specific spheres of Community law by a number of Treaty provisions: for example Article 48 (free movement of workers), Article 52 (right of establishment), Article 59 (free movement of services) and legislation adopted under the Treaty, eg Regulation No 1612/68, which guarantees equality in relation to not only employment and tax, but also "social advantages", a term very widely interpreted by the European Court of Justice.

The scope of free movement and the application of the principle of non-discrimination on grounds of nationality have been progressively extended, by Treaty revision, by legislation and by the case-law of the Court of Justice. Landmarks were:

- the adoption in 1968 of the basic legislation implementing the Treaty provisions on the free movement of workers (Regulation 1612/68 and Directive 68/360);
- the signature in 1986 of the Single European Act providing for an area without internal frontiers in which the free movement of persons was to be ensured;
- the extension by legislation of 1990 of rights of free movement to the economically inactive, thus extending the scope of free movement to virtually all nationals of Member States;
- the Maastricht Treaty in introducing the notion of citizenship of the Union;
- and also, when it enters into force, the Amsterdam Treaty, in incorporating the Schengen Agreement within the framework of the First Pillar.

Just as the personal scope of the rights of free movement has been broadened, so too has the material scope of the prohibition of discrimination. Article 6 prohibits discrimination only "within the scope of application of this Treaty". But most matters, certainly in the economic and social field, now fall actually or potentially within the scope of the Treaty; and a case could be made for saying that virtually all activities of the State are subject to the prohibition of discrimination; in other words, that different treatment of the State's nationals and of nationals of other Member States is always unlawful unless it can be objectively justified.

Although the principle of non-discrimination on grounds of nationality was, in its historical context, essential, there may now be doubts about whether, in at least some contexts, it is sufficient. A more broadly based principle of equal treatment may be necessary for some purposes.

It may indeed be necessary nowadays to ask whether the Community has a blind spot. Is privileged treatment to be limited to Community nationals, and is that consistent with the principle of respect for the fundamental rights of everyone and of equality before the law?

In some respects the principle of equality already goes beyond Community nationals; and that trend may well continue.

There is increasing pressure for legislation to extend the rights of Community nationals to all those lawfully resident in the Union. The Commission has made a number of proposals, for example for free movement within the Community of third-country nationals.

In the commercial field, it may seem more difficult to extend the freedoms of the internal market to third-country nationals. Reciprocity may be necessary. But the increasing liberalization of world trade – particularly under the WTO Agreement – is bringing great changes. In some respects the Agreement has produced greater liberalization than exists in Community law.

But it is for some of the basic social, economic, civic and cultural rights of individuals that the link to nationality of the Member States may be beginning to seem a little dated. Citizenship of the Union, introduced by the Maastricht Treaty, is also linked to nationality of a Member State. Perhaps the general principle of equal treatment, rather than the notion of discrimination on grounds of nationality, will increasingly be seen, in many if not in all areas, to provide a better basis for the development of the law in the future.

This book is concerned not only with Treaty rights, with legislation, and with the legal mechanisms for giving effect to free movement; it is concerned also with the social consequences. These have perhaps received too little attention in the past, both from lawyers and from policy-makers. In bringing together the political, legal and social dimensions of the subject, the book provides a valuable basis for further reflection and for further action.

CHAPTER ONE

FAMILY LIFE IN COMMUNITY LAW: THE LIMITS OF FREEDOM AND DIGNITY

Nicholas Blake QC

The 5th recital of the Preamble to Council Regulation 1612/68 on freedom of movement for workers within the Community provides:

> "Whereas the right of freedom of movement, in order that it may be exercised, by objective standards in freedom and dignity, requires that equality of treatment shall be ensured in fact and law in respect to all matters relating to the actual pursuit of activities as employed persons and to eligibility for housing and also that obstacles to the mobility of workers shall be eliminated, in particular as regards the worker's right to be joined by his family and the conditions for the integration of that family into the host country;"

This was the golden age of implementing measures when it was recognised that Community law must provide for enforceable rights granted to workers and their families (irrespective of the nationality of the latter) as part of the programme for making the right of free movement granted by Article 48 directly effective. It is sufficient to summarise the substantive provisions of Title 3 of this Regulation:

- Under Article 10(1) there is a right to be joined by a spouse and "their descendants" who are either under 21 or remain dependents, or dependent relatives in the ascending line of the worker and his spouse;
- Article 10(2) imposes on Member States the duty to facilitate the admission of any other family member who is dependent or living under the roof of the worker in the country whence he or she comes;
- Article 11 grants the right of family members to work in the host state; and
- Article 12 grants the right of children of a person who "is or has been employed" in the territory of a member state to admission to that State's general educational, apprenticeship and vocational training institutions.

It is also to be noted that Article 7(2) of the Regulation affords to those who have found work (as opposed to mere work seekers)[1] the right to the same social advantages as those enjoyed by the own nationals of the host State.

There has been little advance since then in the Directives and Regulations themselves as to the scope of family rights of EC workers. Other Regulations[2] have provided for family admission of other economic activists, students the retired and the self sufficient but they are in general not more generous in scope than the provisions for workers, which will therefore remain the focus of this

---

1 *Lebon* [1987] ECR 2811

2 Directive 73/148 on establishment and services; the June Directives on residence: 90/364, 90/365, 93/96

chapter. Directive 1251/70 provides for a right to remain on retirement, disablement or death which also extends to non-Community national family members of the worker concerned. But the scope of the family rights has not been broadened. What has changed in the intervening thirty years has been the developing jurisprudence on this Regulation and the Treaty Articles prohibiting discrimination.

Family members who are themselves European Economic Area[3] nationals have an independent right of admission to the territory of other EEA states[4]. Unless they engage in criminal activities which make their deportation conducive to the public good[5] they are unlikely to be removed from the UK at least, whatever the status of the family relationship to the worker. But the limits to 'dignity and freedom' can be best examined with respect to non-Community nationals whose only relevant claim to remain is as a family member of EEA or EU nationals exercising Treaty rights. I will here examine six aspects of the case law.

THE ADJECTIVAL STATUS OF FAMILY MEMBERS

First, it is clear that the rights subsist while the principal is exercising Treaty rights in the Member State and the person remains a member of the family. They are not free-standing rights of entry given to people who happen to be family members; the family rights are adjectival on the exercise of Treaty rights by the principal. Thus in the case of C-267/83 *Diatta v Land Berlin*[6] the Court of Justice explained that whilst the spouses did not have to be cohabiting under one roof for the rights to exist, a spouse's right to remain terminates in the event of either divorce or permanent departure from the host State of the principal. It would appear that divorce means the decree absolute terminating the marriage, a decree nisi or a judicial separation does not terminate the existence of the marriage[7].

The exception to this principle appears to be the right of children to continue in general and vocational education even though the principal has left the territory. Article 12 of the Regulation refers to children of a person

3 The EEA is comprised of the Member States of the European Union and those of the European Free Trade Agreement with the exception of Switzerland. Identical rights accrue to nationals of all these states as regards free movement of persons and family reunion. They are therefore treated as one group although nationals of EFTA states are of course third country nationals (ie nationals of non-EU countries) for the purposes of Community law.

4 In the case of C-64/96 *Land Nordrhein – Westfalen v Kari Uecker* ECJ 5th June 1997 unreported Bulletin 16/97, the Norwegian applicant a spouse of a German national who had exercised no Treaty rights would appear to have done better in relying on her own rights as an EEA national rather than her rights as a spouse

5 *Castelli and Tristan Garcia v City of Westminster* (1996) 3 FCR 383; 28 HLR 616

6 [1985] ECR 567

7 C-370/90 *Surinder Singh* [1992] ECR I-4265

who *has been* employed in the host State. In the case of C-389/87 *Echternach v Minister van Onderwijs en Wetenschappen* [8] the Court concluded that the child's Community law right of residence to pursue education existed even though the father's residence had ceased when his international employment resulted in a transfer elsewhere. This was applied by the UK Immigration Appeal Tribunal in *Gal* [9] where a non-Community national mother and two small children had been abandoned by a French national principal who had returned to France. The children had rights to remain to receive their primary education although the mother had none.

A right to remain for education imports a right to a residence permit to remain for that activity: Community law will not permit a right to be rendered ineffective by a failure of the host State to grant the immigration permission necessary to enjoy the benefit provided[10].

In 1990 the Commission proposed to extend the rights to cover non-Community national spouses who were divorced or separated from the workers concerned and also widows and widowers. Widowers may be substantially covered by Directive 1251/70.

THE TREATY RIGHTS TO BE EXERCISED BY THE PRINCIPAL

The principal must be exercising a Treaty right of free movement and cross national boundaries within the EEA before the adjectival rights of the family members arise. The Court has stressed on numerous occasions that Community law does not arise in situations that are of wholly internal effect. In one of the most noted cases to this effect (C-36/82 *Morson and Jhanjan v Netherlands*[11]) the Court held that a Dutch worker cannot bring his family members into the Netherlands in reliance on Community law if no exercise of Treaty rights of free movement has been made. Many a fine argument seeking to transpose the requirements of "freedom and dignity" from their natural home in the Regulation to a generally applicable principle of either domestic law *simpliciter* or domestic law when confronted when any connecting factor linking it with Community law, has perished on the rocks of "wholly internal effect".[12]

Clearly, there were hopes that this jurisprudence would be re-examined in the light of Article 8A EC[13] inserted by the Maastricht Treaty which appears

---

8 [1989] ECR 723

9 (10620) unreported. Both sides appealed to the Court of Appeal that was minded to make a reference to the ECJ on whether the children had a right to their mother's residence in the UK. The case was settled.

10 C-237/91 *Kus* [1992] ECR I-6781

11 [1982] ECR 3723

12 See 175/78 *R v Saunders* [1974] ECR 1129; *R v Secretary of State for the Home Department ex p Launder* [1997] 1 WLR 839

13 "1. Every citizen of the Union shall have the right to move and reside freely withi the territory of the Member States, subject to the limitations and conditions laid down in this Treaty and by the measures adopted to give it effect."

to grant an immediately effective right of free movement and residence throughout the territory of the EU. It was thought that this would include one's own Member State. After all admission to one's own territory is an essential indicator of citizenship in international law: see the International Covenant on Civil and Political Rights Article 12.4 and the European Convention on Human Rights 4th Protocol Article 3(2)[14]. If one becomes a citizen of the EU by reason of one's citizenship of a Member State of the EU, then surely one's right of residence in the EU extends to the very territory that forms the basis of the citizenship? In the UK cases, the question has arisen in the peculiar context of dual Irish and British nationals[15] and in cases where EU nationals who have not exercised any economic rights in the host State and were dependent on public funds asserted a claim to remain indefinitely on the basis of Article 8A EC[16]. The status and meaning of Article 8A remains open to interpretation, but the UK courts at least have been very shy of making a reference to the European Court of Justice (ECJ). The reference in the well known case of *ex p Adams*[17] was withdrawn when the exclusion order was lifted, although the contrast between the judgments making and removing the reference demonstrates uncertainty in the minds of the UK judges.

In the case of *ex p Phull*,[18] the relevance of Article 8A EC to family members was directly raised. A British citizen who had not worked abroad was precluded from having his non-Community national wife from being allowed to remain with him under national law: she was an overstayer when the marriage took place. He argued that Article 8A EC meant that the situation was no longer of internal effect and the Regulation's Article 10 rights applied to him and his family by analogy. This was rejected, just as earlier had been the suggestion that deportation of the wife was an interference with the principal's Article 8A EC rights of residence and movement. No reference was made to the ECJ despite some dubious observations on the applicability and scope of Article 8A EC not supported by authority. In a sequence of social security cases, the British courts have concluded that Article 8A EC does not give residence rights after the expiry of a reasonable period to find work[19].

The recent judgment of the ECJ in *Uecker*[20] suggests that whilst Article 8A EC may have direct effect subject to the measures to give it effect, it does not apply in situations which are wholly internal and have no Community law link. "Any discrimination which nationals of a Member State may suffer under

---

14 The ECJ referred to this aspect of citizenship in its judgement in *Surinder Singh* (supra) and note the judgment in Case C-171/96 *Roque v Lieutenant Governor of Jersey* 16/7/98

15 *R v IAT ex p Aradi* [1987] ImmAR 359, *R v Secretary of State for the Home Department ex p Adams* All ER (EC) 177 DC, *R v Secretary of State for the Home Department ex p McQuillan* [1995] 4 All ER 400

16 *Ex p Vitale* [1996] All ER (EC) 461; *ex p Remelien* [1996] All ER (EC) 850 CA;

17 Supra

18 [1996] Imm AR 72

19 *Ex p Vitale* [1996] All ER (EC) 461

20 Supra

the law of that state fall within the scope of that law and must therefore be dealt with within the framework of the internal legal system of that state".

The conclusion for the time being is that Article 8A EC will not be of assistance to spouses and children of EC nationals who are not and have never exercised Treaty rights in another Member State.

REVERSE DISCRIMINATION, AND OBSTACLES TO TREATY RIGHTS

It is now clear that the Community link may be established if the principal has genuinely exercised Treaty rights elsewhere in the Community and returns to his/her own country exercising both national and Community law rights of entry[21]. An adjudicator[22] has concluded following the *Surinder Singh* judgment that the relevant date is the date of the British citizen's entry to the UK. If the citizen was then married to a third country national and had previously genuinely exercised Treaty rights in another Member State then the entry of the British citizen engages Community law. The third country spouse is entitled to a Community residence permit even if she has never lived with her husband in, say, Germany at all.

This means that in certain cases where the relationship has not led to a grant of leave in domestic law, the British citizen and the spouse are entitled to travel elsewhere to another Member State and genuinely exercise economic rights for perhaps six months, and then seek to return home under Community law.

The absurd consequence of the law as interpreted to date means that an Irish worker, living in the UK, married to an Asian woman has an indefeasible entitlement to residence with his spouse: whatever primary purpose doubts may have existed, whenever the marriage was contracted or whatever poor immigration history she may have had, and whatever the financial status of the family. The British citizen similarly married working alongside him has no such rights and is confined to the narrow and restrictive measures of national law unless or until he or she travels across a national boundary for six months or more, exercises Treaty rights abroad and seeks to re-enter under Community rather than national law.

Freedom and dignity get lost sight of in this scenario, even before we consider the poor record and inadequate measures for the receipt and speedy grant of visas to non-Community national family members that the duty to facilitate admission would appear to require.

Reverse discrimination has its limits. Thus in *Sahota v Secretary of State for the Home Department*[23] a non-Community national spouse of a British citizen who had exercised Treaty rights was held not to be entitled to indefinite leave to remain as being a period of stay equivalent to the residence rights of the British national under Article 4(4) Directive 68/360, because the unrestricted right of

---

21 *Surinder Singh* supra

22 *Lawler ECO Bangkok* (16th June 1996) THY/21290/96 Professor Counter

23 Times April 30 1997 (1998) 2 WLR 626

entry was inextricably bound up with national citizenship status and the provisions of the Regulation could not be applied in that context. Thus the earlier practice whereby indefinite leave was granted straight away to third country national spouses of British or Irish citizens resident in the UK with Community law rights, has given way to the issue of four year residence permits.

In *Sahota*, the Court did not consider an alternative submission that the third country spouse should be entitled to the "social advantage" of indefinite leave to remain after twelve months, rather than the four years envisaged in the Immigration Rules. The right to equal treatment as regards social advantages arises under Article 7 of Regulation 1612/68 once there has been an actual engagement in employment (as opposed to merely seeking it). In the case of *Reed v Netherlands*[24], therefore, a national provision allowing a residence permit for a co-habiting partner of a Dutch national had to be applied to a British national working in the Netherlands.

If the point falls for consideration again in the UK, the Courts would have to consider whether discrimination requires an exact comparison of like with like, or whether the third country national spouse would have to comply with other applicable national rules before the discrimination in the enjoyment of the advantage arises[24A]. Since the withdrawal of the primary purpose rule, "other national rules" is likely to mean maintenance and accommodation without recourse to public funds and actual cohabitation.

THE RESTRICTED NATURE OF THE FAMILY

If the purpose of Regulation 1612/68 is to remove obstacles to free movement with dignity that would exact the price of family separation for the exercise of Treaty rights then one might expect that a broad and generous interpretation has to be given to the term "family". But evidence of such an approach is currently missing.

It is clear from the *Reed* case that the term "spouse" used in Article 10 of the Regulation [25] does not include an unmarried partner living with a worker as if he or she were a spouse, but no consideration was given to whether such a partner could qualify as another kind of family member to whom the duty of facilitation of entry might apply. It is difficult to see why such people should not be so included.

Certainly the expression family life in Article 8 of the ECHR extends to *de facto* socially existing relationships and not merely relationships recognised by law[26]. Given the regard had to the standards of the ECHR in developing the

---

24 59/85 Netherlands v Reed [1986] ECR 1283

24A The CA have concluded that there is no discrimination contrary to Community Law in such circumstances, *Boukssid v Secretary of State for the Home Department* Times 6th March 1998

25 See supra; Art 10(2) requires Member States to facilitate the admission of "any member of the family not coming within the provisions of para 1 if dependent ..."

26 *Marcks v Belgium* [1979] 2 EHHR 330; *Hendricks* [1982] 5 EHHR 223; *Keegan v Ireland* [1994] Series A No 290; *Kroon v Netherlands* 19 EHHR 263

meaning of Community legislation there may be scope for argument as to non-Community national partner of a Community national. This argument would be strongest in circumstances where there are children or other cogent evidence of the enjoyment of family life together; such as the adoption of married names, joint tenancies, and ownership of property.

If this line of reasoning proves admissible one could work backwards down the line from extra marital children, extra marital partner, to same sex relationships that the Strasbourg Court has hitherto considered only relevant to private life, to conclude that Community law must advance with society and contemporary modes of living if it is to fulfill its objective of removing obstacles to free movement. A Dutch worker will be deterred from moving to the UK if he or she cannot bring his long term same sex non-Community national partner; equally a British national will be deterred from transferring his or her place of work back from the Netherlands to the UK if this means that separation because the British are not required to issue the partner the same residence permit as the Dutch have. There is a hint of a possible shift in the ECHR jurisprudence where it was decided in *XYZ v UK*[27] that a transsexual living with a partner who had children fathered by AID enjoyed family life although in domestic law they were regarded as merely a cohabiting lesbian couple. It remains to be seen how far the landmark decision of *P v S* and other non discrimination cases now pending [28] may affect the approach to free movement cases.

The principal of non discrimination in respect of social advantages assists to a certain extent: if the UK or the Netherlands have a concession for unmarried partners of their own nationals they cannot deny the same concession to other EU nationals. But discrimination has its limits when the state response is to level down to an equality of misery and remove the policy, or status or concession. Many Member States have no concessions for unmarried or same sex relationships, although the system of immigration control may not be so tight as it is in the UK. Other states do not consider themselves bound by the social policies of the most advances states to have to admit same sex partners who have been living together in those other states. Non-discrimination is important but relative. Dignity as a substantive requirement of Community law could be something more absolute. Ultimately, the scope of the Regulation may have to be broadened by new Community legislation.

DISPUTED RELATIONSHIPS

Community law does not permit intrusive inquiries to evaluate relationships. There is no primary purpose test, or similar approach to the reasons why children have been adopted. Spouses do not have to be living together as long

---

27 24 EHHR 143

28 In C-249/96 *Grant v SW Trains,* (1998) ICR 449, 17th February 1998, the Court considered that the prohibition on discrimination on the grounds of sex did not extend to same sex relationships. There was a similarly disappointing decision from the ECHR in the case of *Sheffield and Horsham v The UK* 30th July 1998.

as there is accommodate for them. Independent life styles and disruptions to the continuity of cohabitation are thus irrelevant to the term spouse within the Regulation[29]. *Prima facie* therefore, production of the passport and marriage certificate should suffice to obtain the residence permit.

The European Council has taken an initiative under the Third Pillar[30] that is presently being considered by the House of Lords European Sub Committee[31]. This would seek to exclude marriages of convenience from the ambit of Community law: such a marriage being defined as one which has as its sole purpose the obtaining of a residence permit. This measure is objectionable on a number of grounds, not least the constitutional capacity to promote the Third Pillar something that should below to the First. Further, the action suggests that the authorities could conduct lengthy interrogations, act on hearsay and rely on non-cohabitation, inconsistencies in account, and many other *indicia* of a primary purpose marriage that are irrelevant to a valid Community law marriage. It also reverses the burden of proof in that once grounds for suspicion arise, Article 3 of the Resolution precludes the grant of a residence permit until the state is satisfied that the disqualification does not exist. As is well known, the UK's EEA Order peremptorily precludes a marriage of convenience from the definition of marriage for the purposes of exercise of Community law rights, and even suggests that no right of appeal on that issue would necessarily arise. This is unacceptable meddling with the legal requirements of the Community.

This said, however, a purposive approach to the Regulation does not indicate that Community law would bestow on the parties to a self confessed sham marriage indefeasible rights of residence. There could be little objection in principle if the requisite Member State could establish that there was no other purpose to the marriage than immigration and its conclusion were subject to a pre-removal right of appeal (as the Draft Resolution would afford at Article 5)[32]. It is clear that a right of review or appeal is an integral aspect of Community law: *Heylens*[33] and *Radiom and Shingara*[34], and unilateral declaration of status by the immigration authorities subject only to judicial review of the rationality of their conclusions is an inadequate national remedy to ensure rights are respected[34A]. Existing UK High Court jurisprudence on this question fails to adhere to these standards[35].

---

29 267/83 *Diatta* [1985] ECR 567

30 Title VI Treaty on European Union: Provisions on Co-operation in the Fields of Justice and Home Affairs

31 Draft Council Resolution on Measures to be Adopted on the combatting of Marriages of Convenience 3rd October 1997

32 The ECJ in *Surinder Singh* (footnote 7 supra) excluded "fraudulent marriages" from the operation of the principle there established

33 222/86 *Heylens* [1987] ECR 4097

34 C-65/95 and C-111/95 [1997] 3 CMLR 703

34A Advocate General Colomer's opinion in *Radiom*

35 *Ex p Cheung* [1995] ImmAR 104 see comment in Macdonald and Blake Supplement (1997) para 8.60, but see the decision of the Court of Appeal in *Boukssid v SSHD* Times 6th March 1998

The problem of demonstrable abuse can most readily be addressed in applying the public policy proviso to Community law rights. Such an approach does no violence to the definition of marriage, will not confuse a marriage which has some element of nuptial relations as one of its purposes with a marriage of convenience. It will make it plain that there is both a right of appeal and that the burden of establishing the sham nature of the relationship rests on the party asserting the existence of the sham and not vice versa.

For a nation that has just emerged from the nightmare of twelve years of the operation of the primary purpose rule, British lawyers are well able to understand that the misery and humiliation of couples having to prove why they are attracted to each other and why they married, is incompatible with dignity and freedom.

Turning from marriages of convenience, certain states seem to surround the process of the grant of a residence permit or admission to the territory with bureaucratic formality. In the UK the EEA Order suggests that third country nationals seeking to enter as family members of an EEA national should be in possession of family permit or a pre-entry visa. There is no sound basis for this. Directive 68/360 Article 3(2) refers to "no entry visa or equivalent documents may be demanded save from members of the family who are not nationals of a Member State." Every facility shall be afforded to such persons to obtain the visa. Entry document and visa have a wide meaning and included the stamping of a leave to enter on a passport in *Pieck*[36]. There is no reason therefore why the entry visa cannot be obtained at the port of entry and provided the applicant is in possession of the documents required by Community law to prove the relationship, a refusal to issue a visa (in clear cases where the relationship is established) would be a refusal of every facility. The effective enjoyment of family life of EEA nationals cannot be subordinated to the requirements of strict immigration control sweeping Europe and the wider world. The bitter irony is that the era of a frontier free Europe supposedly heralded by the Single European Act, has in fact led to greater control and bureaucracy for many EU nationals and their families. This is deeply and justifiably resented. If the Council and the Commission are unable to agree on the self evident measures to improve matters, we must at least ensure that the Court does not permit states to renege on their obligations to facilitate entry and admission.

TERMINATION AND EXPULSION

It is a weakness of the Regulations and Directives that save in the cases of retirement and industrial accident, there is no apparent right to permanent residence in the territory of another Member State, merely a right to indefinite renewal of the permit whilst a status: be it employment, self employment or independent means is continued.

---

36 157/79 [1980] ECR 2171

Certainly there is little to suggest that the Treaty was designed to assist the Euro-scrounger or supposed benefits tourist to exist in some illusory state supported idyll innocent of economic activity and self maintenance[37]. Nevertheless there is all the difference between a Community national who never enters economic activity or achieves the status of a worker under the Regulation (as opposed to work seeker) and cannot show genuine efforts to do so and some one who has fallen out of employment after exercising Treaty rights. The Court of Appeal recognised that EU nationals do not become unlawfully present merely by falling out of work, and at least a decision to deport them is needed before that status arises [38]. Deportation decisions are not generally taken against EU nationals in these circumstances save where criminal activity has been engaged in, and any deportation order would be disproportionate insofar as it precludes valid subsequent entries to exercise Community rights.

Nevertheless, over the years, families do break up and separate. Marriages end in divorce, or the principal worker could die[38A]. It is harsh and inappropriate that past residence as a family member is disregarded or of little weight particularly where expulsion of a non-Community national spouse may lead to separation of parent and child in a manner inconsistent with Article 8 ECHR[39]. British practice does permit holders of 5 year residence permits to obtain permanent residence in the UK after four years, and I would certainly suggest that this is a policy that should be reflected in the Directives themselves insofar as the provisions of renewal of residence permits leave room for ambiguity. Free movement with dignity carries with it the expectation of security and indefinite residence without the need for periodic re-qualification.

Long and lawful residence should be its own reward, subject only to requirements of public policy based on criminal conduct of such enormity or such persistence that the continued presence of the person constitutes a threat to public order.

CONCLUSIONS

1998 marks thirty years of the implementation of free movement. I believe Regulation 1612/68 was a bold imaginative and helpful measure when promulgated. It identified standards of dignity which have not diminished with

---

37 C-292/89 *Antonissen* [1991] ECR I-745 applied by the British courts in *Vitale* see above

38 *Castelli and Garcia v London Borough of Westminster* [1996] 28 HLR 616; or an expulsion decision under the Immigration (EEA) Order 1994 Article, see *Chief Adjudication Office v Wolke* [1997] 1 WLR 1640

38A A widow or widower is generably better catered for under Article 3 of Registration 1251/70 than a former spouse who has been divorced

39 "Article 8.1. Everyone has the right to respect for his private and family life, his home and his correspondence." See also the case of *Gal* (supra footnote 9) where a reference would have been made if the case had not settled.

the years and which should not now be downgraded or made less generous: particularly with respect to the extended concept of dependency.

An Europe committed to the principle of non-discrimination should have no difficult in extending the family reunion measures of the Directive to all lawfully settled third country nationals resident within its territory, as well as enabling own nationals to take advantage of the family re-union measures. It seems absurd that the minimum measures to prevent obstacles to free movement thirty years ago seem extravagantly generous when compared with many national policies towards others settled within their territory who cannot pray in aid Community law. There is little to suggest that this call is likely to be heeded by the Council or the politicians and the opportunity for a principled re-statement of family unity for all in the Treaty of Amsterdam seems to have been lost.

But the Regulation needs to be extended in another way in broadening the definition of family beyond the heterosexual institution of marriage which millions of EU nationals now longer find is relevant to their emotional needs and the way of life they chose to express their personalities. The Court has shown courage and imagination in the case of *P v S*. It is to be hoped that that courage will be demonstrated when questions as to the contemporary meaning of family come before them. The evidence suggests that the Council tends to shrink away from measures to implement the respect and dignity that should be shown to all human beings, and finds excuses to delay bringing in the necessary measures to reflect contemporary aspects of the requirements of dignity. The jurist is guided by principle rather than political expediency, whilst that does not place him or her at the forefront of society imposing as settled laws the most advanced thoughts of social relations, it does mean that excessive delay in recognising the actual advances in social relations cannot be indefinitely tolerated. The principle of subsidiarity or the margin of appreciation, defers to how nations implement answers to moral, ethical and socially sensitive questions; it is not a licence to prevent them ever addressing them. It is to be hoped that with the incorporation of the European Convention on Human Rights in British domestic law and policies now reflecting residence rights for same sex relationships, that British lawyers, British Ministers and British judges will contribute to the advance of freedom and dignity.

Chapter Two

What is a Family or Family Life in the European Union?

Linda Hantrais

The concept of 'a family' can take on a wide range of meanings according to the contexts in which it is used (Hantrais and Letablier, 1996). Yet, underlying the 1968 Regulation (1612/68) on the freedom of movement for workers within the Community is the assumption that an agreed definition of the family existed among the six Member States (Belgium, France, Germany, Italy, Luxembourg, Netherlands) in the late 1960s and that such a definition could be operationalised across the European Economic Community.

The concept of the family unit used in European legislation would not, however, be readily recognised in most of the fifteen EU Member States today as a workable definition of a family for administrative purposes, and it would probably not be very meaningful as a description of the everyday living arrangements of families for many Europeans.

The preamble to the Regulation states 'that all obstacles to the mobility of workers shall be eliminated, in particular as regards the worker's right to be joined by his [sic] family and the conditions for the integration of that family into the host country'.

The Regulation goes on to describe what is meant by a worker's family:

1. The following shall, irrespective of their nationality, have the right to install themselves with a worker who is a national of one Member State and who is employed in the territory of another Member State:
   (a) his spouse and their descendants who are under the age of 21 or are dependants;
   (b) dependent relatives in the ascending line of the worker and his spouse.
2. Member States shall facilitate the admission of any member of the family not coming within the provisions of paragraph 1 if dependent on the worker referred to above or living under his roof in the country whence he comes[1].

The same Article in the Regulation affirms that workers and their families, including non-nationals of Member States, have the right to housing under arrangements considered normal for national workers, and that the migrant worker's children are entitled to education and other benefits on the same terms as the children of nationals. In other words, intra-European migrants are to be treated just like workers and their families in the host country, provided

1 Regulation 1612/68 of the Council of 15 October 1968 on freedom of movement for workers within the Community, *Official Journal* no. L 257, 19.10.1968, Title III Workers' families, Article 10

such treatment does not 'give rise to discrimination between national workers and workers from the other Member States'.

This chapter looks at the ways in which the concept of 'a' family is constructed by some of the main institutions concerned with the process of integrating migrants into the host community: statistical agencies, policy makers and public administration. The aim is to show not only that institutions produce statistical definitions and categories, but also that they provide legal and administrative frameworks, each with its own agenda and its own logic. The chapter argues that the cumulative effect of different national and institutional arrangements may be that intra-European family migration will not necessarily appear to be an attractive proposition for migrant workers depending on the working and living conditions in the countries involved, and that the willingness and ability of family members to adapt to, and be integrated into, a new national environment may also be influenced to a greater or lesser extent by these factors. The definition in the Regulation is shown to cover different socio-cultural realities; together, these differences may provide a more convincing explanation of why intra-European migration has remained at a relatively low level even though formal barriers have, in principle, been removed.

STATISTICAL DEFINITIONS OF FAMILIES IN EUROPE

Statistical definitions of a family unit are relevant to an analysis of intra-European family migration for two reasons. Firstly, the production of statistics is a response to the demand by policy makers for accurate data on population trends, which are required in order to predict future needs within society. Statistical conventions are, therefore, an integral part of the policy process, and, as such, reflect political thinking (Desrosières, 1996). Secondly, comparisons of statistical data which take account of national discrepancies are informative about family size and structure and the labour market status of family members among groups of potential migrant workers and in host populations and can, therefore, contribute to an understanding of the issues facing host communities.

The Statistical Office of the European Communities (Eurostat), the organisation charged with synchronising and harmonising the collection and monitoring of national statistical data at European level, has adopted the United Nations' definition of the family unit based on 'the conjugal family concept', and this is widely, though not universally, followed in censuses and surveys across the European Union.

The UN definition presents the family as a subcategory of a household. Accordingly, a family is said to be composed of couples who are or are not related as man and wife, or of singles and their biological or adoptive children, generally for so long as these children remain unmarried. It makes a distinction between couples living in consensual unions and those who are legally married:

> 131. For census purposes, the family should be defined in the narrow sense of a family nucleus, that is, the persons within a private or

institutional household who are related as husband and wife or as parent and never-married child by blood or adoption. Thus, a family nucleus comprises a married couple without children or a married couple with one or more never-married children of any age or one parent with one or more never-married children of any age.

132. The term 'married couple' in the above definition should include whenever possible couples who report that they are living in consensual unions, and where feasible, a separate count of consensual unions and of legally married couples should be given. A woman who is living in a household with her own never-married child(ren) should be regarded as being in the same family nucleus as the child(ren) even if she is never-married and even if she is living in the same household as her parents; the same applies in the case of a man who is living in a household with his own never-married child(ren). 'Children' include step-children as well as adopted children, but not foster children.[2]

Data collected in national censuses generally take private households rather than families as the main unit of measurement. This is the notion more often applied by statisticians and it might correspond more closely to that used in the 'freedom of movement' Regulation, given the emphasis it places on individuals 'living under the same roof', whether or not they are related.

According to the United Nations:

121. A private household is either:

(a) a one-person household, i.e. a person who lives alone in a separate housing unit or who occupies, as a lodger, a separate room (or rooms) of a housing unit and does not join with any of the other occupants of the housing unit to form part of a multi-person household as defined below;

or

(b) a multi-person household, i.e. a group of two or more persons who combine to occupy the whole or part of a housing unit and to provide themselves with food and possibly other essentials for living. The group may pool their income to a greater or lesser extent. The group may be composed of related persons only or of unrelated persons or of a combination of both, including boarders and excluding lodgers.[3]

---

2 United Nations' Statistical Commission/Economic Commission for Europe Conference of European Statisticians, 1987, p. 35

3 United Nations' Statistical Commission/Economic Commission for Europe Conference of European Statisticians, 1987, p. 33

Individual Member States do not, however, all adhere to the UN recommendations for defining families and households. Most EU Member States adopt the notion of the household as the housekeeping unit, based on the pooling of income, but Denmark, Finland, France and Sweden use the concept of household dwelling, which is determined by the main place of residence and, therefore, tends to underestimate the number of actual households. In Italy and Portugal, the household unit is restricted to members related by blood or marriage (Eurostat, 1995b). In addition, Germany counts twice individuals occupying more than one dwelling, thereby inflating the number of single-person households. Ireland and Greece count everyone present in a dwelling on the census date rather than all persons normally resident.

Different practices are also followed to identify the reference person (previously designated as the 'head of household'): the wife is, for example, taken as the reference person in Denmark for households with children, and in Finland this status is attributed to the person who contributes most to household income. The 1968 Regulation refers constantly to the worker and his spouse; households headed by a woman or female workers moving from one Member State to another, although recorded in the statistics, would not appear to be recognised by European law as a reference person.

The UN recommendation is not followed consistently in the identification of consensual unions in national censuses, although the European Community Household Panel study, which has been conducted in twelve of the EU Member States since 1994, does contain data on unmarried cohabiting couples. Statistics are also available on lone-parent families, but they are unreliable, because such families form a particularly unstable and heterogeneous category and because they are conceptualised differently from one society to another. Belgium, Germany and Greece, for example, include lone-parent families with cohabiting couples.

Despite the absence of an age limit in the UN recommendation, some countries do apply an age limit for children, which can create disparities in statistical measures. If information about the age of children is not provided, data on lone parenthood, for example, can be extremely misleading: technically, a widow aged 75 living with her unmarried 45 year-old son could appear in the statistics as a lone-parent family. Nor is it always possible to distinguish between lone parenthood resulting from unmarried, divorced or widowed motherhood, which may be significant if information is being sought about the relative importance of different categories of parents by policy makers concerned about the rights and duties of the absent partner.

Although the UN recommends that stepchildren should be included, statistical tools have proved inadequate for identifying multi-parental or reconstituted families, since most national censuses do not provide details about biological relationships (van Solinge and Wood, 1997). Yet, this could be a key variable in determining rights in cases of family migration or in deciding how to deal with the children of mixed, intra-European marriages following the separation of parents. Clearly, as far as statistical definitions are concerned, a family should not be considered as an immutable and monolithic concept (and even less so the European family), but rather as a generic term concealing a plurality of family forms, which are not always accurately and fully recorded by censuses and surveys.

Notwithstanding the imperfections of measuring tools, data for the 30-year period since the family was enshrined in Regulation 1612/68 suggest that significant changes have occurred in the size and shape of family units as measured by statisticians in the now fifteen Member States of the European Union, compared with the family forms recorded in the original six Member States of the European Economic Community who, together, drew up the Regulation. Average household size has been declining in all fifteen countries but remained largest at the beginning of the decade in Spain, Ireland, Portugal and Greece, which were not among the EEC founding members. By the mid-1990s, completed fertility rates by generation, which have also been falling rapidly, were highest in Ireland, Finland and Denmark. Life expectancy at birth has been growing and was greatest for women in France, Italy, Spain and Sweden (in all Member States, women lived longer than men). Sweden, followed by Greece and Italy, showed the largest proportion of men aged 65 and over, and Sweden and Germany recorded the largest proportions of older women (Eurostat, 1995a). These data are relevant for policy makers interested in the future funding of pensions and in issues concerning long-term care for dependants.

Indicators of what can be called family de-institutionalisation show that marriage rates have been falling over the past 30 years, with Denmark, Portugal and Greece displaying the highest levels; divorce rates have risen and had reached a particularly high level in the UK and Finland; rates of extramarital births have increased markedly in some countries, reaching especially high levels in Sweden and Denmark, which also displayed the highest rates for unmarried cohabitation, another trend which was on the increase. The proportion of lone-parent families with children aged under 15 has been growing steadily, particularly in Denmark and the UK (Eurostat, 1995a).

A broad-brush analysis like this gives an indication of what the family 'commitments' and 'needs' of migrants from different countries might be, but it should not be forgotten that these trends are based on national averages and that within-country differences may be greater than those between countries (East and West Germany, North and South of Italy), or that the majority of intra-European migration would seem to be accounted for by younger males of working age, who are single (Commission of the European Communities, 1993).

If governments are concerned to avoid importing potential social problems associated with the intra-European movement of de-institutionalised family units (unmarried cohabitees, divorcees, lone-parents and children born out of wedlock), the most problematic migrants might be those from the Nordic states and possibly the UK. But if governments are concerned about the influx of large numbers of dependants, the greater problem, according to the terms of the 1968 Regulation, might arise for migrants from countries where the wider kinship group is included in the definition of the family (Italy and Portugal) or for those where household size is largest (Spain and Ireland).

PUBLIC POLICY DEFINITIONS OF FAMILIES IN EUROPE

The review of the definitions of a family applied by statisticians indicated how statistical data feed into the policy process. Like statistical definitions, descriptions of a family and of family relationships in public policy reflect differences in national, philosophical and religious traditions and conventions, and in the conceptualisation of the legal obligations and responsibilities of family members towards one another (Dumon, 1994; Ditch *et al.*, 1996; Hantrais and Letablier, 1996; Millar and Warman, 1996). As both the commissioners and users of statistical data, policy makers require definitions of families and households which can be applied in the administration of public services, but they must also respond rapidly to shifts in socio-economic behaviour and to the demands of pressure groups, so their criteria have to be adapted to meet changing situations. Their response to change, with regard to the redefinition of concepts, is likely to be more rapid than that of statistical services, which are constrained by the need to produce coherent trend data over time and to conform to internationally agreed norms.

In the field of public policy, EU Member States have all developed their own concepts of the family unit as a target for social policy. They broadly agree, however, that social policy should be described as family policy when the family is the deliberate target of specific actions, and the measures initiated are designed to have an impact on family resources and, ultimately, on family structure. The operationalisation of the concept varies considerably, however, from one Member State to another, so that intra-European migrants may find that the rights, benefits and services available for families in another Member States are more or less generous than in the country of origin.

The minimalist view adopted in some countries (Ireland, Italy, the Netherlands and the UK) is that the state should provide no more than a safety net and that families might be expected to have primary responsibility for their own well-being. When external support is necessary, local communities are the first port of call, and collective provision of welfare may come into conflict with informal support structures. At the other extreme, intervention may be legitimised by the national constitution, which places an obligation on the state to support and promote family welfare, or the policy-making process may be used to encourage a particular family type, such as large families in Greece.

By introducing or modifying legislation that affects the status of individuals within families and households, the state has been encroaching further into family life. Such intervention may be justified on the grounds that rules are needed for governing families in a context of rapidly changing social values (Commaille, 1994), to protect members of the family unit from one another (child abuse), or to oblige them to fulfil their obligations to one another (absent father) (Lefaucheur and Martin, 1995), while also carrying out what may be a constitutional duty towards the family as a basic social institution. Policy makers may be faced with the choice of trying to preserve the legitimate family at all costs, or they may be seeking to protect the interests of individual family members, and in particular those of children, irrespective of whether they are born in or out of wedlock (Meulders-Klein, 1993). In the first case, a much more focused definition of the family unit is needed.

Another dimension of the family policy debate, which is relevant to family migration concerns the extent to which the state should intervene to support different family forms: consensual unions, lone-parent families and reconstituted families. While Germany and Ireland are bound by their constitutions to support the legitimate married couple and Greece focuses on the legitimate child, other countries have progressively been removing the distinction between married and unmarried couples and their children (Ditch *et al.*, 1996). The Nordic states have tended to lead the way in legitimising non-traditional family forms (by formally recognising non-institutional relationships), but the Netherlands were among the first Member States to introduce legislation allowing homosexual couples to enter into a cohabitation contract covering property rights and taxation, and the UK and France have more readily recognised consensual unions and extramarital births than Ireland, Italy, Luxembourg and the Southern European countries (Hantrais and Letablier, 1996). A bill brought before the French National Assembly in July 1997 proposed the introduction of a 'contrat d'union sociale', extending to all couples living together, irrespective of sex and family relationships (Théry, 1997).

Lone parenthood and reconstituted families have increasingly become topics of interest for public policy, and, as mentioned above, they are gradually being recorded in the statistics. From being considered as a deviant family form in some countries (Nordic states and France), lone parenthood has been accepted as innovative and deserving of public support (Lefaucheur and Martin, 1993), while recognising that needs will be different according to whether lone parenthood involves a single, divorced, separated or widowed parent. In many countries (including the UK), attention is being focused on measures to enable lone parents to become financially independent of the state (Bradshaw *et al.*, 1996).

Lone parenthood is often a transitional phase into a new relationship, generally involving a reconstituted family. The available literature (for example Meulders-Klein and Théry, 1993) has provided some valuable insights into the complexity and diversity of reconstituted families and has shown the extent to which they have been recognised and accepted as legitimate concerns for public policy in different national contexts. The literature has also shown that the status of step-parents is particularly problematic in terms of rights and duties. The concept of 'living under the same roof' in the 1968 Regulation would not, for example, be recognised in some countries (Belgium and Germany) as a sufficient reason to justify the legal responsibility of a step-parent towards the children of a new partner, unless they are married, whereas in the Netherlands the social responsibility of the step-parent takes precedence over that of the biological parent (Sosson, 1993). Legal obligations towards step-children can involve a moral contract to ensure the upkeep of children, as in Germany, and joint parental authority may be awarded even if the parents are not cohabiting, as in Finland and Sweden (Meulders-Klein and Théry, 1993; Ditch *et al.*, 1996).

The liability to maintain relatives is another area where laws and practices differ. The state generally assumes much greater responsibility for individual family members (older people, children of lone parents) in the Nordic states, while, at the other end of the spectrum, the wider kinship network is expected to provide support for family members in the Mediterranean countries (Millar and Warman, 1996). Analysis of caring arrangements for children and older people also brings out differences between Member States in the conceptualisation of the relationship between the public and private spheres. In Belgium, France and the Nordic states, public provision of childcare is relatively generous, whereas it is relatively poor in Ireland, Luxembourg, the Netherlands, Portugal and the UK. The de-institutionalisation of care for disabled and older people in many Member States, largely for economic reasons, is found to place a heavy burden on family carers. In the Nordic countries, the state has continued to recognise its responsibility for making formal provision for caring, whereas in Germany and the Netherlands there has been a shift towards care insurance as a means of relieving the pressure on both state and families. In the Mediterranean countries, caring has largely remained a duty expected of family members, with relatively little state support (Lesemann and Martin, 1993; Attias-Donfut, 1995). It seems probable that the average Swedish worker with a large number of dependants might be reluctant to uproot family members if relocating to Portugal for example, if his (or her) primary concern is the provision of caring arrangements, whereas an extended family from a Mediterranean Member State might be tempted to take advantage of the facilities provided by the state in the North of Europe.

ADMINISTRATIVE DEFINITIONS OF FAMILIES IN EUROPE

Even if some measure of agreement can be reached at international level about policy objectives, implementation may take very different forms from one national context to another. The definition of the benefit family varies not only between countries but also within countries from one category of benefit to another (Roll, 1991). Eligibility for social protection may differ depending on how relationships within the family are conceptualised, particularly in the case of non-contributory benefits. From a situation, in the immediate postwar period, when the dominant model of the family among policy makers seemed to be the married couple living together with their children, where the husband was the sole or main breadwinner and women did not gain access to benefits in their own right (Lewis, 1992), progressively women have become entitled to receive benefits as individuals, and in some cases (Austria, France and Germany), these rights are extended to recognise unpaid work, for example in pensions, or to cover cohabiting partners (Netherlands).

A good example of the intra-European variations in the definition of the 'benefit family' is the case of family allowances, as they are referred to in Austria and the Latin countries, or child benefit, as it is called in other EU Member States and the UK. Given that the age limit of 21 is used to define dependent children in the 1968 Regulation, it is interesting to look at age as a defining characteristic for entitlements to family benefits. Portugal imposes the lowest age limit: benefits are paid for all children up to the age of 15 and extended up to 25 for those who continue in education. In Germany, Ireland, Sweden and the UK, children up to 16 are considered as dependants for the purpose of child benefit, and up to 17 in Finland and the Netherlands. The age limit is extended to the age of 27 in Germany, Luxembourg and Austria for children undergoing vocational training and further education. Unemployed or jobseeking children are covered in Austria and Germany up to the age of 21 years, as in the 1968 Regulation (MISSOC, 1996).

Children are also treated differently from one country to another depending on their rank: in the UK, child benefit rates are higher for the first child, whereas in France no family allowance is paid for the first child; larger families receive higher benefits in Austria, France, Greece, Ireland, Luxembourg and Sweden.

Different rates of child benefit for larger families may be justified and accepted on economic grounds, although pronatalist reasons are also evoked for supporting larger families as a means of stemming population decline (Lenoir, 1995). Belgium, France, Francoist Spain and Sweden have all followed pronatalist policies at particular times in their history, whereas pronatalism has been rejected in Germany, post-Franco Spain and the UK. France in particular provides more generous benefits for larger families. It is perhaps worth noting that Regulation 1408/71 on the application of social security schemes to employed persons and their families moving within the Community, in a section which covers family benefits and family allowances for employed and unemployed persons, identified France as a special case in the rules governing the distribution of benefits and drew attention to the fact that some benefits are aimed at encouraging an increase in population:

> Whereas, moreover, the current restrictions on the granting of family benefits should be abolished, and whereas in order to ensure payment of benefits for the maintenance of the members of separated families, leaving aside those benefits aimed largely at encouraging an increase in population, it would be preferable to lay down rules common to all the Member States and efforts should continue to this end; but in the face of great variations between national legislations a solution should be adopted to take this situation into account: payment of family benefits of the country of employment in respect of five countries, and payment of family allowances of the country of residence of members of the family where the country of employment is France....[4]

Taxation is another area where the family unit is conceptualised differently. For the purposes of levying taxes, the unit of assessment may be the family (France and Luxembourg, *quotient familial*), thereby focusing on the unit of consumption. It may be the legally constituted married couple (Belgium and Germany, *Ehengattensplitting*), or the individual (Austria, Denmark, Finland, Greece, Italy, Netherlands, Sweden and the UK), although in this case most countries offer tax relief for spouses. In another grouping are Member States

---

4 Regulation 1408/71 of the Council of 14 June 1971 on the application of social security schemes to employed persons and their families moving within the Community, *Official Journal* No. L 149, 05/07/1971, chapter 7, Article 73

where earnings are aggregated (Ireland, Portugal and Spain). The individualisation of tax liability, which has become increasingly widespread in the 1990s, emphasises the productive capacity of family members and can be considered as an inducement for women to enter paid employment and gain control over their earnings. Children may or may not be recognised for tax relief. At one extreme, no tax relief is granted (Denmark, Ireland, the Netherlands and the UK) while, at the other, in addition to tax relief, allowances are granted towards childcare costs (Belgium, France, Greece and Spain).

Non-marital cohabitation has been recognised to different extents in tax law. The shift towards individual taxation has removed or reduced disparities between married and unmarried partners, but in most cases unmarried cohabiting couples continue to pay more than married couples, particularly when only one partner is an earner (Ditch *et al.*, 1996).

In sum, a few countries (France, Germany and Luxembourg) conceptualise the family as an administrative unit to be supported and promoted by the state. Another group of countries pledge themselves, in their constitutions, to support the family unit (Greece, Italy, Portugal and Spain), but they may not possess the means required to do so (Mediterranean countries), while others may be reluctant to intervene formally in the private lives of families (Ireland, Netherlands and UK). The Nordic states tend to focus on individual needs, rather than on the family as a unit.

Paradoxically, as social protection budgets have become stretched, emphasis has been placed increasingly in many countries on the responsibilities of biological parents to maintain their children and on family means, irrespective of formal relationships, as a substitute for public provision, thereby reinforcing the importance of the family as an administrative unit, and in principle reducing the potential burden on the state to support family members. If migrant workers are aware of these different approaches, the degree of state support for family life could be a factor they would want to take into account in deciding whether to relocate their family or whether to 'commute' to another EU Member State. The living conditions available for family members might even be a reason for not seeking employment elsewhere in the European Union.

SOCIO-CULTURAL FACTORS AS AN INCENTIVE OR DETERRENT TO INTERNATIONAL LABOUR MOBILITY

It is by no means obvious to what extent public policy provision influences or determines behaviour. Some economists and demographers argue that decisions about marriage, family size, family dissolution, female economic activity and the timing of life events are the outcome of rational choices based on careful consideration of financial and personal interests (Becker, 1981), and that policies affecting the level of income and benefits can, therefore, influence decisions (Ekert-Jaffé, 1986). If this were the case, it would be possible to calculate the probability of worker mobility based on the relative financial gains and disadvantages of moving a family from one EU Member State to another. The rational choice approach has been criticised for not taking account of cultural factors (Allsopp, 1995), and some studies suggest that differences in socio-economic behaviour cannot be explained by rational choice alone (Grignon and Fagnani, 1996).

In the absence of an econometric model which incorporates a range of socio-economic factors, it may be hypothesised that the Nordic states, France or Luxembourg would be popular destinations for family units from Southern Europe or Ireland among migrant workers with a number of dependent children and ageing relatives, or that most French families in the medium-income range, with three children would not find it a very attractive proposition to uproot and establish a young family in a country where public provision for children was less extensive than in France.

Socio-cultural and economic factors may go some way towards explaining why intra-European migration of workers and their families has remained at a relatively low level. By the early 1990s, it was estimated that about 1.4% of the Union's citizens lived in another Member State. The proportion of nationals of working age from another Member State did not exceed 3%, except in Belgium (5%), and the figure was well below 1% in Portugal and Spain. The UK and Germany together received about 70% of intra-European migrants (Commission of the European Communities, 1993).

There is little evidence to suggest that the removal of formal barriers to freedom of movement through binding European legislation has provoked large-scale family migration between Member States. European regulations have not been sufficient to remove the informal socio-cultural and language barriers (Hantrais, 1995), which most probably continue to act as a much greater obstacle to freedom of movement. The lack of a shared understanding of what a family is could well be one of the many components shaping cultural identity which contribute to an explanation of the limited take-up of opportunities for intra-European mobility.

REFERENCES

Allsopp, V. (1995) *Understanding Economics* (London and New York: Routledge).

Attias-Donfut, C. (ed.) (1995) *Les solidarités entre générations: vieillesse, familles, État* (Paris: Nathan).

Becker, G.S. (1981) *A Treatise on the Family* (Cambridge MA and London: Harvard University Press).

Bradshaw, J., Kennedy, S., Kilkey, M., Hutton, S., Corden, A., Eardley, T., Holmes, H. and Neale, J. (1996) *Policy and the Employment of Lone Parents in 20 Countries* (York: European Observatory on National Family Policies, Social Policy Research Unit).

Commission of the European Communities (1993) *Employment in Europe* (Luxembourg: Office for Official Publications of the European Communities).

Commaille, J. (1994) *L'esprit sociologique des lois* (Paris: PUF).

Desrosières, A. (1996) 'Statistical Traditions: An Obstacle to International Comparisons', in L. Hantrais and S. Mangen (eds), *Cross-National Research Methods in the Social Sciences* (London: Pinter), pp. 17–27.

Ditch, J., Barnes, H. and Bradshaw, J. (1996) *A Synthesis of National Family Policies 1995* (York: European Observatory on National Family Policies, Social Policy Research Unit).

Dumon, W. (ed.) (1994) *Changing Family Policies in the Member States of the European Union* (Brussels: Commission of the European Communities, DG V and European Observatory on National Family Policies).

Ekert-Jaffé, O. (1986) 'Effets et limites des aides financières aux familles: une expérience et un modèle', *Population*, vol. 41 no. 2, pp. 327–48.

Eurostat (1995a) *Demographic Statistics 1995* (Luxembourg: Office for Official Publications of the European Communities).

Eurostat (1995b) 'Households and Families in the European Economic Area', *Statistics in Focus. Population and Social Conditions*, no. 5.

Grignon, M. and Fagnani, J. (1996) 'Transferts de revenus et activité féminine en Europe', *L'espace géographique*, no. 2, pp. 129–44.

Hantrais, L. (1995) *Social Policy in the European Union* (Houndmills and London: Macmillan).

Hantrais, L. and Letablier, M-T. (1996) *Families and Family Policies in Europe* (London/New York: Longman).

Lefaucheur, N. and Martin, C. (1993) 'Lone Parent Families in France: Situation and Research', in J. Hudson and B. Galaway (eds), *Single Parent Families: Perspectives on Research and Policy* (Toronto: Thompson Educational Publishing), pp. 31–50.

Lefaucheur, N. and Martin, C. (1995) 'Qui doit nourrir l'enfant dont le père est "absent"? Rapport de recherche sur les fondements des politiques familiales européennes (Angletere – France – Italie – Portugal)', (Rennes: École nationale de la santé publique).

Lenoir, R. (1995) 'L'invention de la démographie et la formation de l'État', *Actes de la recherche en sciences sociales*, no. 108, pp. 37–61.

Lesemann, F. and Martin, C. (eds) (1993) *Les personnes âgées: dépendance, soins et solidarités familiales. Comparaisons internationales* (Paris: La Documentation Française).

Lewis, J. (1992) 'Gender and the Development of Welfare Regimes', *Journal of European Social Policy*, vol. 2 no. 3, 159–73.

Meulders-Klein, M-T. (1993) 'The Status of the Father in European Legislation', in Danish Ministry of Social Affairs (ed.), *Report from the Conference: Fathers in Families of Tomorrow, June 17–18, 1993* (Copenhagen: Danish Ministry of Social Affairs), pp. 107–50.

Meulders-Klein, M-T. and Théry, I. (eds) (1993) *Les recompositions familiales aujourd'hui* (Paris: Nathan).

Millar, J. and Warman, A. (1996) *Family Obligations in Europe: The Family, the State and Social Policy* (York: Joseph Rowntree Foundation).

MISSOC (1996) *Social Protection in the Member States of the Community: Situation on July 1st 1995 and Evolution* (Brussels: Commission of the European Communities).

Roll, J. (1991) *What is a Family? Benefit Models and Social Realities* (London: Family Policy Studies Centre).

Sosson, J. (1993) 'Le statut juridique des familles recomposées en Europe: quelques aspects de droit comparé', in M-T. Meulders-Klein and I. Théry (eds), *Les recompositions familiales aujourd'hui* (Paris: Nathan), pp. 299–312.

Théry, I. (1997) 'Le contrat d'union sociale en question', *Esprit*, no. 236, pp. 159–211.

United Nations Statistical Commission/Economic Commission for Europe Conference of European Statisticians (1987) 'Recommendations for the 1990 Censuses of Population and Housing in the ECE Region: Regional Variant of the World Recommendations for the 1990 Round of Population and Housing Censuses', *Statistical Standards and Studies*, no. 40 (New York: United Nations).

van Solinge, H. and Wood, J. (1997) *Sample Surveys as a Potential Data Source for the Study of Non-Standard Household Forms and New Living Arrangements: An Inventory of Data Sources on European Households and Families* (The Hague: NIDI).

Chapter Three

Equal Treatment, Social Advantages and Obstacles: In Search of Coherence in Freedom and Dignity

Robin Allen QC

Professor Bhikhu Parekh has recently discussed[1] the role and meaning of 'national identity' in multi-cultural Britain. He pointed out that individuals and societies usually go about their daily business in a largely unselfconscious manner, well adjusted to their environment. This continues until they are confronted with unusual problems and painful choices, their environment undergoes rapid and extensive changes or their way of life faces unexpected internal or external threats. When this happens the result is disorientation and confusion and conduct which lacks coherence and a sense of direction. In those circumstances he said that consciously or unconsciously their members are then led to ask deeper questions about who they are, what they stand for, what values are central to their way of life, how they are changing, and if and how they should reconstitute themselves.

This chapter tries to pose and answer some of the questions that have come with the confusion about another kind of national identity – that of citizen of Europe. Its aim is to look at the one of the main foundations of European citizenship – free movement – and to seek a coherent understanding of a particular but very important part of that right: the principle of non-discrimination in relation to social advantages. As a result it is hoped that some contribution will be made to a deepening of the understanding of what is this new citizenship.

The multi-cultural nature of Britain with which Professor Parekh was most concerned was the result of immigration from the Commonwealth in the early post war years. There is however an important link between the impact that this immigration had on national identity and the impact of membership of the European Communities. Indeed arguably the two greatest changes to British national identity post war have been caused by Commonwealth immigration and membership of the European Communities.

Free movement into the UK for Commonwealth citizens was brought to an end progressively but most notably and finally with the Immigration Act 1971[2]. However the abolition of such rights was accompanied with increasing and deepening rights of equal treatment for persons of different racial groups[3]

---

1 In the Kapilla lecture given at the Bar Council on the 19th November 1997 entitled "National Identity in a Multi-cultural Society".

2 See eg the discussion in Chapter 1 of McDonald's Immigration Law and Practice 4th Edition by McDonald and Blake, Butterworth 1995.

3 In this paper 'racial groups' is used as defined by section 3 of the Race Relations Act 1976: persons defined by reference to colour, race, nationality or ethnic or national origins.

already lawfully in this country through the Race Relations Acts of 1965, 1968 and 1976. The political prejudice against further immigration was in large part the progenitor of laws against discrimination for the benefit of those who had already immigrated.

By one of those ironies of history, while Britain was closing doors, the Member States of the European Communities, were developing the rights of free movement throughout the Community for migrant workers. Indeed, perhaps the most important secondary legislation to give effect to this, was adopted in the same year as the Commonwealth Immigrants Act 1968, when the Council of the European Communities adopted Regulation 1612/68 on freedom of movement for workers within the Community.

So, it is a double irony, that just one year after the UK closed the doors finally to Commonwealth immigrants it opened them to Europeans exercising free movement rights, because the European Communities Act of 1972, had the effect of introducing not only a directly effective Article 48 but also this Regulation. It is to the effect on citizenship of this Regulation that this chapter is principally directed. The purpose of this Regulation is set out in its extensive recitals. In essence it was designed to make directly enforceable provision[4] in the field of free movement of workers to give a greater substance to the free movement rights in Articles 48 and 49 of what was then the Treaty of Rome[5].

One key recital to the Regulation sets the tone of what follows

> "Whereas the right of freedom of movement, in order that it may be exercised, by objective standards, *in freedom and dignity*, requires that *equality of treatment* shall be ensured in fact and in law in respect of all matters relating to the actual pursuit of activities as employed persons and to eligibility for housing, and also that *obstacles* to the mobility of workers shall be eliminated, in particular as regards the worker's right to be joined by his family and the conditions for the integration of that family into the host country;"(emphasis provided)

Freedom and dignity are at the heart of these free movement rights. They are plainly an essential ingredient of substantive equal treatment. Above all else as concepts they resonate with the political concept of citizenship. But it may be asked: *What do they really mean in law?*

Article 7(2) of the Regulation makes it clear that a person exercising free movement rights is to enjoy the same *social advantages* as national workers, and later Articles extend these provisions to worker's families, covering education and housing[6]. So the rhetorical question may be developed: *How precisely, is equal treatment in matters of social advantages to be enjoyed in freedom and dignity?*

---

4 It is significant that the Council chose to legislate by means of a Regulation so that the legislation has general application and is binding in its entirety and directly applicable in all Member States: see EC Article 189.

5 For an extensive consideration of this subject see 'Free Movement of Persons in the European Community' by Martin and Guild, published in 1996 by Butterworths.

6 See Title III, Articles 10 to 12, of Regulation 1612/68.

The answers to these questions have a double significance for those in the UK: firstly they go to explain the content of free movement rights and secondly they illuminate and may well affect the content of overlapping municipal rights. Moreover both of these consequences relate to our deepening and changing concepts of citizenship.

The legal concept of citizenship of the Union is expressly stated in Part II of the EC Treaty [7], but there is a problem. While the content and meaning of that citizenship is still under debate[8] even by those with knowledge of the Single European Act, the Treaty of European Union and the Amsterdam Treaty, the outline of the concept remains, at worst unknown, or a best, a shadow or cipher for most citizens of the UK.

While ordinary citizens in the UK know that they can vote in European elections, they probably do not read that part of the form on which they register for the electoral roll which tells them that non-UK nationals can also register. If they have travelled abroad recently, they may know that their passport has changed colour, but they will probably neither know why, nor know the relationship between their passport and those of other Member States. Indeed even the existence of the right of free movement is probably understood by only a few.

Moreover any deeper understanding of this new citizenship has been seen by some governments as politically dangerous and even nationally divisive. Thus the European Commission declined to extend to the UK in its full form the recent advertising campaign entitled "Citizens First" for reasons of pre-election sensitivity[9]. The response to the campaign among those countries that did receive it is also instructive: out of 969,000 enquiries Italy produced 78,000, France 60,000 and Spain 53,000; the Germans and Dutch produced proportionately many fewer. On average 12 households in every 100,000 responded, approximately 0.1%.

These figures do not suggest that the rights that go to make up European citizenship are so well understood in Germany and Holland that they have little need to make enquiries or that the higher figures in Italy, France and Spain reflect a deeper wish to understand what it is to be a citizen of the European Union. Rather these figures probably reflect social facts about the degree to which workers from these countries wish to move within the Union for purposes connected with work.

Yet knowledge of this newly described if yet largely undefined concept will increase among those living and working among the Member States. What seems likely is that as workers move around the Union they will find increasingly that they both need and expect equal treatment. As they pursue and discuss those needs with their friends, and colleagues, as well as with officials, they will self-educate and provoke discussion about what it means

7 See Articles 8, and 8A - E.

8 See eg O'Leary, S and Tiilikainen, A (eds), Citizenship and Nationality Status in the New Europe (1998), London, Institute of Public Policy Research and Sweet and Maxwell.

9 See the Guardian 26 November 1997.

to have the rights of free movement. This reflects the author's own small experience.

I am not personally a stranger to free movement in practice. I have worked briefly abroad. My family have a young French woman living with us as a lodger in our home. Last year she worked as a French assistant at my children's school. This year she has obtained a part-time post in a translation company. At the same time she has been accepted on a course at University for an MA in translation. Like most students she needed a loan to pay for her tuition fees. I gave her some help in filling in a form for a student loan. The intriguing fact is that both she and I were surprised to discover that under a Government backed scheme the loan would be interest free while she was at college. Our surprise, despite our different nationalities, was the same: why were taxes I paid to the United Kingdom Government used to underwrite a loan to a French student and worker. Of course the answer lies in Article 48 EC and Regulation 1612/68; in the principle of equal treatment of European citizens in matters of social advantage. However my instant reaction of surprise shared by my French friend, reflects the extent to which our European citizenship has not yet permeated our deeper sense of personal identities. This is an issue of awareness – of self-identity as fellow 'Europeans'.

In the late 1970s and early 1980s and indeed even now, many officials and even managers went on race awareness training, discussing their deepest attitudes to persons not sharing the same colour, racial, ethnic or national origin as themselves. Such race awareness training was controversial and accused sometimes of being divisive. However it did serve to make attitudes in the UK to Commonwealth immigrants more reflective and less instinctive. Such training continues today for instance in a more sophisticated form it plays a part in judicial training. However there is little equivalent in the field of European identity. What is needed is training to help us to be more reflective and less instinctive in our attitudes to Europe and to celebrate our common citizenship. It is one thing to confer rights and another to ensure that they are understood.

When I reflected further I located this loan to my French friend in its deeper legal context – I quickly realised that though I may help pay for this loan this obligation is not without benefit to me. For, of course, the equal treatment that the UK affords her merely reflects the extent to which I can expect equal treatment for myself and my family in other Member States.

So what is behind the key concept of social advantage and obstacle? In *Peter De Vos v. Stadt Bielefeld*[10] the European Court held:

> "'Social advantages' should be understood to mean all those advantages which, whether or not linked to a contract of employment, are generally granted to national workers because of their objective status as workers or by virtue of the mere fact of their residence on the national territory and the extension of which to workers who are nationals of other Member States therefore seems likely to facility their mobility within the Community"[11].

10 Case C-315/95 [1996] ECR I-1417.

11 See also Case 207/78 Ministère Public v. Even [1979] ECR 2019, para 22 and Case C-310/91 Schmidt v. Belgian State [1993] ECR I-3011 para 18).

There is a limit to the scope of the concept when it meets social security benefits. Indeed the same report of the Commission's Citizen's First campaign states that most enquiries it received related to social security. There is no doubt that Regulation 1408/71, on the application of social security systems to persons moving within the Community, serves to enhance the free movement of workers for the very diversity of social security systems is itself an obstacle to free movement. It is important to note the line between the concept of social security benefit and social advantage as it appears in Article 7(2) of Regulation 1612/68. Dimitrios Gouloussis has rightly stated in a recent paper[12] that either the two concepts are alternatives or they must overlap, yet the case law of the Court shows that even where the Court has adopted an alternative approach it has not refused to consider a problem from both sides. Thus he concludes on this point[13]:

> "...the Court of Justice even where it adopted the alternative relationship hypothesis, did not refuse to examine the matter from the angle of Regulation 1612/68 whenever it ruled out the application of Regulation 1408/71[14]. There have even been cases[15] in which the Court, without examining the problem in the light of 1408/71, though referred by the national court, approached it directly and exclusively from the angle of Regulation 1612/68...In conclusion, the case law of the Court of Justice, though fluid at a theoretical level, has effectively contributed to providing efficient protection of the rights of migrant workers."

However a wider discussion of equal treatment in matters of social security benefits is outside the scope of this chapter. A Celex search shows that there are no less than 47 occasions in which the concept of "social advantage" in the context of Regulation 1612/68 is discussed either in the rulings of the Court or the Opinions of the Advocates General. So there is more than enough to discuss in relation to equal treatment in matters of social advantage.

Turning to the extent and content of the concept of social advantage in Article 7(2) of 1612/68 and the related but more specific rights detailed in that Regulation, these might be analysed by reference to each of the 47 reports. However it is quite sufficient to note how the case law has demonstrated that "social advantage" can cover most of the more serious rights of passage. A consideration of 9 of the leading cases show that the ECJ has recognised a very wide range of social advantages, covering situations extending from before the cradle and up to the grave, and discovering important areas beyond Shakespeare's seven ages of man[16]!

---

12 See 'Equal Treatment and the Relationship Between Regulations 1612/68 and 1408/71' in the report of the conference 'Social Security in Europe - Equality between Nationals and Non-Nationals' at Oporto November 1994 (1995) Brussels, European Commission.

13 See paragraph 7 on page 81 op. cit.

14 Case 249/83 Hoeckx [1985] ECR 973 and Case 122/84 Scrivner [1985] ECR 1027.

15 Case 261/83 Castelli [1984] ECR 3199.

16 'As you Like It' Act 2 Scene 7.

The first case concerns attempts by a Member State to promote its domestic birthrate and to discourage abortions. In *Francesco and Letizia Reina v. Landes Kreditbank Baden-Württemberg*[17] the Court was concerned with a dispute on a matter of administrative law concerning the grant of a childbirth loan. The Reinas were a married couple of Italian nationality living in Germany. The Landes Kreditbank had the right to grant loans upon application on the basis of guidelines laid down by the State of Baden-Württemberg. The childbirth loans were free of interest and reasonably large. The municipal German condition for the grant of the loans was that they would be provided to married couples only where a least one of the spouses was a German national and the family income did not exceed a specific amount. The evidence before the Court was that this system of childbirth loans was introduced with a view to stimulating the birth rate of the German population and in order to reduce the number of voluntary abortions.

It was argued on behalf of the Landes Kreditbank that the loan was not in the scope of Article 7(2) and did not concern a social advantage. They said that there was an absence of any connection between the grant of the loan and the recipient's status as a worker and on that ground the refusal to grant the loan to the Reinas was in no way a hindrance to the mobility of workers within the Community.

The Court rejected this approach. It held that[18]:

> "Childbirth loans such as those referred to by the National Court satisfy in principle the criteria enabling them to be classified as social advantages to be granted to workers of all the Member States without any discrimination whatever on grounds of nationality. In particular in view of their aim which is to alleviate in the case of families with a low income the financial burden resulting from the birth of a child."

The Court made short shrift of the Landes Kreditbank's argument that the purpose of the loan took them outside the scope of Article 7(2) on the ground that they were principally for reasons of demographic policy in order to counteract the decline in the birthrate of the German population. The Court said[19]:

> "It should be stated that since the Community has no powers in the field of demographic policy as such the Member States are permitted in principle to pursue the achievement of the objectives of such a policy even by means of social measures. This does not mean however that the Community exceeds the limits of its jurisdiction solely because the exercise of its jurisdiction affects measures adopted in pursuance of that policy. Accordingly childbirth loans of that kind may not be considered as falling outside the scope of the rules of Community law relating to the free movement of persons and more specifically of Article 7(2) of Regulation 1612/68 solely because they are granted for reasons of demographic policy."

---

17 Case 65/81 [1982] 33.
18 Para. 13.
19 Para. 15.

The Landes Kreditbank tried a second tack alleging that the loans in question were voluntary benefits arguing further that it was proper to take into account the fact that many foreign workers returned to their countries of origin before the expiry of the period prescribed for the repayment of the loan so that the repayment is put in jeopardy. This point of view was equally rejected by the Court[20].

While *Reina* was concerned principally with stimulating the birth rate the case of *Commission v. Luxembourg*[21] was concerned with the very act of conception itself. In that case the Commission brought an action for a declaration that Luxembourg by imposing residence requirements for the grant of childbirth and maternity allowances had failed to fulfil its obligations under Article 7(2). The allowance was split into three instalments. The first instalment was paid when the mother to be had undergone the last of medical examinations required by the legislation. It was a condition for such payment that the mother to be should have been 'officially resident' in Luxembourg for a year preceding the birth of the child and to have attended all the medical examinations required by the legislation. In effect in most cases the child had to be conceived in Luxembourg. The Court held that this was a case of covert discrimination applying *Sotgiu v. Deutshe Bundespost*[22]. Perhaps unsurprisingly it held[23] :

> "that ... the requirement that the mother reside on the territory of the Grand Duchy for a year preceding the birth of the child [was discriminatory] because such a requirement is in practice more easily met by Luxembourg nationals than by nationals of other Member States."

Birth is soon followed by the need to educate the offspring. As every parent knows educational needs can go on for a long time; some children never seem to leave home! However in *Carmina Di Leo v. Land Berlin*[24] the problem started when Ms Di Leo wanted to leave her parent's home and to return to her native country to complete her education. Ms Di Leo was the daughter of an Italian migrant worker who had been employed for 25 years in Germany. Ms Di Leo had received her primary and secondary education in Germany and indeed that was her principal place of residence. When she came to pursue further education she applied to study medicine at the University of Sienna in her native country of Italy. She applied to the State authorities in Berlin for a grant under the Federal Law on Grants for Training and Further Education. However this law was construed initially within Germany as being limited so that grants could only be applied to Germans, stateless persons and foreigners entitled to asylum.

---

20 Para.16.

21 Case C-111/91 [1993] ECR I-817.

22 Case 152/73 [1974] ECR 153 at para 11.

23 Case C-111/91 [1993] ECR I-817 at para. 10.

24 Case C-308/89 [1990] I-4185.

The Court reminded itself that Article 12 of Regulation 1612/68 referred not only to the rules relating to admission to education but also to general measures intended to facilitate educational assistance[25]. The Court held[26]:

> "... the status of a child of a Community worker implies in particular that it is recognised in Community law that such children must be eligible for study assistance from the State in order to make it possible for them to achieve integration in the society of the host country. This means ... that the children of Community workers are entitled to assistance granted to cover the costs of student education and maintenance under the same conditions as apply to the host country's own nationals."

Ms Di Leo's case raised the question whether her claim for a grant to study in a country other than the host State of Germany was nevertheless within Article 12 of Regulation 1612/68. It was argued for Germany simply that studies in another country, Italy, would not secure integration within the host State. This argument was roundly dismissed by the Court[27]:

> "It must also be borne in mind that the aim of Regulation 1612/68 namely freedom of movement for workers, requires, for such freedom to be guaranteed in compliance with the principles of liberty and dignity, the best possible conditions for the integration for the Community worker's family in the society of the host country. If such integration is to be successful, it is essential for the child of a Community worker who resides with his family in the host Member State to have the opportunity to choose a course under the same conditions as a child of a national of that State."

Advocate General Darmon in his opinion[28] set the position out in a way which underlines the comprehensive nature of the coherence sought by Community institutions:

> "Let us consider for a moment a situation in which two young people, one of whom is a national of the Member State and the other a child of a migrant worker from another Member State, have both completed their primary and second education and wish to enrol for the same course at University, but only the first of whom obtains a grant from the State in order to pursue that course abroad, whilst the other is refused such a grant. Is the latter, at the time when the refusal is notified to him, likely to experience a feeling of being integrated in the host Member State, a feeling that he was being treated by that State no differently from his fellow student whose nationality is different from his own? Integration is not simply a legal concept; it is also something which must be lived and experienced personally and intimately. Hence it is far from certain, in my view, that the actual possibility of a migrant worker's child pursuing a course outside the host State, which may depend on the award of a grant by the State, is *a priori* unconnected with the aim of integration in that State."

---

25 See joint Cases 389 and 390/87 Echternach and Moritz v. Minister for Education and Science [1989] ECR 723.

26 Case C-308/89 [1990] I-4185 at para 9.

27 Para. 13.

28 Para. 14.

The next big step in life is the move from education to work. In *Commission v. Belgium*[29] the Court was concerned with the social advantages in that transition. The action was brought by the Commission against the State of Belgium which had introduced tideover allowances which were paid in relation to young people seeking their first employment. The relevant provision provided that to[30]:

> "... qualif[y] for the unemployment allowances, young workers seeking their first employment must in all cases have completed full-time secondary education or technical or vocational training at a centre run, recognised or subsidised by the State or have obtained in respect of such studies a diploma or school leaving certificate from the Central Board."

The Commission argued before the Court that this provision was indirectly discriminatory against nationals of other Member States. The Court accepted that argument reminding itself of the test it had set in *O'Flynn v. The Adjudication Officer*[31] that:

> "A provision of national law must be regarded as indirectly discriminatory if it is intrinsically liable to affect migrant workers more than national workers and if there is a consequent risk that it will place the former at a particular disadvantage. It is not necessary to find that the provision in question does in practice affect a substantially higher proportion of migrant worker. It is sufficient that it is liable to have such an effect."

Turning to the provision in question the Court ruled[32]:

> "Conditions applied without distinction which may be more easily fulfilled by national workers than migrant workers are prohibited. ..."

The Court ruled[33] that the condition at issue was:

> "akin to a condition of prior decision .... which will be fulfilled more easily by the children of Belgian nationals than by those of nationals of another Member State ..."

A modern Shakespeare's list of the ages of man or woman would almost certainly include an eighth – *unmarried cohabitation*. The Court had to consider this new 'age' in *State of the Netherlands v. Anne Florence Reed*[34]. Ms Reed wished to obtain a residence permit from the Dutch Secretary of State. In some circumstances the Netherlands permitted an alien with a stable relationship with a Dutch national or an alien who is the holder of a permanent

---

29 Case C-278/94 [1996] I-4307.

30 Para. 4.

31 Case C-237/94 [1996] ECR I-2617 paras. 20 and 21, discussed below.

32 Para 28.

33 Para 29.

34 Case 59/85 [1986] ECR 1305.

residence permit to obtain a residence permit in consequence of that relationship. The rules were that the persons concerned must live together as one household or have lived together as such before arriving in the Netherlands, be unmarried and possess adequate means of support for the foreign partner and appropriate accommodation. Ms Reed's first argument was that she was to be treated as married to her co-habitee Mr W. This was rejected by the Court. However it was further submitted that there was discrimination in the key provision between the treatment afforded to Dutch citizens whose co-habitees claimed residence permits and those from other Member States. The Court ruled that[35]:

> "Article 7 of the Treaty in conjunction with Article 48 of the Treaty and Article 7(2) of Regulation 1612/68 must be interpreted as meaning that a Member State which permits the unmarried companions of its nationals who are not themselves nationals of that Member State to reside in its territory cannot refuse to grant the same advantage to migrant workers who are nationals of other Member States."

And so to marriage! There are numerous cases which are concerned with discrimination in respect of social advantages which accrue to spouses. One such case is *Sandro and Marisa Forcheri v. The Belgian State*[36]. Mr Forcheri, an Italian, was an official of the European Commission, working in Brussels. His wife wished to pursue further education. Mrs Forcheri enrolled in the Institut Supérieur de Sciences Humaines Appliquées. This Institute like others in Belgium required a "fee for foreign students" from all students not of Belgian nationality and whose parents were not resident in Belgium. A partial exemption stated that the fee was not required in particular from students whose parents were foreign officials working in Belgium with the European Communities or whose spouse was resident in Belgium, was in paid employment there and paid taxes to the Belgian Treasury. The point which gave rise to the action was that Mr Forcheri, as an official of the European Communities, was not required to pay taxes to the Belgian Treasury.

One can see again in this case, as in *Carmina Di Leo*, some of the considerations which went through the author's mind when helping his French friend apply for a grant in this country! The State of Belgium plainly considered the payment of taxes to fund such grants as these to be of considerable importance and the Municipal Court referred a question as to whether this was relevant or not. The Court ruled[37]:

> "It must be observed that the legal position of officials of the Community in the Member States in which they are employed comes within the scope of the Treaty on a dual basis by reason of their post with the Community and because they must enjoy all the benefits flowing from Community law for the nationals of Member States in relation to freedom of movement, freedom of establishment and social security."

---

35 Para 30.

36 Case 152/82 [1983] 2323.

37 Para. 9.

The Court reminded itself that Article 48 prohibited discrimination and that Regulation 1612/68 provided fundamental rights for workers and their families. It then said[38]:

> "According to the Fifth Recital in the Preamble to the said Regulation the right of freedom of movement, in order that it may be exercised, by objective standards, in freedom and dignity, requires that equality of treatment should be ensured in fact and in law in respect of all matters relating to the actual pursuit of activities as employed persons and to eligibility for housing and also that obstacles to the mobility workers shall be eliminated, in particular as regards the workers right to be joined by his family and the conditions for the integration of that family into the host country."

The Court reminded itself of a Decision[39] concerning a common vocational training policy and concluded that while educational and vocational training policy were not part of the areas which the Treaty had allotted to the competence of the Community institutions, the opportunity for such kinds of instruction fell within the scope of the Treaty. It said[40]:

> "Consequently if a Member State organises educational courses relating in particular to vocational training, to require of a national of another Member State lawfully established in the first Member State an enrolment fee which is not required of its own nationals in order to take part in such courses constitutes discrimination by reason of nationality which is prohibited by Article 7 of the Treaty".[41]

Our new 'ages' must certainly recognise that other modern phenomenon – *the two income family.* This arose in the case of *Emir Gül v. Regierungspräsident Düsseldorf*[42]. Emir Gül was a doctor of Cypriot nationality whose wife was British. They both lived in Germany where she worked as a hairdresser. He too wished to work. A complicating factor was that when Dr Gül arrived in Germany in 1976 to undertake further training as a specialist in anaesthesia, the authorisation granted to him (renewed on a number of occasions) was subject to an express condition that Dr Gül undertook to return to his own country, or to another developing country, after completing or discontinuing his training. On the 25th October 1982 Dr Gül was awarded a Certificate as an Anaesthesiologist. The following year he sought permanent authorisation to practice in Germany relying on the fact that his wife and the children of their marriage were of British nationality and that his wife was exercising free movement rights.

---

38 Para. 12.

39 EEC Decision no. 63/266 of 2nd April 1963 .

40 Para. 18.

41 Additionally, it pointed out in para 19 that although Commission staff did not pay taxes they were in fact liable to a particular Community Tax on their salaries which was of indirect benefit to the Member State.

42 Case 131/85 [1986] ECR 1573.

The Court ruled that[43]:

> "The rights granted to the spouse of a migrant worker by Articles 10 and 11 of Regulation no. 1612/68 are linked to the rights which that worker enjoys under Article 48 of the Treaty and Article 1 et seq of the Regulation insofar as the spouse can rely on such secondary rights and those rights include the right to take up any activities an employed person pursuant to Article 11, he must be able to pursue that activity under the same conditions as are applicable to a worker entitled to freedom of movement. Article 3(1) of the Regulation thus requires the authorities of the host Member State to treat the spouse in a non-discriminatory fashion. The "national treatment" to which workers from Member States are entitled in that regard is thus extended to their spouses."

It is interesting to look further at the reasoning of the Court in disposing of this case. It ruled[44]:

> "As the Preamble to Regulation 1612/68 points out, in order that the right of freedom of movement may be exercised, by objective standards, in freedom and dignity, equal treatment must be ensured "in fact and in law" (Fifth Recital). In that context the first indent of Article 3(1) of the Regulation prohibits the application of discriminatory legal provisions and "administrative practices" which make access to employment subject to conditions not applicable to nationals of the host State. Furthermore, the very concept of equal treatment presupposes not only that the same laws should be applied to nationals and to foreigners but that those laws should be applied to both categories of persons in the same manner."

Thus in *Gül* the Court was underlining the essential nature of freedom and dignity as equal treatment under the law. This theme of equal treatment under the law can be seen in the cases cited above and in the two which follow to complete this conspectus of the Court's approach. It can also be seen in the case of *Konstantinidis*[45] which is so important it merits a special and more detailed consideration below.

A brush with the law is all too often an aspect of modern manhood. This too is within the scope. In *Mutsch*[46] the Court had to consider whether a municipal right for a national of a Member State to have criminal proceedings in a language other than that normally used before the Court was a social advantage which must be extended to a migrant worker.

Mr Mutsch was a Luxembourg national residing in Belgium in Saint Vith which was a German speaking municipality within Belgium. Had Mr Mutsch been a Belgian national he would have been entitled to have proceedings against him in German; the question was therefore whether as a Luxembourg national he was entitled to the same treatment. The ruling of the Court was simple[47]:

---

43 Para. 20.

44 Para.25.

45 Case C-168/91 [1993] I-1191.

46 Case 137/84 [1985] ECR 2681.

47 See op part.

> "The principal of free movement of workers as laid down in Article 48 of the Treaty and more particularly in Regulation 1612/68 of the Council requires that a worker who is a national of one Member State and habitually resides in another Member State be entitled to require that criminal proceedings against him take place in a language other than the language normally used in proceedings before the Court which tries him, if workers who are nationals of the host Member State have that right in the same circumstances."

It is plain that the reasoning of the Court applied not just because the proceedings were criminal proceedings but because the administrative use of translators was a social advantage extended to workers of the Member State which must be equally extended without discrimination to workers from other Member States.

Finally we are all mortal, yet there are also social advantages in the way in which Member States deal with this. In *O'Flynn v. The Chief Adjudication Officer*[48] the Court had to address the treatment afforded to Mr O'Flynn an Irish national resident in the UK as a former migrant worker. Mr O'Flynn's son had died in the UK. After the funeral in the UK he was buried in the Republic of Ireland. Mr O'Flynn applied for a funeral payment which was refused on the ground that the burial had not taken place in the UK. Mr O'Flynn appealed alleging that the relevant municipal regulations in respect of such payments indirectly discriminated against migrant workers and were in breach of Article 7(2) of Regulation 1612/68.

The Court held that Article 7(2) of Regulation 1612/68 precluded the provision in the municipal regulations which made grant of a payment to cover funeral expenses incurred by a migrant worker subject to the condition that burial or cremation took place within the territory of the Member State whose legislation provided for that payment.

This short study demonstrates how important freedom and dignity is. The way in which the Court has dealt with these cases signposts the answer to the question what do freedom and dignity mean. That freedom and dignity plays a central role in Regulation 1612/68 is of course clear because it is found in the Recitals. To transpose the words of the Recital somewhat : the right of free movement requires that equality of treatment shall be ensured in fact and law *precisely so that* it may be exercised by objective standards in freedom and dignity.

Objectivity in relation to freedom and dignity must necessarily strip out considerations of instinct such as the author's in relation to his French lodger. It must strip out considerations of local form and rules. It must focus foremost on the point of contact through common European citizenship rather than the point of difference through differing nationality. It is concerned with the identity of the individual in the fullest sense approaching points of difference not as barriers unworthy of further consideration but as in need of sensitive and fair consideration.

48 Case C-237/94 [1996] ECR I-2617.

Perhaps the best example of such sensitive and fair consideration is to be found in the approach taken by the Court to the case of *Konstantinidis*[49]. Mr Konstantinidis was a Greek national who worked in Germany as a self-employed masseur and assistant hydrotherapist[50]. Inevitably his name was written on his Greek birth certificate in Greek orthography. When he came to marry a German woman his name was entered in the Marriage Register as Christos Konstadinidis. This was written using letters from the Roman alphabet. In due course he made the simple application to the Registry Office for the rectification of the entry in relation to his surname on the Marriage Register. For the removal of the first letter "d" and its replacement by "nt". He can hardly have known that such a simple request would end up in the European Court of Justice.

The response by the District Office to this request was to obtain a transliteration of his name as found in the Greek alphabet on his birth certificate into the Roman alphabet using a system developed by the International Organisation for Standardisation.

Mr Konstantinidis' application, which came 7 years after his marriage, led to the surprising result that the District Office proposed not to accede to his request nor maintain the entry that had been on his Certificate but to replace it with yet another name – written thus: Hrēstōs Konstantinidēs. Subsequently it was suggested that these inflexions should be replaced by acute accents. The relevant Court then had to consider whether it should approve such an amendment. One accent was replaced from that suggested by the District Office but the Court concluded that under German law it was powerless to do anything else. However it is some consolation to note that it was concerned that his rights under Community law may have been affected.

Advocate General Jacob was confronted with an argument that the issue was not particularly profound. He commented[51]

> "I do not think that actual damage of a tangible nature need be proved in order to bring into operation the prohibition of discrimination. Community law does not regard the migrant worker (or the self-employed migrant) purely as an economic agent and a factor of production entitled to the same salary and working conditions as nationals of the host State; it regards him as a human being who is entitled to live in that State "in freedom and dignity" (see the Fifth Recital in the Preamble to Regulation 1612/68 on freedom of movement for workers within the Community) and to be spared any difference in treatment which would render his life less comfortable physically or psychologically than the lives of the native population. There is support for that proposition in the case law of the Court for example in *Mutch*[52]. If Mr Konstantinidis

---

49 Case C-168/91 [1993] ECR I-1191.

50 As a self-employed person Mr.Konstantinidis was exercising rights of free movement under EC Article 52 not Article 48 with which this paper is principally concerned. The approach, as can be seen below, is obviously similar.

51 Paras. 24 and 25.

52 See footnote 48 supra.

is compelled to call himself Hréstos Konstantinidés when dealing with the German authorities with his clients or with firms from which he himself buys goods or services (for example when he insures his car or opens a bank account), then I should say that, even without proof of actual financial loss, the inconvenience and unpleasantness thus inflicted on him are sufficient to entitle him to invoke the prohibitions laid down by the Treaty."

Advocate General Jacobs approached the argument that the objectionable spelling was limited only to certificates of civil status a matter of dusty archives. This was an argument which he rejected in his opinion roundly in terms which go to the very core of concepts of identity as a European citizen, freedom and dignity. He said[53]:

"Birth, marriage and death are the most significant and sacred events in a person's existence. The entries made in official registers to record such events and the corresponding certificates issued to the person concerned are of such obvious importance that the migrant worker should be entitled to demand that he, like any citizen of the host country be properly identified in those documents and have his name written in a manner that is not insulting and offensive to him. From a purely practical viewpoint it should in any event be noted that even if Mr Konstantinidis is legally free to write his name as he pleases for social and professional purposes, he would inevitably feel some pressure to use the spelling prescribed for official documents; discrepancies between those documents and his everyday practice, regarding the spelling of his name, might cause him inconvenience and embarrassment and would a source of unnecessary confusion for all concerned."

Advocate General Jacobs approached the issue also from a question of fundamental right. This raised issues both under German constitutional law[54] and Articles 5[55] and 8[56] of the European Convention on Human Rights. After a consideration of constitutional traditions in relation to personal identity Advocate General Jacobs concluded[57]:

"It is possible to infer ... from the constitutional traditions of the Member States in general, the existence of a principle according to which the State must respect not only the physical well being of the individual but also his dignity, moral integrity and sense of personal identity. I do not think that there can be any doubt that those "moral rights" are violated if a State compels someone to abandon or modify his name, unless at any rate it does so for a very good reason." (For example if the name when used for commercial purposes creates confusion with the goods of another trader it may be legitimate to restrict the use of the name for those purposes.)

53 Para. 26.
54 Article 1 of the Grundgesetz.
55 The right to liberty and security
56 The right to private and family life
57 Para 18.

> "A persons right to his name is fundamental in every sense of the word. After all, what are we without our name? It is our name that distinguishes each of us from the rest of humanity. It is our name that gives us a sense of identity, dignity and self-esteem. To strip a person of his rightful name is the ultimate degradation, as is evidenced by the common practice of the repressive penal regimes which consists in substituting a number for the prisoner's name. ..."

These are issues which are familiar to many who work with the concept of equality and it is on that concept that this chapter now concludes. Equality is a fundamental right recognised as central to European law. Schermers and Waelbroeck point out[58], that in Community law great care is taken to guarantee equality or prevent discrimination, that the principle of equality is a superior rule of law.

What is noteworthy that Community law protects equality for migrant workers in a way which is even more rigorous than the protection afforded to equality between different genders. In *O'Flynn* the European Court of Justice brought together its case law in relation to indirect or disguised discrimination in the field of free movement rights [59]. It pointed out that merely a risk that a provision may operate to the particular detriment of migrant workers was sufficient to require the provision to be justified.

There is no doubt at all that this test goes further and is more stringent than anything found in discrimination laws of the UK. Neither of the first two Race Relations Acts of 1965 and 1968 dealt with anything other than direct discrimination. In the leading textbook at the time, written after the 1968 Regulations came into force there was no reference to European concepts of covert discrimination[60]. Indeed the White Paper[61] leading to the Sex Discrimination Act of 1975 did not even mention the idea of outlawing indirect discrimination[62], requiring provisions which had a covert or disguised discriminatory effect to be justified.

It is well known[63] that Section 1(1)(b) of the Sex Discrimination Act of 1975, which contains the first British legislative statement of indirect discrimination, was only introduced into after Anthony Lester[64] together with

58 Schermers, H and Waelbroeck, R Judicial Protection in European Communities by 4th Edition 1987 (1992), The Hague, Kluwer Law International at para. 116.

59 Para. 18.

60 Lester, A and Bindman, G, Race and Law (1972) London, Penguin.

61 Equality for Women – Command 5724.

62 Interestingly the concept of indirect discrimination Case 2/56 Geitling Selling Agency [1957] ECR 3, see also Case 14/59 Societes des Fonderies de Pont-à-Mousson [1959] ECR 215.

63 For a description of the fortuitous events that lead to this change see 'The Concept of Discrimination' by David Pannick published in 1985 by Oxford University Press at page 39 et seq.

64 Now Lord Lester of Herne Hill QC.

Roy Jenkins[65] visited the United States of America and heard of the Supreme Court judgment in *Griggs v. Duke Power*[66].

That case was seminal in the development of what has come to be known as adverse impact theory. As a result of that visit first the Sex Discrimination Act 1975 and the next year the Race Relations Act 1976 adopted a formulaic approach[67] which has led subsequently to detailed statistical considerations.

It is intriguing that this formulaic approach has permeated European sex discrimination law following a submission adopted by Advocate General Jean-Pierre Warner in *Jenkins v. Kingsgate (Clothing Productions) Ltd*[68] which was adopted and taken up by the Court in its ruling. This approach which can be seen in numerous subsequent cases has led to detailed statistical considerations in the field of sex discrimination law and to some extent in race relations law applying municipal statutes. Some attempts to stem the formulaic approach was taken by the Court of Appeal in *R v. The Secretary of State for Employment ex parte Seymour-Smith*[69] when they expressed their view that the collective result of the European Court's rulings in indirect sex discrimination cases was that[70]:

> "Before a presumption of indirect discrimination on a ground of sex arises there must be a considerable difference in the number of percentage of one sex in the advantaged or disadvantaged group as against the other sex and not simply a difference which is more *de minimis.*"

That ruling will come up for consideration by the European Court of Justice in 1998 following a reference made by the House of Lords on the appeal by both parties[71].

The contrast between the approach taken in European law in relation to indirect discrimination between nationalities in free movement cases (epitomised by *O'Flynn* and *Commission v. Belgium*), where even a risk of discrimination is sufficient to require justification, is obvious. What is not at

65 Now Lord Jenkins of Hillhead.

66 401 US 424, (1971) 3 Fed 75.

67 Thus the test for indirect discrimination in the Race Relations Act of 1976 is as follows.'A persons discriminates against another if (a) if he applies for that other a requirement or condition which he applies or would apply equally to persons not of the same racial group as that other but (I) which is such that the proportion of persons of the same racial group as that other who can comply with it is considerably smaller than the proportion of persons not of that racial group who can comply with it; and (ii) which he cannot show to be justifiable irrespective of the colour, race, nationality or ethnic or national origins of the person to whom it is applied; and (iii) which is to the detriment of that other because he cannot comply with it'.

68 Case 96/80 [1981] ICR 592.

69 [1995] ICR 889

70 See page 950 C.

71 [1997] ICR 371.

all obvious is why there should be such a difference of approach[72]. Why should the protection from indirect or disguised discrimination in the provision of social advantages to those exercising Article 48 rights (or in the case of for instance Mr Konstantinidis, Article 52 rights) be so much greater than those exercising Article 119 rights? Surely the right to equality between the different sexes is a universal fundamental human right having content independent of the construct of laws which give rise to European citizenship. Why should it be protected so much less favourably than the protection from discrimination in the exercise of free movement rights? A possible though unsatisfactory answer lies in the role that Article 48 has in creating both the need for an European citizenship and providing meaning for the concept.

So a possible further irony may be posed[73]. If the Race Relations Act 1996 were to be construed in a way which was consistent with *O'Flynn*, as it would have to be in cases where Community law were concerned[74], might this not lead to a reversal of the *Jenkins* doctrine at least in Great Britain?

In such a way the law develops and each succeeding generation of European citizen acquires a deeper understanding of the fundamental nature of freedom and dignity. The economic consequences for migrant workers are agnostic affecting the affairs of those who are naturally Euro-sceptic as much as those that are Euro-enthusiasts. However these social consequences, such as the right to use a language of choice, to express personal identity, to dignity in death, will come to be seen as enhancing the development and understanding of the concept of European citizenship.

---

72 In his opinion in O'Flynn, Advocate General Lenz tried to reconcile these different approaches: the one requiring statistical proof and the other using an almost intuitive assessment of risk of discrimination.

73 This possibility was raised but not finally determined by the Employment Appeal Tribunal in Bossa v Ansett Worldwide Aviation Services; [1998] ICR 694.

74 See eg. Amministrazione delle Fiananze dello stato v Simmenthal SPA Case 106/77 [1978] ECR 629, paras 17 and 22.

Chapter Four

Insiders and Outsiders in the Euopean Union: The Search for a European Identity and Citizenship

Zig Layton-Henry

The Member States of the European Union are engaged in a momentous project to create a European identity, a European citizenship and an ever more perfect European Union. The drivers behind this project want the European Union and its institutions to have popular support and legitimacy among the peoples of the Union, as well as among its elites. They are thus concerned with the growing scepticism about European initiatives and directives, and are anxious about the democratic deficit but they are determined that the momentum should be maintained. The progress in building the European Union project has been astonishing and after Maastricht, Amsterdam and the likely creation of European Monetary Union it does not appear fanciful to be discussing the construction of a European Union identity and citizenship.

In a recent article Soledad García[1] asked the question, "why do we need a European Union identity?" Identity like most concepts is difficult to define and involves the creation of boundaries – some are included within a specific identity and others are excluded. One could argue that a common unified identity has never existed in European societies and the idea that it has is as much a myth as the concept of the nation-state itself. Identities have always been multi-faceted – fragmented by class, gender, religion, language or dialect but also by local, regional, national and transnational senses of belonging. In Britain multiple national identities are the norm. One can feel English in England, Scottish in Scotland and British in both without feeling that these identities are incompatible or in conflict. In the Imperial period one could be Canadian and British or Indian and British. However, as nationalism grew in strength local identities were increasingly asserted against the imperial identity, resulting in the formation of independent states. This transition was most difficult in the territory closest to Britain so that in Ireland, while Nationalists wished to assert that Irishness was incompatible with Britishness, Unionists asserted the reverse. However, for English, Scots, British and Irish a European identity could be an acceptable and welcome additional identity that could bring with it positive benefits of greater co-operation, partnership and prosperity.

However, if a European identity is to be constructed around the European Union to create a sense of belonging, loyalty and legitimacy for economic and political union, does it have to be built on a bedrock of a common European heritage and culture? Can Europe be said to have a common cultural heritage

---

1 S García, European Union Identity and Citizenship: Some Challenges, in M Roche and R Van Berkel (eds) European Citizenship and Social Exclusion, Ashgate 1997.

based on a shared history, religion, values, political institutions, myths and symbols?

No doubt many people believe that there is a common European cultural heritage and history, though it might be hard to pin down its defining characteristics. However, attempts to define a common European culture quickly run into insuperable problems. For example, one might argue that a defining characteristic of European culture and identity is its Christian tradition. This definition ignores the historic Muslim legacy in Spain and Portugal and the long standing and contemporary presence of Islam in the Balkans and Russia. Moreover it could be interpreted as a deliberate attempt to exclude Muslim immigrants from being accepted as European and to exclude Albania, Bosnia and Turkey from future membership of the European Union. This would also apply to North African countries which might also wish to become full members of the European Union in the future. This example underlines the danger that a European Union identity would be asserted against other identities and cultures. In practice there is no common European language, political tradition, religion or history. Rather there exists a mosaic of cultures and traditions. This mosaic could be a strength in allowing for an even greater plurality of cultures and traditions to be constructed as European in the future or it could lead to a search for a kind of lowest common European cultural denominator which might exclude many life-long residents of the European Union and countries close to western Europe which might wish to become associated with it.

National identity and nationality are closely related to the concept of citizenship and many writers believe that by redefining citizenship in a broader and more all-embracing way we can arrive at a fairer and more inclusive society – a society that is more equal and democratic. Citizens after all are insiders. They formally possess the full range of civil, political and social rights and it is their duty to participate in society and its institutions. In the French Republican tradition citizens are the masters. They have the right to govern the state and society.[2] Citizens, of course, have duties and responsibilities too but these tend to be downplayed compared with the rights and benefits of citizenship.

This view that by, broadening and deepening citizenship, problems of inequality and marginalisation can be overcome may be over-optimistic. The Western tradition of citizenship and its related concept of nationality tend to be highly restrictive – to be rooted in national closure with a double meaning of limited access from outside and cultural homogeneity within. In this tradition citizenship is seen as a form of identity that acts as an anchor situating

---

2 W R Brubaker, Citizenship and Nationhood in France and Germany, Harvard University Press 1992.
A Favell, Philosophies of Integration: Immigration and the Idea of Citizenship in France and Britain, Macmillan 1997.

oneself in society.[3] I am a British citizen. This means I am not only a citizen of the UK but a member of an imagined British community. It could be an imagined UK community but the concept is rarely stretched across the Irish sea. In some countries this issue of identity is considered to be so important that one needs to be accepted as a member of the community before one can become a citizen. You therefore have to be born into the community or be fully assimilated and accepted before you can join it through naturalisation. The Swiss example comes to mind – you need the support and approval of your local commune before you can become a naturalised Swiss citizen.

The restrictive view of citizenship is described most clearly by Rogers Brubaker who argues that citizenship today means membership of a nation-state.[4] He argues that the nation-state model of citizenship remains deeply influential. It combines the concepts of citizenship and nationality and in its extreme form assumes the following six ideals:

1. Egalitarian – all citizens should have equal status.
2. Sacred – citizens should be prepared to make sacrifices for their state and not regard citizenship in an instrumental way.
3. National – membership of the political community should be simultaneously membership of a cultural community.
4. Democratic – citizenship should carry with it rights to political participation and in the long run residence and membership must coincide.
5. Uniqueness – every person should belong to one and only one state.
6. Socially consequential – membership should be valued both directively and subjectively – that is there are material and psychological benefits from citizenship.[5]

Brubaker's description of the nation-state model shows the blending of citizenship and national identity. Some of the criteria he outlined in this ideal type such as sacredness, cultural membership and uniqueness are highly restrictive and even unrealistic in the modern world. International migration and transnational marriages are increasingly common and many people see considerable advantages in dual nationality or even multiple citizenships and rarely feel conflicts of loyalties or duties caused by their membership of more than one State. It would be impossible to accept the European Union's aspiration for a European citizenship if the nation-state model is accepted. The ideas of a transnational citizenship and even of a transnational identity are both ruled out.

---

3 P Conover, I Crewe and D Searing, Conceptions of Citizenship Among British and American Publics: An Exploratory Analysis, Essex Papers in Political Government, No 73, Department of Government, University of Essex, March 1990.

4 W R Brubaker (ed) Immigration and the Politics of Citizenship in Europe and North America, University Press of America, 1989.

5 *ibid.* p3-4

This discussion does illustrate the two traditions that underlie definitions of citizenship: the contractual and the communal. The contractual model of citizenship tends to be legalistic and has at its core a strong emphasis on individualism and individual rights. Citizenship is linked to access to rights – civic, political and social. The duties of citizenship in this liberal view tend to be relegated to the background as they are seen as illiberal, restricting the individual's freedom of action. Many traditionalists at the present time are concerned that citizenship has become increasingly unidirectional, emphasising rights or entitlements from the state and no longer stressing the obligations and duties traditionally expected from citizens.

The second view is communitarian. It sees citizenship as rooted in the community. People share common traditions and understandings with their neighbours and come together to pursue a common good. They have a common identity and it is their duty to participate in public affairs and activities. The duties of citizens are much more prominent in the communitarian view. In Anglo-Saxon debates, the United States is often given as an ideal type of a country where contractual citizenship is most important, and Britain is given as an example of the communitarian case.[6]

However there is no clear distinction between the two traditions. Those countries which emphasise citizenship through descent from a citizen (ius sanguinis) would seem to fall in the communitarian tradition but these countries are often republican, with an emphasis on the sovereignty of the people and the rights of citizens, which seem closer to the liberal contractual view. Those countries like the United States which fall into the liberal contractual tradition can place strong emphasis on the duties of citizens and demand a high degree of citizen participation and loyalty.

One way of emphasising the difficulties of creating an European identity and citizenship is to examine the problems of distinguishing between people who can be considered to be full members of the European Union and those who are not. Which people can be considered to be European Union insiders and which are outsiders? There would seem to be a clear distinction between insiders and outsiders, just as there seems to be between citizen and alien in sovereign states but in practice the distinction is far from clear. This is obvious if, for simplicity, we develop a straightforward two by two matrix of insiders and outsiders in the European Union.

Insiders and Outsiders in the European Union

The two by two matrix gives us four categories insiders who are really insiders; insiders who are outsiders; outsiders who are insiders and outsiders who are beyond the Pale. The first category, insiders who are really insiders in modern Europe, seems to be straightforward enough, though it is tempting to confine this group to members of the Council of Ministers or members of the

---

6 P. Conover, I Crewe and D Searing, op cit.

European Commission or even MEPs, though the latter group might well consider themselves to be outsiders and of less importance than members of national parliaments. They are insiders in European institutions but outsiders in national politics. However this is too narrow a definition as far as citizenship is concerned. We can broadly define citizens/insiders in the European Union as those with full civic, political and social rights – that is citizens of the Member States. But when we take into account the ability to *exercise* these rights, then residence becomes important as well, as it is only citizens of a Member State residing within the borders of their national state who enjoy full civil, political and social rights. EU citizens residing in another Member State face significant restrictions on their rights – for example they cannot vote in national parliamentary elections, take employment in the civil service and do not necessarily possess full access to social welfare benefits.

The second category, insiders who are really outsiders, draws attention to two dimensions of citizenship: membership of the community and the ability to exercise citizenship rights. Every society has members/citizens who are regarded as not really full members of the national community. In some societies these groups can be very large. In pre-war Poland, Jews, Gypsies, Ukrainians, Germans, White Russians, and people who belonged to the Protestant and Orthodox faiths were not fully accepted as members of the Polish national community. They were not fully Polish. To be fully Polish you had to be of Polish descent, speak the Polish language and be a Roman Catholic. In modern Europe there is a struggle taking place over who is to be considered a European. Is it people who are of European descent or people born in Europe, speak European languages, and have the legal citizenship of a Member State? Or can African Muslims be European? Was the Queen correct in saying on her recent trip to Pakistan that we are pleased that we have developed the new identity of British Muslim? An intense debate has been going on in France as to whether Muslims can be really French. Discrimination, non-acceptance, or racist attacks can turn insiders, defined as people with citizenship, into outsiders because of rejection by their fellow citizens. All over Europe Gypsies are disliked, stigmatised and rejected. They provide a good example of people who may legally be citizens and insiders but everywhere are treated as outsiders.[7]

Inability to exercise citizenship rights does not only occur because of racial or ethnic discrimination. Unemployment, poverty, physical disability, sexual orientation or gender may marginalise groups of people and cause them to be treated as second class citizens. The European Commission has argued that unemployment is the greatest source of social exclusion and marginalisation in the European Union.

The third group I mentioned seems really anomalous – outsiders who are accepted as insiders. There are some non-citizens who have a range of privileges

7 I Bohn, F Hamburger and K Roch, The Racist Portrayal of Gypsies in the Media in Z Layton-Henry and C Wilpert, Challenging Racism in Britain and Germany, Macmillan 1999.

and receive such a positive welcome that they can be considered more like insiders than outsiders. This is very obvious in Britain where citizens of independent Commonwealth countries, especially citizens of 'Old Commonwealth' countries like Australia, Canada and New Zealand, have traditionally been considered part of the British community. All Commonwealth citizens have almost all of the privileges of citizenship in terms of civic, political and social rights. Some of these rights have gradually been lost as post-war immigration and nationality laws have been introduced but they are still able, for example, to vote in national Parliamentary elections, a right which is denied to citizens of other European Union countries. Citizens of Old Commonwealth countries face no social discrimination and on the contrary have traditionally been welcome as 'kith and kin' and allies in two World Wars. The entry of Britain into the European Union and post-war nationality and immigration legislation has eroded the privileged position of British subjects in Commonwealth countries but Commonwealth 'patrials', that is people descended from a British grandparent, are still largely treated as insiders even though they may be citizens of another country.

Some other non-citizens like Americans and Japanese may for political and economic reasons be treated more like insiders than outsiders. They are often businessmen or investors and in either case are welcome. In general non-citizens who have permanent residence and employment rights are more like insiders than outsiders. They have considerable civic and social rights and so are treated almost as though they are citizens. In some European countries: Netherlands, Denmark, Ireland, Norway, and Sweden, permanent residents have been granted local and regional voting rights, so the distinction between citizen and non-citizen becomes even less significant. The European Commission wishes to place permanent residents on the same footing as citizens of Member States on the grounds that they are part of the European Union's labour force and working population, so free movement of workers, for example, should apply to them equally as to citizens of Member States.

The final category, outsiders who are really outsiders, seems to be clear and straightforward. This category would apply to citizens of non-Member States who reside in states outside of the European Union. They don't possess any citizenship rights and so have no claim on the countries of the European Union. This of course is not correct. The countries of the European Union have historic ties and obligations to many countries outside of the Union. Moreover outsiders may be potential insiders so while Africans, East Europeans, Asians and Latin Americans may all appear to be outsiders who are really outsiders, in practice they cannot necessarily be ignored and excluded. Trade, international migration and historic ties, particularly those involving imperial and colonial obligations, mean that the links between these countries and modern Europe are very strong.

International obligations also complicate the distinction between the citizen and the outsider. Are refugees outsiders or people whom European countries are obliged to admit and protect under UN Treaty obligations? Convention refugees are entitled to admittance and protection and so in theory have rights in modern European countries, that is, providing they can travel to Europe in order to exercise these rights. In practice refugees like immigrants are often considered to be illegitimate competitors for scarce European resources such as jobs, welfare benefits, housing and security. Research by the Home Office shows that refugees are generally well educated and skilled people, eager to work and repay the country that gives them refuge and also eager to return to their own country when conditions allow.[8] The picture of refugees portrayed in the media and by some politicians is very different. They are castigated as 'bogus refugees', people who are using asylum as a means of circumventing firm but fair immigration controls to gain entry to the prosperous states of the European Union.

In looking at the citizen and the outsider in modern Europe what I have tried to show is that there is no sharp distinction between being a citizen and an insider and being an alien and an outsider. It is possible to be a citizen and an outsider because your way of life, your language, your colour, your religion, your disability cause you to be rejected by your fellow citizens most of the time. It may also be that lack of a job, poor education or poverty may make it very difficult for you to exercise your citizenship rights. You can also be legally an outsider but for reasons of kinship, skills, or money for investment be warmly welcomed and considered to be a valuable member of the community even though you are not formally a native or a citizen.

It may be that the modern European Union that is developing will be better able to develop a broad inclusive notion of citizenship and individual membership of the European Union and European society because of the plurality of cultures, languages and religions that already exist. Respect for other peoples' culture and traditions may come more easily to the new generation of young Europeans. They also are more used to the global village that the modern world is fast becoming. The problem is that defining membership of a club, a country or even a European Union involves the creation of boundaries and limits to membership. It is inconceivable that the European Union's policy of enlargement can continue indefinitely. No matter how many countries are allowed to join there must be limits to membership or else the costs will start to outweigh the benefits and the legitimacy of the European Union project will be undermined. This will raise once again the issue of who is to be included and who excluded. So the problem of insiders and outsiders will always remain.

---

8 J Carey-Wood, K Duke, V Karn and T Marshall, The Settlement of Refugees in Britain, Home Office Research Study No. 141, HMSO 1995.

Part II:

Third Country Nationals in the European union: Coming to Terms with Partial Rights

Introduction

Professor C S R Russell

For an amateur, the papers in this conference have been a real intellectual treat, both to hear and to read. They are also, to a historian, a vivid demonstration of the cultural unity of the countries of the European Union. With a few exceptions, of which Greece is a conspicuous and distinguished example, the countries of the European Union are the countries of Latin Christendom. It is not for nothing that the European Union's most distinguished prize is the Karlspreis, or Charlemagne Prize.

The countries which make up the Union are the heirs of that remarkable growth of European civilization which stretches roughly from Charlemagne to Erasmus, and the competing cross-currents we see in these papers mostly have their springs far back in the Middle Ages. In recent years they have flowed faster, and other currents have flowed into them. In the years since 1990, some of these competing currents have met hard enough to generate intellectual whirlpools, through which these contributors, each equipped with their own skills, are warily paddling their way.

Nationalism extends, far back into the Middle Ages, and it was in 1106 that the Abbot of St Denis declared that "it is not right that the English should be governed by the French, nor the French by the English". The great Mediaeval monarchies, especially those of France, England and the Holy Roman Empire, were always trying to give such sentiments political embodiment in state institutions whose purposes were essentially competitive. Yet at the same time mediaeval Christendom had, through the papacy and canon law, an international system of law and an international system of courts, which attempted to impose a legal order on these competing states. The European Court of Justice is the heir of a long intellectual tradition. While human law was seen as based on natural law, it was always easy to see 'rights' as based on principles of supra-national origin. Against that idea, the great national kings, like Edward I and Philip The Fair, struggled, and sometimes fought with fury.

Developments within our own lifetimes have put these ancient struggles onto a higher plane of intensity. The Treaty of Rome revived what was familiar to our mediaeval ancestors, a Europe-wide system of law, with its own courts to enforce it. This created a series of rights, justiciable on a supra-national basis. Among these, in Title III of the Treaty of Rome, were rights to freedom of movement. Any competent lawyer, given a right expressed in unambiguous general terms, can make a ratchet of it, as the history of the US Constitution illustrates.

That ratchet effect seeps across the European Union's borders by the process of osmosis and is extended, bit by bit, to peoples with associate status under a series of agreements. Elspeth Guild's analysis of the Association Agreements with Eastern Europe, and Julia Onslow-Cole's description of the cases of *Rush Portugesa* and *Vander Elst* show that ratchet in operation. What Julia Onslow Cole calls "the overriding principle of nondiscrimination", and the dislike of 'social dumping' which follows from commitment to the single market, then operate to confer further social rights on those so protected.

At the same time, we have had economic trends which should have been complementary to this process, but which have so far proved antithetical to it. The growth of the world global market rests on thinking which is often very close to the Treaty of Rome, yet it sometimes makes not only the EU's Member States, but even the EU itself, behave like an old-fashioned nation state.

If the EU's concept of the level playing field were extended to the global market, it would involve freedom of movement of labour, equally with freedom of movement of capital. It is only if that is so that there can be genuinely equal competition between them. In practice, this is not easy to achieve. Money can be moved round the world in seconds, yet labour is not nearly so easily uprooted. Even a full determination to achieve a level playing field between capital and labour in the global market would leave it very difficult to achieve. In fact there is no such determination, for the interest of each country differs from the interest of all. A level playing field between capital and labour is in the interest of all, but it is not in the interest of each. A country which shows greater willingness to admit cheap labour from abroad than its competitors do risks becoming the victim of what is a form of social dumping. Indeed, if GATT were to enjoy the services of a court with equivalent powers to the ECJ it might wish to hold men like Radovan Karadzic, who send large numbers of their subjects as destitute refugees into another country, guilty of social dumping as well as of war crimes. In fact, Germany's reaction to the opening of the borders in Eastern Europe, described by Dariusz Stola, shows that we are still far away from this way of thinking. Freedom of movement and fortress Europe sit very uneasily together, and until this paradox is resolved, global markets will not work as they should. The pillars of Maastricht, as Douglas Hurd almost told the House of Commons in 1992, mark the fightback of the nation state. I always think of them as the Pillars of Hercules.

That, of course, was not the end of the story. The European Commission's Communication on Immigration of 1991, quoted in Elspeth Guild's paper, stressed that too tight a control of migration can build up an irresistible pressure of illegal migration, creating a rightless class of excluded non-citizens, like the abused maids who occasionally appear in the English courts. Joanna Apap and Hans van Amersfoort have stressed how much such a development threatens a democratic notion of citizenship, and therefore the rights of all other subjects. The existence of 'lesser breeds without the law' must, in any democratic society, threaten the law itself.

The emergence of a class of rightless people is something to which good lawyers are likely to be allergic: it threatens the very being of their subject. If those good lawyers are armed with a series of treaties embodying a set of overriding general principles, they are able to put their allergies to good effect.

I remember reading, more years ago than I care to count, an Agatha Christie story, most of it thoroughly implausible, in which a group of people had been captured and concealed by the villain in the invisible parts of a sanatorium in the Atlas Mountains. The intrepid hero, having discovered them there, burst out to tell the story to a distinguished visiting deputation inspecting the visible parts of the establishment. The politicians, wishing to avoid the embarrassment, tried to brush the story under the carpet. Only the judge, almost eighty and very deaf, insisted on hearing the story, because his training taught him to listen to evidence before he decided anything. Having heard the story, he arrived at the truth. That part of the story, if nothing else, is in line with experience as I have known it since.

The least ineffective weapons for controlling over-mighty executives are courts. Judges, no doubt, are and have always been full of faults. Yet those very faults, because they make them allergic to bullies, may become part of their strength. In England, judges have been restricted by the luxuriant growth of the doctrine of Parliamentary sovereignty. It is only recently that Lord Woolf has had the courage and the ingenuity to come up with the brilliant maxim that "if Parliament wishes to confer a power to act unfairly, it must say so in express words" – a challenge to which no politician will ever rise. (*Court of Appeal, R -v- Secretary of State For the Home Department, ex parte Mohammed Fayed*, 13 November 1996).

As the American experience shows, once endow judges with a rights-based law based on principles the legislators lack the sovereign power to repeal, and they become a formidable force for human rights. They still need control, of course, as all powers do, but that control comes then from other judges.

Mediaeval and seventeenth century common law was a far more rights-based system of law than modem lawyers sometimes realize. That strand of the law has been diminished by Parliamentary sovereignty in its English incarnation as much as it has been magnified by the constitution in its American incarnation. Now, thanks to the careful wording of the European Communities Act 1972, European law has something of the status of a constitution: Parliament cannot alter it.

The intellectual excitement of the world that Act opened up was felt at once by Lord Scarman (Sir Leslie Scarman, *English Law: The New Dimension*, 1974). That intellectual excitement has been a long time feeding through into the daily substance of the law. Here, in this collection, we see quite how right Lord Scarman was.

Chapter Five

The Right of Establishment and Provision of Services: Community Employers and Third Country Nationals

Julia Onslow-Cole

Introduction

This chapter will focus on the situation of third country nationals with Community employers, who are exercising the right of establishment and the provision of services. The approach here will be practical – what are the rights and how are they exercised? This time last year my firm, Cameron McKenna, had one of the first cases in the UK where the principles established in European case law concerning the provision of services and the movement of third country nationals were invoked.

I am going to take a brief look at the Treaty provisions relating to the right of establishment and the right to provide services. I will then look at the well-known cases of *Rush Portuguesa*[1] and *Vander Elst*[2]. I will then explain how we applied the Vander Elst principles on behalf of a client in the UK and the Home Office Guidelines which were laid down for such cases. Finally, I will look at developments, principally the Simone Veil Report and the proposals for a Convention on the Admission of Third Country Nationals.

Articles 52 – 58

Article 52 of the Treaty states that "restrictions on the freedom of establishment of nationals of a Member State in the territory of another Member State shall be abolished". The abolition shall also apply to restrictions on the setting up of agencies, branches or subsidiaries by nationals of any Member State established in the territory of another Member State.

Freedom of establishment includes "the right to take up, maintain or pursue activities as self-employed persons and to set up and manage undertakings, in particular, companies or firms", under the conditions laid down for own nationals by the law of the country where such establishment is effected.

Article 58 extends the right of establishment to companies or firms formed in accordance with the law of a Member State which have their registered office, central administration or principal place of business within the

1 C-113/89 [1990] ECR I-1417
2 C-43/93 [1994] ECR I-3803

Community, saying that for the purposes of the right of establishment they are to be treated in the same way as individuals who are of that state nationals.

ARTICLES 59 – 66

Article 59 provides that restrictions on the freedom to provide services within the Community shall be abolished in respect of nationals of Member States who are established in a Member State other than that of the person for whom the services are intended.

The intention is to allow EEA[3] nationals established as service providers within one Member State, temporarily to provide services in another Member State, without going as far as to establish themselves in that second Member State under Article 52. So long as there is a cross-border element the provider may either move to the second Member State in order to provide the service, or may simply remain in his own Member State, whilst providing a service to a recipient in a second Member State. In addition, it is now generally accepted that Article 59 also covers situations such as those where a national doesn't actually provide services in his home Member State because he is economically inactive, or because he is actually an employee there. As in the case of the right of establishment, companies established as service providers in Member States have the same rights as individual EEA nationals.

At the heart of the provisions on both establishment and the provision of services is that those exercising the rights must be able to do so without suffering any discrimination on the grounds of their nationality, covert or overt, direct or indirect. They must be treated in all respects in the same manner as nationals of the Member State. The only exceptions to the freedoms are on the grounds of public policy, public security, public health or an imperative reason in the general interest.

THIRD COUNTRY NATIONALS

The basic provisions are clearly limited to nationals of Member States or companies established in Member States. How then, and to what extent can third country nationals benefit from these provisions?

Businesses established in the EEA can either set up a branch in another Member State under Article 52 or provide services on the basis of Article 59, whatever the nationality of their owners and shareholders. However, in practice the most effective means of taking advantage of these rights is by physically transferring personnel to the second Member State. If those personnel are EEA nationals then they can come as workers under Article 48, but if the personnel are third country nationals, there would appear to be no direct basis for them

---

3 This last subject will be dealt with more fully in the final chapter of this book, Raising Minimum Standards or Racing for the Bottom? The Commission's Proposed Migration Convention by Steve Peers

to transfer. In addition, third country nationals who wish to provide services or establish themselves on an individual basis have no rights either.

The second indent of Article 59 gives the European Council the power to extend the provisions on the freedom to provide services to third country nationals who are established within the Community, but this power has not yet been put to use. Therefore, it has been up to the European Court of Justice to extend the principle by means of its jurisprudence.

JURISPRUDENCE OF THE EUROPEAN COURT OF JUSTICE

The ECJ used its typically creative interpretation of Treaty provisions to further the fundamental freedoms of the Community. Basing its decisions on the overriding principle of non discrimination it has reached two important judgments which served to extend the basis of the freedom to provide services.

The first decision came in 1990, in the case of *Rush Portuguesa*[4] . *Rush* was a building and public works company governed by Portuguese law with its registered office in Portugal. *Rush* entered into a sub-contract with a French company for works on several sites in France. In order to carry out the works, *Rush* brought its Portuguese work force from Portugal.

As the case occurred during the transitional period of Portugal's membership of the Community, whilst Portuguese businesses could rely on Article 59, Portuguese workers could not rely on free movement as workers under Article 48. Although the workers all obtained the necessary short stay visas to enter France, France claimed that according to their *Code du Travail,* the workers needed French work permits, following spot checks by the labour inspectorate on a couple of the sites which *Rush* were working on. *Rush* claimed that Articles 59–66 prevented the application of the *Code du Travail* to its employees. The French authorities contended that the freedom to provide services did not extend to all the employees of the supplier of services and that such employees remained generally subject to the requirement of a work permit unless they could rely on the Article 48 free movement of workers, which, in Portugal's case, did not apply until the transitional period ended on 1st January 1993.

The Court held that Articles 59 and 60 of the Treaty and the provisions of Spain and Portugal's Act of Accession must be interpreted as meaning that an undertaking established in Portugal providing services in the construction and public work sector in another Member State may move with its own work force which it brings from Portugal for the duration of the works in question. Moreover, the authorities of the second Member State may not impose conditions relating to the recruitment of manpower *in situ* or the obtaining of work permits for the Portuguese work force on the service provider.

---

4 The EEA comprises the Member States of the European Union and those of the European Free Trade Agreement. Identical rights on free movement of workers, establishment and service provision apply to all these states by vitue of the European Economic Area Agreement.

The case created a lot of publicity at the time, but certainly the Home Office in London and other authoritative and administrative bodies throughout Europe said that the principles of that case were unique because they concerned Portuguese workers during a transitional period. However, the Court rejected this interpretation in the case of *Vander Elst*. In that case, Mr Vander Elst, an Belgian employer established in Belgium, operated a specialist demolition business. In addition to Belgian nationals, he employed Moroccan nationals who were legally resident in Belgium and who held Belgian work permits. In 1989, his business carried out demolition works in France. He put a team of eight people on the site who were regular employees, four Belgian and four Moroccans. The French employment inspectors made a check at the site and said that the Moroccans should have permits.

Mr Vander Elst appealed that decision and the Court held that Articles 59 and 60 prohibited Member States from requiring businesses established in another Member State but providing services in that first Member State to obtain work permits for non EEA nationals which it lawfully and habitually employs in the home State, and to pay the cost of obtaining a work permit or a fine if the requirements were not complied with.

The Court took the view that because the workers were legally resident in Belgium with Belgian work permits, and had obtained short stay visas they had complied with all the necessary steps. The French requirement that they obtain a work permit went beyond the preconditions which can be imposed on service providers. Work permits are intended to regulate access to the French labour market for third country nationals, and the Court considered that workers employed in an undertaking established in one Member State seconded temporarily to another Member State and who will return to the home State on completion of the work do not seek access to the labour market in the second State in any way, as was the case here.

The Court reiterated that Article 59 of the Treaty requires not only the elimination of all discrimination on the grounds of nationality against a service provider established in another Member State, but also the abolition of any restriction, even if it applies without distinction to national service providers and those of other Member States, when it is liable to prohibit or otherwise impede the activities of a provider of services established in another Member State where he lawfully provides similar services.

Similarly, the Court had previously held that national legislation requiring such service providers to be subject to the issue of an administrative licence or to pay fees in respect of employees transferred to the second State, when they already pay similar fees in the home State, constitutes a restriction on the freedom to provide services.

Finally, the Court ruled that as one of the fundamental principles of the Treaty, the freedom to provide services may be restricted only by rules which are justified by overriding reasons in the general interest and which are applied to national and non-national service providers in the Member State without distinction, insofar as that interest is not already protected by the rules which cover the service provider in the Member State where he/she is established.

WORKING CONDITIONS

One of the main concerns in relation to workers temporarily seconded under Article 59 is that their social protection may be undermined as workers seconded to a second Member State may fall outside that State's social legislation. Many states, and in particular, France and Belgium, fear "social dumping", where organisations use the freedoms to avoid social protection legislation, employing third country national workers from States with low labour costs and seconding them to work in countries with high labour costs. Not only does this exploit third country nationals but is also anti-competitive.

To this end the ECJ held in *Rush Portuguesa*[5], and confirmed in *Vander Elst*, that such seconded personnel could be made subject to national legislation and collective agreements entered into by the social partners as regards working conditions. However, any such legislation is obviously a restriction and can only be permitted if it can be justified in the overriding public interest. The operation of this principle can be seen in the case of *Michelle Guiot, Climatec SA*[6]. Mr Guiot was the managing director of Climatec SA, a construction company based in Luxembourg and governed by Luxembourg law, which decided to second temporarily four workers to Belgium.

Belgian law required Climatec to make employer's social security contributions. However, Climatec was also required to make certain social security contributions in Luxembourg in respect of all the workers it employed, including those temporarily working in another Member State. Climatec refused to make the additional social security contributions in Belgium. The ECJ held that in this case the imposition of the conditions were not justified, because the interest the Belgian social security legislation aimed to protect was already safeguarded by the Luxembourg legislation, as this extended to posted workers.

The problem is likely to be resolved, at least in part, by the adoption of the Posted Workers Directive last year. This Directive, which must be implemented by Member States by September 1999, applies to workers who are temporarily posted by a company in one Member State to work in another Member State. The Directive provides that workers seconded to another Member State must be given the same core employment rights as workers who are permanently based in that State, whatever law their employment contract is governed by. The key rights cover matters such as maximum work periods, minimum wage and health and safety at work. However there are many derogations, for example, Member States can choose not to apply the provisions on minimum pay to postings of less than one month.

EXERCISE OF THE RIGHTS IN PRACTICE

Entry Conditions

It is well established that EEA nationals exercising their rights under Articles 52 and 59 must benefit from the corollary right to enter the second Member

---

5 *Supra*

6 C-272/94 judgment of 22.6.96

State and to stay there in order to take advantage of their rights. However, what conditions of entry can be imposed on third country nationals?

In *Vander Elst* the ECJ held that because the Moroccan workers had obtained short stay entry visas to enter France, French immigration rules had been complied with. Although the point was not made directly, this suggests that compliance with national immigration requirements is a legitimate precondition which may be imposed on service providers. However, this cannot be the case as surely such a requirement amounts to discrimination which could not be justified purely on the basis that Member States wish to monitor population flow into its countries. It has been suggested that a simple notification procedure where the service provider notifies the authorities in the Member State would be more appropriate, but to date this system has not been adopted and the requirement is yet to be tested in practice.

APPLICATION IN THE UK

Certainly in the case of the UK, it is envisaged that an application for entry clearance should be made to a British diplomatic post overseas. The application will then be considered in accordance with guidelines, which the Home Office say were drawn up shortly after the *Vander Elst* judgment, but which were not published until my firm's case last year.

The guidelines state that, in order to take advantage of the principles the applicant worker must be:

- lawfully resident in the first Member State;
- lawfully and habitually employed by the employer in the first Member State for 12 months;
- required to be transferred to the UK for a short period to provide a service;
- intend to take no other employment in the UK; and
- intend to leave the UK at the end of the fixed period.

As I have explained, Cameron McKenna were involved in one of the first cases in the UK where the Home Office had to implement the *Vander Elst* principles. A large UK banking client wanted to install a computer software system and had contracted the project out to a German company. The German company employed an Indian national in Germany who was to be instrumental in the one year project. The Indian national went to the British-Consulate General in Dusseldorf to obtain a visa, but was told that she must obtain a work permit. We then invoked the *Vander Elst* principles, liaising with the Home Office and the British Consulate-General. Unfortunately, the Indian national did not have a full 12 months' experience with the employing company in Germany. The Home Office recognised that the guidelines were to be applied flexibly, to ensure that full effect is given to the fundamental principle of free movement, and the Indian national was permitted to come to the UK under the *Vander Elst* principles. Arguably, the guidelines themselves are more restrictive than the Court of Justice intended in the *Vander Elst* judgment.

I understand that the Home Office have since been involved in a small number of similar cases, and have only refused applications where they clearly fell well outside the rules. For example, one application was made for an EEA national's third country national maid to come on the basis that the maid was providing services to the woman. The Home Office took the view that this was not covered by the rules as the maid was not really providing services in the terms of the Treaty, but was really an employee and the application was refused. This raises the question of the applicability of the employer's rights under Article 52 EC, the right of establishment, to move third country national staff from the place of employment in one Member State to a place of employment in another Member State. However, this involves the exercise of a different right from that of service provision which is under consideration here.

Whilst the UK generally gets a bad press for compliance with European law, it seems that it was actually one of the first countries to draw up guidelines for the implementation of the principle in practice. In fact, as the Chair of the International Bar Association Migration Committee, one of my tasks is to write a newsletter updating our members of recent developments. Literally a few days ago I received a fax from one of our members in Belgium, headed "Newsflash", stating that by virtue of a Royal Decree passed in August 1997, and which had come into force on September 1997, Belgium had introduced guidelines implementing the *Vander Elst* principle! These guidelines are slightly different from the UK's, for example the third country national must have a "staying permit" from the Belgian consular services in the country in which he/she is employed and the Consular services will then verify the facts with the Brussels Ministry of Interior Affairs. Like the UK guidelines, the Belgium guidelines require the individual to have been employed by the company for 12 months without interruption. They also require the third country national to hold a work permit issued in the country "of origin" valid for the period of employment in Belgium, to hold a passport and to be authorised to stay for a period equal to the period of services plus three months. Other countries impose a requirement that the third country national must have been employed by the service provider for 2 years, and others, such as Austria, make it very difficult for service providers to exercise the right because they don't recognise the *Vander Elst* principle and require the third country national to go back to their original country in order to make an application. For example a German company employing Russian nationals in Germany wanted to provide services in Austria. The Austrian authorities said that the Russians had to go back to Russia and apply for visas from the Austrian Consulate there.

FUTURE DEVELOPMENTS

So far, the cases have centred on the right of the service provider to transfer third country national personnel on the basis of Article 59 and have involved the exercise of the right to provide services on a temporary basis. There has been much speculation as to whether the principles laid down will be extended to the more permanent situations envisaged by Article 52. If an organisation established in one state wishes to set up a branch in another state, it is more than likely that it will want to transfer some of its senior personnel to that branch office on an indefinite basis, and it is inevitable that in some cases these personnel will be third country nationals. If the business were unable to effect an inter-company transfer on this basis without obtaining a work permit, this is surely equally a discriminatory restriction likely to impede the business. In my view one could apply Article 52 in exactly the same way as Article 59. There was, however, no hint as to how such situations would be considered in the *Vander Elst* judgment, but there have been various recent developments.

SIMONE VEIL: HIGH LEVEL PANEL REPORT ON FREE MOVEMENT OF PERSONS

In March 1997 the High Level Panel on Free Movement of Persons, appointed by the European Commission and chaired by Simone Veil, presented its lengthy report to the Commission, setting out a series of concrete measures to ensure that individuals can take full advantage of their Treaty rights to free movement.

In relation to third country nationals the Panel recognised that the situation of third country nationals already legally resident in a Member State could be improved, irrespective of Member State's immigration policies. The Panel made a number of recommendations, for example, relating to visa requirements for third country national family members and to extend the situations in which third country national spouses of EEA nationals who work in a second Member State can pursue a professional activity on a self-employed basis.

However, more relevant to my talk today are the Panel's proposals in relation to workers covered by the *Vander Elst* principles. The Panel reported that the difficulties encountered by such firms are due to the burdensome, slow and extensive formalities imposed on them (e.g. the requirement that a worker should be employed for at least one or two years by the same undertaking before he is seconded) and that this type of procedure creates a *de facto* obstacle which undertakings might find difficult to overcome. The Panel recognised that such workers sent temporarily to another Member State to supply services do not in any way seek access to the labour market of the second State if they return to their first State after completion of their work, and therefore action should be taken to reduce the requirements imposed.

The Panel stated, "Whilst there is no question here of creating new rights for third country nationals as such, the Panel considers…that Community action should be undertaken to clarify the situation concerning the temporary presence of these workers in the Member State where the services are supplied and to try to reduce the obstacles facing their employer. The purpose of such a measure should be to strengthen the rights which Community employers derive from Community law… with particular reference to the handling of visa, residence and work permit problems."

On 12 November 1997 the Commission adopted a Communication to the

Council of Free Movement of Workers which contains an action plan following the Simone Veil Report, including improving the situation of third country nationals. It is also understood that the Commission is considering proposing a Directive to address the problems in implementing the *Vander Elst* principles in countries like Austria.

PROPOSAL FOR A CONVENTION ON RULES FOR THE ADMISSION OF THIRD COUNTRY NATIONALS TO THE MEMBER STATES

Finally, the Commission recently adopted a Proposal on a Convention concerning rules for the admission of third country nationals to the Member States. Whilst the Proposal does not create any automatic rights for admission, leaving individual decisions to be made by the Member States, it sets out very important, and certainly revolutionary, rules which must be applied by the Member States in deciding whether admission should be granted to establish a coherent framework for immigration from third countries.

The Convention is very wide-ranging, covering third country nationals who want to stay more than 3 months in a Member State for employment, self-employment, study, training, and non-gainful activity. It also creates rights for third country nationals' family members and a right for third country nationals who have been resident in a Member State long term to move to any other Member State to take employment. In fact, only asylum seekers are excluded from its ambit, although those granted refugee status with long term residence will be covered. As a general rule, the Proposal requires all applications for first admission to be made from outside the Community.

The provisions are very precise and include valuable rights in all categories. With particular reference to the subject of this chapter, in relation to establishment, admission for an independent economic activity may be granted if the individual has sufficient resources to undertake the activity which he/she wants to undertake and if the business will have a beneficial effect on the employment in the Member State in the initial period of leave granted, which will be at least 2 years. The article in the Convention concerning admission for third country nationals supplying services (where they are doing so on their own account, rather than as employees under the *Vander Elst* principle, which is not covered by the Convention), merely provides that implementing measures may be adopted. This, of course would have implications for the Community's commitments under the General Agreement on Trade in Services Annex to the World Trade Organisation Agreement.

According to the way the Proposal is drafted it will be more akin to an international treaty than European law and only those countries which ratify it will be subject to its terms. However, in the notes to the Convention the Commission advises that once the Amsterdam Treaty has come into force it will present the contents of the draft Convention as a Directive, which, if adopted, would obviously be a major step in terms of European immigration policy as a whole.

CHAPTER SIX

INTERNATIONAL MIGRATION AND CIVIL RIGHTS: THE DILEMMAS OF MIGRATION CONTROL IN AN AGE OF GLOBALISATION

Hans van Amersfoort

INTRODUCTION

The aim of this paper is to explore the dilemmas that arise out of the combination of two secular trends in the social and political development of those west European states which form the European Union.

The first trend has its starting point in the Enlightenment. It can be briefly described as the 'extension of rights' in theory and practice. Extension means in this context the inclusion on the base of equality of ever larger sections of the population into society. In practice it means in this context that these rights were no longer only formulated as 'ideals', as 'utopian landmarks' but were enacted in political institutions and laws. This development finds its political expression in the welfare states. All EU Member States belong to the family of welfare states. This does not mean that they are the same in every respect. As in every family there are dissimilarities along side the common family characteristics. In this chapter the focus is on the similarities, but I shall also have to point out some dissimilarities that are important with regard to the discussion.

The second trend is the growing population mobility in the world, particularly during the past decades. Several modern developments, in transport technology, in scale of economics, in growth of the world population, have contributed to the increase in migration flows. International migration affects all countries of the European Union. It is an important factor in their demographic development, it leads to cultural diversity, it has consequences for the functioning of labour markets and has an impact on the functioning of state financed welfare institutions such as schools and hospitals.

The political response to the growth in population mobility is ambivalent. We see on the one hand a positive attitude towards international migration reflected in measures to remove restrictions on population mobility and on the other hand we witness an outright negative evaluation leading to a search for more migration control. In the negative response immigration is seen as a threat to the welfare state. In every welfare state a balance has to be found between 'rights' and 'duties', between services provided and taxes collected. This balance is seen as in danger of becoming fundamentally upset by international migration processes, or at least by some of them, hence the political saliency in all EU Members States of the immigration issue.

It is the aim of this chapter to point out that this search for control over population mobility brings to a halt the further extension of civil rights and even threatens to reverse recent articulations of these rights.

In the second section the historical developments around citizenship and the articulation of rights, leading to the welfare state are briefly sketched. In the third section I will take a closer look at the relation between welfare states and immigration, especially at the paradoxes that have become visible when, after the oil crisis of 1973/74, immigration did not come to a halt, as expected, but actually increased. Consequently, I will describe the search for more effective intervention mechanisms in international migration flows. Finally I will come to some conclusions with regard to the intended and unintended effects of the migration policies of west European states.

I have not the aim to contribute to the already voluminous descriptive literature on migration development and migration control. I will of course use descriptive studies and examples, especially of the Dutch case which I know best, but it is not my pretension to offer the reader new descriptive material. The sole aim of this chapter is to point out the threats that the pressure for more migration control in an age of globalisation pose for the civil rights which we have become accustomed to see as cornerstones of a civil society.

CITIZENSHIP, CIVIL RIGHTS AND THE WELFARE STATE

State, Nation and Citizenship

In one of his essays that has been seminal to the idea's expressed in this section T.H.Marshall has remarked that it is difficult to find a definition of 'Welfare State', that satisfies both its friends and its enemies (Marshall, 1965: 238). This could be equally well said for the 'State' in general or for the 'Modern State'. However, essential characteristics are clear and have to be spelled out as far as they are relevant to this subject.

An essential process leading to the establishment of states as we now know them has been the amalgamation of government, territory and people. We are so used to see this trio as a unity that we tend to forget that this unit has come into being only relatively recently. Legitimate rule was up until quite recently based on dynastic rights, leading to entitlements and claims over often widely scattered territories. Non territorial organizations, especially the church had jurisdiction over certain kind of affairs, regardless the territorial jurisdiction. Peoples were expected to regard with due respect the overlords which the matrimonial policies of the ruling class had bestowed on them.

It was only late in the Middle Ages that patrimonial rulers started to rationalize the government of their realm. They created a class of modern bureaucrats, men with formal training whose duty it was to rationalize the administration and ground justice in clear procedures. The foundations of the modern state were laid by these servants of centralizing absolute power, who gradually ousted the aristocracy and the clergy from their administrative strongholds. It is ironical that once the absolute monarchs had succeeded in overcoming the territorial fragmentation and had amalgamated territory and government, the third factor, 'people' came to the fore. Once the logic of the dynastic rights and loyalties was questioned as a source of legitimate authority, the idea arose that sovereignty rested not in the ruler, but in the entity of territory and people. Hence we use the strange expression 'sovereign state'. The legitimation of authority was no longer based on the 'will of the king' but in the 'nation'.

States that claim to have their foundation in the will of the nation, are understandably in need of a definition of 'the nation'. In the ethnic conceptualization the nation is seen as a primordial given, as a deeply rooted entity characterized by common history, descent and destiny. A different way of conceptualization sees the nation as based on 'social contract'. In this line of reasoning citizens, who came together out of their free will to pursue their common interests founded the nation (Van Amersfoort, 1991, 1995). In German political thinking the ethnic conception has been dominant, the American tradition is dominated by the second ideology. Summarizing the arguments around the ideological foundation of the nation state we can say that there are two ways in which the link between people and state is conceptualized. The first can be paraphrased as: "The nation precedes the state." A historically already existing ethnic community organizes itself in a state. Membership of the nation is given by "the blood". We can call this the ethnic definition of the nation. The second way can be paraphrased as: "The state is the creation of free citizens". Membership is acquired by the will and the capacity to fulfil the rights and duties of a citizen. We can call this the contract definition of the nation.

Modern historians do not accept these visions as valid descriptions of the process of state formation. But that does not mean that they are not relevant for this discussion. They form part of the legitimation of the relation between state, nation and foreigner and have therefore great relevance for the legitimation of migration policies.

CIVIL RIGHTS AND SOCIAL RIGHTS

The legitimation of government by the will of the people made it necessary to find ways in which "the people" could express its political will. The first aspect of citizenship is therefore the right to take part in the process of decision making, the right to vote and being eligible for public office. In the process of democratization this aspect has been extended from a restricted circle of men to the whole adult population. It is clear however that this political aspect forms only part of the totality of 'rights'. The 'nation' has always been thought of as being more comprehensive than the electorate. In this sense we can distinguish between nationals and citizens, but the two words have become in fact synonyms. As we will see in the next section, with regard to migration policies the right of abode has become an even more fundamental aspect of citizenship than the right to vote. Marshall has distinguished two other types of rights, which have developed alongside the political rights (Marshall, 1965: 71–134). Civil rights are rights necessary for personal freedom such as liberty of person, freedom of speech, of faith, the right to own property and the right to justice. Social rights are described by Marshall as the right to a modicum of economic welfare and to live according to the standards prevailing in the society.

Civil rights are predominantly rights of 'non interference' by the state. They belong to the dawn of liberalism when the individual citizen sought protection against absolute rulers. The role of independent courts and the principle of equality before the law are crucial for an effective implementation of these rights. There is one more aspect that is not mentioned by Marshall, but relevant for the discussion of migration control mechanisms – this is the specification, and thereby limitation, of the competencies of state officials. Specification of roles has perhaps led to the horror of bureaucratic red tape, but it certainly has strengthened the position of individuals in their dealings with state officials.

It is important to note that what Marshall still described as aspects of citizenship have become extended much further. Civil rights are not only extended to all people remaining on the territory, regardless if they are considered to belong to the nation or not, but they are even extended beyond the territory. With the ratification of international conventions and treaties, such as the UN Convention relating to the status of refugees 1951 and the UN Convention on the Rights of the Child 1989, these rights are declared universal. States recognize them even out of their own territory and take on responsibilities in case of violations by other states or authorities. This is an amazing leap into the unknown as far as responsibilities are concerned and it is not surprising that the rhetoric of these extension of rights tends to run well ahead of practical implementation.

The social rights as described by Marshall differ in an important way from civil rights in so far as they are not about protection from state interference but instead give the individual a claim to positive state interference to secure the provision of facilities such as education, health care and housing. The implementation of these rights has as a logical consequence the transformation of the Nightwatch state into a Welfare State. Just as civil rights have been expanded beyond the boundaries of territory and citizenship, social rights are increasingly seen as 'universal human rights'. However the welfare states have been more cautious to take on responsibilities worldwide in this case. It is however important to note that in all welfare states 'legal residents' (non citizens) have been included in the civil and in the social rights. For this 'nearly citizenship status' of the legal permanent residents the term 'denizens' has been coined by Tomas Hammar (Hammar, 1990). In the case of illegal residents the situation is more complex as we shall see below on immigration control.

WELFARE STATES AND IMMIGRATION

Regulating Migration in Democratic States

The success of the nation state ideology and the stabilization of the state as the dominant institution regulating a growing number of fields of social interaction, made the distinction between *nationals* and *foreigners* increasingly relevant. Government for the people by the people contributed to the saliency of the divide between the insiders and the outsiders. In this process state frontiers became important barriers to population mobility. We have become accustomed to accept the assumption that 'international' migration is of a different order than 'internal' migration. Governments feel that they have the right if not the duty to regulate migration. Here we come up one of the paradoxes of state interference in present day population mobility. When a state prohibits its citizens from leaving the country, it is seen (at least in our Western democracies) as an infringement of the civil rights of its subjects. At the same time however the prohibition to enter a territory is seen as a perfectly normal legal measure.

To regulate migration democratic states have developed a construct of legality around entry, residence and work. Although all EU Member States use this construct there are substantial differences in the way it is applied in practice. The practice of migration regulation is the outcome of a combination of 'principles' and 'interests' and European states have not the same perception of what the principles in this respect are neither do they (always) define their interests in the same ways.

The principles we find directly back in the legal framework for the regulation of migration. The interests are more diffuse, they are defined in the ongoing discourse around migration and we find them back in the ways laws and regulations are applied in practice.

The first and paramount base for migration regulation is between 'citizens' *cq* 'nationals' and 'non citizens' or 'non nationals'. The most important aspect of citizenship in this regard is the right of abode. All EU Member States accepted this principle in the period after World War II, even when this consequence of citizenship status or definition of nationality had unforeseen and far reaching consequences. Only the UK has, for instance in the case of the Ugandan Asians, refused the automatic settlement of British citizens. In this regard we see an important distinction between the countries with an 'ethnic' conception of the nation and countries with a 'social contract' conception of the nation, mostly described as countries following *ius sanguinis* or *ius soli* respectively. Germany's policy with regard to the 'ethnic Germans' from Eastern Europe (the Aussiedler) has its base in the idea that 'Germanness' can not really be lost; just as it is almost impossible for 'foreigners' ever to become "real" Germans. This basic idea has resulted in very high numbers of immigrants from Eastern Europe and extremely low numbers of naturalization among immigrants settled in Germany, even among the second and third generation. France has always applied *ius soli,* the result of which is not only relatively high numbers of immigrants, from oversees 'departments', holding French citizenship but also regarding French citizenship as a matter of birthplace and culture. Recent changes of the law, under extremist political pressure, have not really changed this character. The Dutch have in this respect the same flexible attitude towards citizenship as the French, resulting in relatively high numbers of post colonial immigrants and a high number of naturalisations. An interesting difference is that the French actively recruited labour in their colonies whereas the Dutch never did this and have accepted (however reluctantly) the settlement of Eurasians and West Indians with Dutch citizenship as a consequence of their colonial past. The UK the former colonial power *par excellence*, has followed a somewhat different course in this respect (Cornelius et alii,1995; *Baldwin-Edwards* & *Schain*, 1994; Heckmann & Bosswick, 1994).

Just as we can say that citizenship implies the right of abode, being a foreigner implies that there is no automatic right of entry and settlement in a country other than one's own. That is not to say that foreigners cannot have a right, but this is always a 'negotiated' right. Such a right can be acquired in a personal capacity, such as a work permit or recognition as refugee. But such a right is also often the consequence of bilateral or multilateral agreements. States form an international system with subsystems. Within these, interstate agreements are made about the rights of the respective citizens on entry, residence and work. In our case the most obvious example is that of the European Union regulations with respect to the free movement of European citizens within the Member States. The actual implications of the rights of European citizens in the Member States are as yet not completely clear. The right of entry is not in dispute, but the right to reside and the social rights that may be claimed in this capacity are given different interpretations. The dissimilarities between the EU Member States in their conception of citizenship and the importance of citizenship for the entitlement to further rights still seems to be very large, even between neighbouring countries such as Germany and the Netherlands (see, for instance, the legal dispute around the rights of the Spanish woman, Martinez Sala, in Germany, Migration News Sheet, September 1997.)

Foreigners from countries outside the European Union immigrate under a great variety of regulations. An overview of commonly found headings of residence, gives a first orientation:

Visitors

These are not considered to be or to become residents, but only to stay for a limited period of time. Visitors are obliged to have valid papers (passports, in some cases visas) and sufficient resources, but are otherwise welcome. As visitors do not enter the migration statistics it would be possible to disregard them in a discussion of migration control. However, not all visitors behave as visitors: overstaying is a source of illegal residence. The regulations for visits have been modified in the past decades in an attempt to prevent 'prospective immigrants' from entering the country as 'visitors'. Here we are right on the border of migration policies.

Foreigners with a Temporary Residence Permit

This permit is valid for a restricted time, usually a year, and has to be renewed when it expires. This temporary status, however, cannot be lengthened indefinitely. In most countries temporary residence permits lead, where there is continued residence, to permanent residence permits. In the Netherlands, for example, further residence must either be refused after 5 years or permanent resident status granted. Other countries have similar regulations, in the end leading up to the status of permanent resident.

Permanent Residence Permit Holders

The status of permanent resident implies practically all civil rights and social rights. It is often described as 'denizen status' (Hammar,1990).

Refugees

Persons who are recognized as entitled to protection in accordance with the UN Convention relating to the status of refugees 1951 and its 1967 Protocol.

Asylum Seekers

People who have managed in one way or the other to enter the country and claim an entitlement to protection under the UN Convention relating to the status of refugees, but whose claim is still under consideration.

Tolerated Residents

Foreigners who come within no specific residence category, but whose residence has nevertheless to be accepted. For instance asylum seekers whose claim has been refused, but who can not be deported because of international complications or personal circumstances. This 'in between' status is now even institutionalized in most countries under labels such as 'Temporary Protection Status'.

Finally we have *'illegal residents',* who run the risk of being deported when detected.

This overview neglects niceties such as 'temporary dependent residence status' but reflects sufficiently the legal framework for the regulation of migration. These labels are the outcome of the legal construct that regulates entry, residence and work, for people not belonging to the nation. It is however clear that the practical application of these definitions is not always easy, as is demonstrated already by the existence of the category of 'tolerated persons'. The way the legal instruments are put into practice is influenced by the evaluations and perceptions of the general public, journalists, scholars and, finally, of the government of certain migration flows or certain migrants.

The actual implementation of laws and regulations depends on a general evaluation (rightly or wrongly) of the following consequences of immigration:

1. numerical consequences (does the country need more people ?)
2. economic consequences (is immigration contributing to our economy, or at least to sectors of it ?)
3. social consequences (what are the consequences for social housing programmes, the education system etc?)
3. cultural consequences (what are the consequences for our basic values and norms?)

The answers to these questions are rarely straightforward. For instance the Netherlands is preoccupied with being a densely populated country. The general notion is that there are already more than enough people, but this has had no effect on actual immigration policies that were either based on labour market needs or consequences of Dutch citizenship. Even when there is a general agreement that immigration should be regulated according the interests of society, it is not always easy to say what this interest is in a concrete case. A high level of unemployment, may still leave certain sectors of the economy in need of immigrant labour.

The construct of legality has as its unavoidable counterpart: illegality. The problem of illegal residence is politically very sensitive. In the general discussion of 'illegals' the term is often used in a simplistic way. It is important to note that 'illegals' do not form a single category. In relation to the construct of legality with regard to immigration we must at least distinguish between:

a. Illegal residents: people who have either entered the country illegally or who have overstayed the period permitted as a visitor or on the basis of a temporary residence permit;
b. Illegal workers: people who have entered legally, reside legally, but have no work permit (for instance tourists or students) and nevertheless enter the labour market.

From the point of control these are very different categories. Overstaying and illegal working are not affected by border control, however rigorously applied. Illegal working by immigrants is in many instances connected with the existence of a 'black labour' market, which is certainly not exclusively the domain of immigrant labour.

PARADOXES OF WEST EUROPEAN IMMIGRATION

The past decades have confronted the countries that form the European Union with the unsettling experience of continuous mass immigration. This experience did not fit into the way these countries saw themselves. They defined themselves rather as emigration than immigration countries. Only France from the European countries has from the nineteen century onwards regarded immigration as a salutary strengthening of its population. It regarded this demographic impulse as a necessary remedy against a low fertility rate and the population loss resulting from World War I. At the same time France was confident that all immigrants wished to become 'real Frenchmen' and could become so in the course of time by contact with the superior French culture. This 'assimilationist' assumption is not any longer accepted, not by all immigrant groups and certainly not by the French extreme nationalists united in the Front National.

What made it difficult for the EU countries to accept the reality that they had become immigration countries, was the coincidence of immigration with rising unemployment.

After the oil crisis of 1973/74 the west European countries had to restructure their economies, which caused a loss of jobs in particular in the sector of unskilled manual labour. At the same time the various migration flows, for different reasons gained momentum. This was not only against the common sense logic of the general public and politicians, it was also contrary to the classical migration literature in which developments in the labour market were seen as the motor and *ultimo ratio* of international migration processes. It has been in particular the development of immigration after the end of the demand of unskilled manual labour that has made immigration a political sensitive issue and forced the EU countries to come to terms with it. The policy with regard to immigration has evolved over time in the countries of the European Union mainly in direct response to actual situations. There was little long term planning, let alone that there was an idea that all these countries were confronted with basically similar, long term global developments. It is especially in the crisis around asylum seekers that the urge to come to a common migration policy at the EU level has become manifest. In general terms we can divide the immigration policies of the west European countries in three stages.

Limited Measures to Regulate a Temporary Phenomenon (Post World War II until 1975)

During the first post-war period European countries did not see immigration and the regulation of migration as an important field of policy making. The idea was that, when necessary, classical instruments such as work permits could be used to stop migration. An important element of the policy was the firm belief, stressed over and over again, that there were no immigrants, but only 'temporary foreign workers'. The most generally known example of this is of course the German word "Gastarbeiter', that has been taken over into other languages. But also in French and Dutch there existed a whole series of terms, the primary function of which was to avoid any association with immigration. As far as policy measures were taken to regulate the recruitment of labour, these were *ad-hoc* measures, responses to direct problems with regard to housing, health care, etc.

The Acceptance of Immigrants as a Permanent but Limited Phenomenon (1975–1990)

After 1975 it gradually became impossible to maintain that there were no immigrants, but only temporary 'foreign residents'. Nevertheless it remained more or less the official point of view of most European countries. Germany has never departed officially from this line, the Netherlands did reluctantly in 1983. In the mean time it became obvious that the immigrants were there to stay. This brought to the fore the question whether there was a need for a special policy with regard to the integration of the immigrant population into society. Some west European countries like Sweden and the Netherlands went pretty far in that direction, but no country could really neglect the presence of immigrant populations and their consequences for the wider society. However this development did not diminish faith in the state's capacity to guide migration processes. On the contrary we witness a further articulation of the classical control migration instruments to manage migration processes. We can (roughly) summarize the attitude of the west European countries as an acceptance of the immigration of the recent past and its consequences such as family reunion, but at the same time a determination to prevent further mass immigration in the future.

The Asylum Seekers Crisis and its Consequences (1990-Present)

The tremendous rise in asylum requests marks a break point in migration policy. The intensification of classical migration control instruments such as visa requirements, the introduction of new ones such as carriers' liability had not prevented the development of new immigration flows. The reaction to these unwanted flows of immigrants has been ambivalent, because measures to fence them off effectively were also contradictory to the ideology of liberal democracies and even of concrete international treaties such as the UN Convention relating to the status of refugees. In this period the ability of liberal democracies to intervene successfully in migration processes was seriously thrown into doubt, whereas at the same time political pressure to do so increased. The electoral success of parties that made the immigration issue the core of their political propaganda enhanced the moral panic of the parties of the democratic centre.

The attitude towards migration of the EU countries in this period has become highly ambivalent. On the one hand we see a firm belief that the flow of people, information, capital and goods is an asset for the further development of economies and societies. On the other hand immigration from the Third World and the former communist countries is seen as a threat to European welfare states. Migration regulations reflect this division into 'good' and 'bad' migration flows, between welcome and unwelcome immigrants.

Gould and Findlay have divided population mobility in the age of globalisation into three broad patterns: migration within the Third World, migration within the developed world, and migration from the Third World to the developed world (Gould & Findlay, 1996; Macura & Coleman,1994). This is obviously a very rough first classification. However for our purpose it has something to offer. This classification helps to explain why countries take measures to make migration easier, for EU citizens, for international student exchange, for staff members of Japanese firms and are at the same time building a growing control apparatus to hamper other population mobility. The 'good migration' contributing to economic growth is obviously thought to be the migration within the developed world, the 'bad migration', posing a threat to the very survival of the welfare state is obviously the migration from the less developed to the developed world (New Community,Vol.22 no.2; King, 1993 a; King 1993 b.;Miller, 1994; van Amersfoort & Doomernik, 1998).

IMMIGRATION CONTROL IN A GLOBALIZED WORLD

Introduction

The measures taken by governments to mange international migration and to curb unwanted migration flows have been analysed in several ways. A useful distinction has been made by Grete Brochmann into internal and external control mechanisms, even when there are measures which extend into both areas (Brochmann, 1993; 1998). External controls are measures taken to keep unwanted people out of the territory, internal control is directed at people already in the country, to detain them when found illegally residing, to prevent them from settling, bringing family members over and to induce them to return.

It is important to note that internal control measures are not always only aimed at immigrants, employers sanctions, for instance, are part of the wider social control thought to be necessary in a welfare state to prevent tax evasion, unhealthy work conditions etc.

The Expansion of External Control

In several ways governments have tried to prevent further immigration. Not all measures have been relevant in all countries of the European Union, nevertheless a general picture may be drawn.

Limitation of Citizenship and /or Citizenship Rights

Several governments have redefined citizenship rights with regard to unwanted immigrants. The UK has a whole well documented history of citizenship legislation primarily centred on the right of abode. The French have made the application of their *ius soli* tradition less automatic. The Dutch have persuaded Surinam to become a Republic with separate citizenship but failed to persuade the Antillian islands to do the same. The Germans are carefully trying to limit the unquestioned right of settlement of ethnic Germans of the countries of the former communist block. These redefinitions have or have had great consequences for the people involved. The main purpose is of course to make them subject to the same measures of migration control which apply to foreigners.

Extra-territorialization and Articulation

In the period 1975–1990 we have described above we see the regular expansion of external control. The measures taken can be characterized as extra-territorialization and articulation. In the process of extra-territorialization entry formalities are pushed away from the border to the embassies and consulates in the countries of origin. In the past such procedures could often be fulfilled at the border or in the country of residence. Turks living in Germany could apply for a work permit or visitors visa for the Netherlands in a Dutch consulate near their place of residence, nowadays such procedures have to be fulfilled in Ankara or Istanbul.

The articulation of control measures have put the work permit into a central place. Originally the work permit was not intended as an instrument for migration control, but as a mechanism to protect the working class from competition from outsiders. In the course of time a work permit and residence permit were made dependent on each other. At the same time a great number of 'risk' countries were brought under visa regulations that made it more difficult to visit family members or friends, or even just an academic institution in one's field of study.

The articulation of control measures in combination with extra territorialization was meant to prevent people from even coming to the border, let alone entering the territory. This aim was however not achieved. A great number of people still arrive at borders and airports without the necessary visas or documents, either because they were not well informed or because they have decided to take a chance.

Carrier Liability

To diminish the chance that people 'illegally' present themselves at the border a further measure was taken: carrier liability. The carriers were saddled with a responsibility which does not belong to their job. The travellers are confronted with a strange infringement of their civil rights. Why should anyone be obliged to show identity papers, visitor's visas, work permits etc. to whoever sits at that moment at the counter of a transport company ? It is amazing that this measure has become accepted so widely. Leaving aside the, in some situations, quite real opportunity for corruption, this form of control is also not effective. Really effective control of identity documents requires training and equipment, which is generally not even available to immigration officers, let alone to staff at airline counters. Forged documents are only rarely detected.

Restricting Asylum Rights

The measures mentioned so far were already taken in the period following the oil crisis. They contributed to the rise in asylum requests because this was almost the only way open to people who wanted to emigrate to do so within a legal construct. The other cause of the rise in asylum requests lies in the combination technical easy means for population mobility and the severe political tensions in countries such as Iran, Iraq, Somalia, Bosnia etc. To bring the asylum crisis under control we see the same measures taken as mentioned before but focused on asylum seekers. The introduction of the notion 'safe countries' or even 'passage through safe countries' in combination with the demand to be able to show valid papers, makes one wonder how anybody from countries such as Iraq can ever manage to make a valid request in the Netherlands or any other country of the EU for that matter. It comes often down to an infringement of the right to protection of refugees without formally retreating from the UN Convention relating to the status of refugees 1951 and the 1967 Protocol.

Trafficking of Migrants

Finally some words on the opaque subject of migrants as contraband. The trafficking of migrants who lack legal ways to migrate, seems to have come to a large extent into the hands of criminal organisations, with more or less close links to governments and organisations such as airlines. It is by no means clear how far migrants are the victims or the villains in the whole process of migrant smuggling. It is, however, clear that without cooperation of the governments of the sending societies there is little chance of success in blocking trafficking routes effectively.

THE EXPANSION OF INTERNAL CONTROL

The stepping up of external control measures did not achieve their objective. The flows of passengers is today simply to great to be controlled effectively, without great harm to economic sectors such as tourism and international transport. The costs in personnel and equipment are also more than states want or are able to pay for border control. Those are important reasons behind the wish to abolish those costly obstacles to the movement of persons and goods inside the European Union. Moreover illegal entry is only one source of illegal residence, just as illegal residence is only one of the factors in 'informal employment'. This has directed attention towards internal control.

Identity Control

The first form of internal control is of course the identification of 'illegals' and the detention of the trespassers. It has led in several countries to the formalization of personal identity papers and the obligation to show them.

The Limitation of Civil Rights

These measures have been aimed generally at permanent residents to limit their possibilities to bring over spouses and children. Germany has not only lowered the age limit for children eligible for family reunification with their parents, but also restricted the period during which the decision has to be taken to bring over the family or not. The Netherlands has taken only the first step. A specific measure to discourage immigration by internal control is the exclusion from the labour market during four years for spouses and two years for children after their settlement in Germany.

These measures are typically half way measures between internal and external control, they regard people in the country but are aimed at preventing people coming to the country. One motive behind these measures is to induce immigrants to return home. The assumption that making life difficult for immigrants would send a message out to deter others from coming and induce even settled immigrants to go home, is taken for granted by many policy makers. However this assumption seems to reflect more the hope of the politicians than statistically substantiated reality.

Exclusion from Society

Internal control measures that go even further than a limitation of civil rights are aimed at the rigorous exclusion of immigrants from social rights, at least so long as they are not legitimate permanent residents. The most known example of such a measure is of course Clause 187 in California. It is a tendency that runs counter the whole development of rights in welfare states, certainly fields of health care and education will not be brought under such restrictions without great resistance from the agencies which administer these institutions.

The tendency to exclude unwanted immigrants from society, when they cannot be excluded from the territory has become particularly visible in the asylum crisis after 1990. All EU governments have taken measures to exclude asylum seekers from society so long as their request is not decided upon, and this may take a very long time, often more than a year. The Netherlands, for instance, excludes them from the labour market and from meaningful schooling that would prepare them for life in the Netherlands.

Employer Sanctions

Finally we have to consider employer sanctions as a measure for internal control. Although not only aimed at illegal immigrants they are thought to be an important mechanism for migration management. In reality the role of the 'black labour market' in migration processes is not so clear. It is obvious that for people excluded from regular work the black labour market offers the only opportunity to stay alive in the long run. It is also obvious that the knowledge that there is a way to earn money may influence the decision to migrate, legally when possible, illegally when necessary. It is also obvious that the presence of a non-unionized reserve labour pool forms an asset for employers in the shadow economy. It is however not clear how far those factors in practice interact. It is, for instance, questionable if illegal immigrants are indeed a major factor in the 'informal labour force', which consists in any event of students, housewives, people on unemployment benefit, weekend workers etc.

This brings us back to the issue of the effectiveness of internal control measures. Making the identification system more uniform seems to be a general tendency. But it is questionable if those measures indeed lead to a greater number of expulsions, let alone that the more indirect aims of the internal control measures will be reached.

The Scandinavian countries have, for a long time, had the system of a personal number that is used throughout the administrative system. In the Netherlands such a system did not exist which made it impossible to link the various administrative systems. Over the years such an administrative system has now been developed. In the meantime a law is being prepared (Koppelingswet, "Linkage Law") which requires the inspection of various administrative systems to combine residence papers with entitlement to welfare benefits. An interesting point is that education has been left out of the original draft law, because it was contrary to the UN Convention on the Rights of the Child 1989, and school boards and headmasters had announced they would carry out a massive sabotage of this aspect of the law if enacted.

CONCLUSIONS

Summarizing the west European experience we can say that although more rigorous external control measures have been taken, the management of international population mobility has not really been successful. The lack of efficiency of external control and the marginal impact of the classical internal control mechanisms (identification, detention, expulsion) has led to a quest for internal control measures.

External control has already in some cases led to a violation of civil rights. Two points stand out in this respect: making procedures unduly complicated and difficult to fulfil and the power of persons with no official or state capacity to decide over identity papers, visas etc.

Internal control measures show even more severe infringements of what were thought to be civil and social rights. Restrictions on family reunification, exclusion from the labour market and even from more essential social services are certainly a break with the secular development of the extension of rights.

The moral foundation of the extension of rights is rooted in the whole concept of the welfare state. It is contrary to this concept that immigrant groups should develop into a marginalized sub-category, into what is sometimes called 'an underclass'. Such a development would not only be to the detriment of the immigrants and their descendants, but also to the detriment of society as a whole. Because permanently marginalized groups are likely to form sources of tension and conflict. The great danger of the intensification of external and internal control is that when these measures do not contribute to a more successful management of population mobility, they may well contribute to the coming into being of such an excluded underclass.

There is no easy way out of the dilemma of migration control in a globalized world. The two secular trends I have sketched in the introduction seem to have come to a cross-roads from where it is difficult to find the right way. Precisely because the way out seems difficult the pressure on politicians to advocate symbolic measures is great. In these circumstances I think that scholars, and particularly people engaged in the study and application of the law should point out the great dangers of the present course.

It is an inherent characteristic of the welfare state that it has to balance rights and duties, and this will become even more accute in the coming decades. It is, however, unfair and against the essential development of the extension of rights that certain groups, in this case immigrants are singled out and made the prime, symbolic object of this balancing act. I think it is essential if we want to preserve civil society as we have come to know it over the past decades, that civil rights of immigrants are respected. A necessary first step in that direction is a uniform European regulation of permanent residence status, which includes those settled immigrants as fully as possible in society, giving them the same rights to relocate inside Europe as 'true European citizens'.

REFERENCES

Baldwin-Edwards, Martin and Martin A Schain (ed) 1994, *The Politics of Immigration in Western Europe*, Frank Cass & Co, Ilford.

Brochmann, Grete, 1993, Control in immigration policies: a closed Europe in the making., in R. King (ed.), *The New Geography of European Migrations*, Belhaven Press, London, 100–115.

Brochmann, Grete, 1998, Controlling immigration in Europe: nation-state dilemmas in an international context, in Hans van Amersfoort & Jeroen Doomernik (ed.), *International Migration: Processes and Interventions,* Het Spinhuis, Amsterdam, 22–41.

Cornelius, Wayne A., Philip A. Martin and James F. Hollifield, (eds.) 1995, *Controlling Immigration, A Global Perspective,* Stanford University Press, Stanford.

Gould, W.T.S. and A.M. Findlay, (1996, 2nd pr.) *Population Migration and the Changing World Order,* John Wiley & Sons, Chichester, New York.

Hammar, Tomas, 1990, *Democracy versus the Nation State: Aliens, Denizens and Citizens in a World of International Migration*, Avebury, Aldershot.

Heckmann, F and W. Bosswick (eds), 1994, *Migration Policies: a Comparative Perspective*, European Forum for Migration Studies, Bamberg.

King, Russell (ed.),1993 a, *Mass Migration in Europe*, Belhaven Press, London.

King, Russell (ed.), 1993 b, *The New Geography of European Migrations*, Belhaven Press, London.

New Community, Vol. 22/2, 1996, Special Issue, New Migration in Europe: dilemmas of mobility and control.

Marshall, T.H. 1965, *Class Citizenship and Social Development*, Doubleday & Company, Garden City, New York.

Macura Miroslav and David Coleman (ed.) 1994, *International Migration: Regional Processes and Responses*, United Nations, Geneva.

Miller, Mark (ed.), 1994, Strategies for immigration control: an international comparison. *Annals the American Academy of Political and Social Science 534, July.*

Van Amersfoort, Hans, 1991, Nationalities, Citizens and Ethnic Conflicts: Towards a Theory of Ethnicity in the Modern State, in Hans van Amersfoort and Hans Knippenberg (ed.), *States and Nations,* Netherlands Geographical Studies no. 137, KNAG, Utrecht, Amsterdam, 12–29.

Van Amersfoort, Hans, 1995, Institutional Plurality: Problem or Solution for the Multi-ethnic State?, in Sukumar Periwal (ed.), *Notions of Nationalism*, Central European University Press, Budapest, London, 162–181.

Van Amersfoort, Hans and Jeroen Doomernik (ed.), 1998, *International Migration: Processes and Interventions,* Het Spinhuis, Amsterdam.

Chapter Seven

The Third Country Agreements: The Right to Work and Reside in the First Generation Agreements

Tim Eicke

Introduction

This chapter is concerned with a look back over the application of what has been referred to as "First Generation Agreements" despite the fact that the Agreements covered fall into two very distinct categories which do not, on their face, have very much in common at all.

The first of these categories is the Agreement establishing an Association between the European Economic Community and Turkey (EEC-Turkey Association Agreement) which was signed – more than thirty years ago – in Ankara on 12 September 1963[1]. This was designed to prepare Turkey for eventual accession to the European Community – a purpose expressly set out in its Preamble:

> "*Determined* to establish ever closer bonds between the Turkish people and the peoples brought together in the European Economic Community;[2]
>
> *Recognising* that the support given by the European Economic Community to the efforts of the Turkish people to improve their standard of living *will facilitate the accession of Turkey to the Community at a later date;"* (emphasis added)

The second category of Agreements is made up of the so-called "Maghreb" Co-operation Agreements concluded in 1976 between the EC and Tunisia[3], Algeria[4] and Morocco[5]. These latter agreements are far less ambitious and "only" seek to "maintain and strengthen their friendly relations in accordance with the principles of the United Nations Charter" and to "to promote ... economic and trade co-operation between Morocco and the Community and to provide a sound basis therefore in conformity with their international obligations.[6]

---

1 OJ 1973 C113/2.

2 This wording is surprisingly close to that in the Preamble to the EC Treaty "Determined to lay the foundations of an ever closer union among the peoples of Europe".

3 Co-operation Agreement between the European Economic Community and the Republic of Tunisia, signed in Tunis on 25 April 1976 – OJ 1978 L265/2.

4 Co-operation Agreement between the European Economic Community and the People's Democratic Republic of Algeria, signed in Algiers on 26 April 1976 – OJ 1978 L263/2.

5 Co-operation Agreement between the European Economic Community and the Kingdom of Morocco, signed in Rabat on 27 April 1976 – OJ 1978 L264/2.

6 Preamble.

It is important to note at the outset, that the European Court of Justice (ECJ) has expressly accepted that it has jurisdiction to interpret the (free movement) provisions of Association and Co-operation Agreements and any Additional Protocol thereto (adopted under Articles 228 and/or 238 EC Treaty) and any decisions of Association Councils made thereunder. The ECJ held that such agreements are such as to create "special, privileged links with a non-member country which must ... take part in the Community system."[7] This jurisprudence has been developed primarily in the context of the EEC-Turkey Association Agreement[8] and has since been extended – by reference to the EEC-Turkey Association Agreement jurisprudence – to the provisions of at least the Maghreb Agreements[9].

THE EEC-TURKEY ASSOCIATION AGREEMENT

When considering the EEC-Turkey Association Agreement it is always important to keep in mind the objective behind the Agreement as set out in the Preamble. It is in this context that it may be explicable that the EEC-Turkey Association Agreement has an almost unique feature amongst all the Association Agreements. Unlike any of the other (later) Association or Co-operation Agreements, it expressly links the "three freedoms" (freedom of movement of workers, freedom of establishment and freedom to provide services) to the respective provisions of the EC Treaty[10]. Articles 12, 13 and 14 of the Agreement expressly provide that "the Contracting Parties agree to be guided by ..." the relevant provisions of the EC Treaty[11]. The ECJ has expressly confirmed that "it is essential to extend, as far as possible, the principles enshrined in those Treaty articles to Turkish workers ...."[12] It is, however, clear that:

> "As the law stands now, however, Turkish nationals are not entitled to move freely within the Community but merely enjoy certain rights in the host Member State whose territory they have lawfully entered and where they have been in legal employment for a specific period."[13]

---

7 Case 12/86 *Demirel v Stadt Schwäbisch – Gmünd* [1986] ECR 3719, para 9.

8 See eg. Case 12/86 *Demirel v Stadt Schwäbisch-Gmünd* [1986] ECR 3719 at paras. 6 to 12; see also Case 30/88 *Greece v Commission* [1989] ECR 3711.

9 It is highly likely, though yet untested, that this approach will also apply to the provisions of the Europe Agreements with the countries of Central and Eastern Europe.

10 Article 9 of the Agreement furthermore provides for a prohibition "within the scope of this Agreement" of "any discrimination on grounds of nationality... in accordance with the principle laid down in Article 7 [now 6] of the [EC] Treaty".

11 Arts. 48 to 50, 52 to 56 and 55, 56, 58 to 65 EC Treaty respectively.

12 Case C-434/93 *Bozkurt v Staatssecretaris van Justitie* [1995] ECR I-1475, at paras. 14, 19 and 20; Case C-171/95 *Tetik v Land Berlin* [1997] ECR I-329, at para. 20 and Case C C-36/96 *Günaydin v Freistaat Bayern*, judgment of 30 September 1997, para. 21.

13 *Tetik*, para. 29 and *Günaydin*, para. 22, Case C-98/96 *Kasim Ertanir v Land Hessen*, judgment of 30 September 1997, para. 22.

The desire to achieve full freedom of movement for workers expressed in the Agreement was, however, further confirmed by the 1970 Additional Protocol to the EEC-Turkey Association Agreement[14]. This provides at Article 36 that the freedom of movement of workers

> "shall be secured by progressive stages in accordance with the principles set out in Article 12 of the Agreement of Association between the end of the twelfth and the twenty-second year after the entry into force of that Agreement."

ie between 30 November 1974 and 30 November 1986. This aim was to be achieved, at least in part, through decisions of the Association Council set up by the Agreement[15].

In *Demirel v Stadt Schwäbisch-Gmünd*[16], the ECJ, however, held that these provisions are essentially programmatic and therefore:

> "are not sufficiently precise and unconditional to be capable of governing directly the movement of workers."

This was partly justified by the fact that Article 36 provides that the Association Council has exclusive power to "decide on rules necessary to that end". The question of direct effect of Articles 12 and 36 is again the subject of a reference to the ECJ from the Immigration Appeal Tribunal where the ECJ is asked:

> "Did Article 12 of the Agreement ... become directly effective at the end of the transitional period (31 December 1993) in accordance with Article 36 of the Additional ... Protocol ... ?"[17]

In addition to the progressive achievement of freedom of movement of workers, Article 37 of the Additional Protocol further provides for a prohibition on discrimination on grounds of nationality in relation to "conditions of work and remuneration" between Turkish workers and those who are nationals of the EC Member States[18]. Though there is no case law directly applicable to Article 37, the ECJ jurisprudence in relation to virtually identical provisions

---

14 Signed in Brussels, 23 November 1970, OJ 1973 C113/18.

15 Arts. 22 and 23 Additional Protocol.

16 Case 12/86 [1986] ECR 3719.

17 *Secretary of State for the Home Department v. Mustafa Saglam*, reference from the IAT madein October 1997; AG Darmon in *Demirel* at para. 23 seems to suggest that "the passage of time ... has no legal implications. Progressive implementation depends on decisions of the Council of Association.
Any other solution would, indeed, be incompatible with the consensual nature of an international convention ..." – see also R. Plender QC in Vaughan, *Law of the European Communities Service,* at para. 15[61] citing the decision of the Court of Appeal in *R v Secretary of State for the Home Department ex parte Unal Nadir* [1990] 2 CMLR 233.

18 In this respect it differs slightly from the Co-operation Agreements and the Europe Agreements which prohibit discrimination with own nationals rather than with those of EC Member States.

in the EEC-Morocco Co-operation Agreement would suggest that Article 37 does have direct effect and can be relied upon by the individual in the courts of the Member States[19].

In order to achieve the principles laid down in Article 12 of the Agreement and Article 36 of the Additional Protocol, the Association Council adopted a number of Decisions. The first of these (of relevance to the issue of free movement of persons) was Decision 2/76[20] . Article 2 of Decision 2/76 provided for preferential rights of Turkish workers after three or five years of legal employment in a Member State[21]. The Decision further granted Turkish children "legally resident with their parents" the right of access to courses of general education[22]. Article 7 of Decision 2/76, for the first time, provided a standstill clause, preventing Member States from introducing new restrictions on the "conditions of access to employment applicable to workers legally resident and employed in their territory." However, the validity of Decision 2/76 was expressly limited to a duration of four years as from 1 December 1976, ie until 1 December 1980[23]. The only case law relating to Decision 2/76 relevant for present purposes is the decision of the ECJ in *Sevince*[24]. In that case the ECJ first held that the standstill clause in Article 7 did have direct effect and that the term "legal employment" in Article 2 of the Decision did not cover a situation where the only reason for the Turkish worker to be able to work legally was the fact that he benefited from the suspensory effect deriving from an appeal against a decision refusing him a right of residence. Though now irrelevant in the context of Decision 2/76, this judgment laid the basis for the now constant jurisprudence of the ECJ in relation to Decision 1/80.

The next relevant Association Council Decision is Decision 1/80 which, in the field of free movement, is probably the one Association/Co-operation instrument that has occupied the ECJ[25] the most. Out of Decision 1/80 Article 6 is the most litigated provision. This provides:

> " 1. Subject to Article 7 on free access to employment for members of his family, a Turkish worker duly registered as belonging to the labour force of a Member State:
>
> – shall be entitled in that Member State, after one year's legal employment, to renewal of his permit to work for the same employer, if a job is available;

19 See Case C-18/90 *Office national de l'empoi v Bahia Kziber* [1991] ECR I–199 at para. 22; see further below.

20 adopted on 20 December 1976.

21 Art.2.

22 Art. 1(2).

23 Art. 1(2).

24 Case C-192/89 [1990] ECR I-3461.

25 Mainly at the instigation of the German courts.

- shall be entitled in that Member State, after three years of legal employment and subject to the priority to be given to workers of Member States of the Community, to respond to another offer of employment, with an employer of his choice, made under normal conditions and registered with the employment services of that State, for the same occupation;
- shall enjoy free access in that Member State to any paid employment of his choice, after four years of legal employment."

In its judgments in *Sevince* and *Kus v Landeshauptstadt Wiesbaden*[26] the ECJ made clear that Article 6 of Decision 1/80 does have direct effect. The rights provided thereunder, however, only benefit those Turkish workers who fulfil the requirements of that provision:

1. Legal employment;
2. Duly registered as belonging to the labour force; and
3. The time requirement.

This approach by the ECJ is in direct contradiction to a whole series of earlier German decisions which had held that Turkish nationals do not derive any rights directly from the Agreement or provisions adopted thereunder[27]. This provision has been described a "further stage in securing freedom of movement for workers on the basis of Articles 48, 49 and 50 of the Treaty.". It is for that reason that the ECJ has stated that it is:

> "... essential to transpose, so far as possible, the principles enshrined in those Treaty articles to Turkish workers who enjoy the rights conferred by Decision No. 1/80."[28]

Article 6 does not expressly provide Turkish workers either with a right of entry or with a right of residence in EC Member States, but only with a right of renewal of his/her permit to work. Though the right to regulate the right of access, the first grant of a right of residence and the right to regulate access to the national labour market are retained by the individual Member States[29] once a Turkish worker fulfils the requirements of one of the indents of Article 6, his/her right to have his/her work permit renewed carries with it an automatic right of residence. As the EC stated in *Kus*:

---

26 Case C-237/91, ECR.

27 *VerwGH Baden-Württemnerg* [1982] NJW 676 and *BverwG* [1981] NJW 1919; see also C Vedder *Rechtswirkung von Assoziationasratsbeschlüssen – Die Kus-Entscheidung des EuGH* [1994] EuR 202.

28 See case C-434/93 *Bozkurt v Staatssecretaris van Justitie* [1995] ECR I-1475, at para. 20; Case C-171/95 *Tetik v Land Berlin* [1997] ECR I-329 at para. 20; Case C-98/96 *Kasim Ertanir v Land Hessen*, judgment of 30 September 1997, para. 21; Case C-36/96 *Günaydin v Freistaat Bayern*, judgment of 30 September 1997, para. 21.

29 *Kus*, para. 25; *Günaydin*, para. 23.

> "... even though that provision [Article 6(1)] governs the situation of the Turkish worker only with respect to employment and not the right of residence, those two aspects of the personal situation of a Turkish worker are closely linked and that, by granting to such a worker, after a specified period of legal employment in the Member States, access to any paid employment of his choice, the provision in question necessarily implies – since otherwise the right granted by it to the Turkish worker would be deprived of any effect – the existence, at least at that time, of a right of residence for the person concerned."[30]

The Member States, furthermore, do not have the power to "make conditional or restrict the application of the precise and unconditional rights which Decision No. 1/80 grants to Turkish nationals who satisfy its conditions"[31] eg. by issuing residence permits or work permits "restricted to temporary paid employment by a specific employer and prohibiting that person from changing his employer within the Member State concerned."[32] Nor are the rights subject to any condition connected with the reason for which the right to enter, work or reside was initially granted[33]. A worker cannot therefore be denied his/her rights under Article 6 because he/she "allegedly stated that he wished to pursue his professional career in his country of origin after being employed for several years in the host Member State with a view to perfecting his vocational skills and that he initially accepted the restriction placed upon his permit to reside in that State"[34] or because he/she initially entered as the spouse of a national. The only exception to this is where the national court finds that he/she made such statement "with the sole intention of inducing the competent authorities to issue the requisite permits on false premises"[35]. The provision of Article 6(3)[36] does not affect this position. Article 6(3) merely provides that Member States may adopt such national legislation as may be required to give effect to the rights of Turkish workers under Article 6(1) and (2)[37].

The concept of *legal employment* "is a concept of Community law which must be defined objectively and uniformly in the light of the spirit and the purpose of the provision"[38]. According to the case law of the ECJ, legal employment, though not conditional upon the possession of a properly issued residence permit, presupposes a "stable and secure situation as a member of the labour force"[39]; this implies the existence of an undisputed right of

---

30 Para. 29, see also *Sevince* para. 29, case C-355/93 *Eroglu* [1994] ER I-5113; Case C-434/93 *Bozkurt* [1995] ECR I-1475 and *Günaydin.*

31 *Sevince* para. 22l *Kus* para. 31 and *Günaydin*, para. 39.

32 *Günaydin*, para. 35.

33 *Kus*, paras. 21 to 23; *Günaydin*, para. 52.

34 *Günaydin* paras. 54 and 57.

35 *ibid*, para. 60.

36 "The procedures for applying paragraphs 1 and 2 shall be those established under national rules."

37 *Ertanir*, para. 30.

38 *Ertanir*, para. 59.

39 *Sevince* para. 59.

residence[40]. The ECJ has made clear that administrative documents issued by the authorities of Member States only constitute evidence of the existence of the rights enjoyed by Turkish workers and cannot constitute a condition for their existence[41]. The following do *not* fulfil the requirement of legal employment:

- Those who benefit from the suspensory effect deriving from an appeal against a decision refusing a residence permit[42];
- Those who benefit from a retroactive suspension (ordered by a court) of a decision refusing a residence document[43].

These "exclusions" are justified on the basis that they are "effective only for the duration of the proceedings and has the effect of allowing the person *who initiated them* to remain and work on a provisional basis pending a finale decision on his right of residence."[44]

> "The reason for which, ..., the Court declined to regard as periods of legal employment those completed while the decision refusing the person concerned the right of residence was suspended as a consequence of proceedings brought by him against the decision was to prevent a Turkish worker from being able to contrive to fulfil that condition ..."[45]

- Those who have been employed in a Member State under a residence document issued to them as a result of fraudulent conduct "in respect of which they have been convicted"[46].

The fact that under the national legislation a residence and/or work permit was expressed to have been merely provisional or conditional does not, in principle, affect the legality of the worker's employment[47].

In order for a worker to have been *duly registered as belonging to the labour force* it is important to ascertain whether:

- The legal relationship of employment can be located within the territory of the Member State; or whether
- It retains sufficiently close links with that territory (this is for the national court to decide taking into account *inter alia* where the Turkish worker was hired, the territory on which his paid employment was based and the applicable legislation in the field of employment and social security law)[48].

---

40 Case C-285/95 *Suat Kol v Land Berlin*, judgment of 5 June 1997, para. 21.

41 Case C-434/93 *Bozkurt v Staatssecretaris van Justitie* [1995] ECR I-1475, at para. 30.

42 *Sevince.*

43 *Kus* para. 13.

44 *Kus* para. 13, emphasis added.

45 *ibid.* para. 15.

46 *Stuat Kol*, para. 29.

47 *Ertanir*, paras. 54 to 59.

48 *Bozkurt*, paras. 22 and 23; in setting down these criteria, the ECJ applied its own judgment in Case 9/88 *Lopez de Veiga v Statssecretaris van Justitie* [1989] ECR 2989 relating to Regulation 1612/68; see also *Günaydin*, para. 29; *Ertanir*, para. 39.

Once these criteria have been fulfilled, the courts will then have to ascertain, whether:

- the worker is bound by an employment relationship covering a *genuine and effective economic activity* pursued for the benefit and under the direction of another person for remuneration[49].

Where a worker voluntarily leaves his/her employment after four years of legal employment in order to seek new employment he/she may not be treated as having definitively left the labour force of the Member State. In case he/she is unable to secure such new employment immediately he/she will remain a member of the labour force:

> ... only in so far as the person who finds himself without employment satisfies all the formalities that may be required in the Member State in question, for instance by registering as a person seeking employment and remaining available to the employment authorities of the State for the requisite period."[50]

This also makes it possible to ensure that the worker is not abusing his/her right of residence and is genuinely seeking new employment.

By contrast, where a worker is permanently prevented from ever engaging in subsequent employment (be it by reason of an accident at work or otherwise) or has reached retirement age he/she is to be regarded as having definitively ceased to belong to the labour force of that Member State and the right of residence which he/she seeks therefore has no connection with paid employment, even in the future[51]. In the absence of any specific provisions conferring such rights on Turkish citizens[52], they cease to enjoy a right of residence under Article 6 of Decision 1/80.

Article 6(1) makes the enjoyment of the rights thereunder dependent upon certain *time requirements.*

The first indent provides that after *one year's* legal employment, the Turkish worker is entitled to a renewal of his/her work permit "for the same employer", and therefore to an extension of his/her residence permit. The one year requirement has been interpreted to be fulfilled only where the worker has completed one year's uninterrupted legal employment with the same employer[53]; ie where the worker changes employer before completion of one year's legal employment with that employer, the requirements of the first indent will only be fulfilled after he/she has spent one years legal employment with another employer.

The first indent will, furthermore, only be applicable where the worker seeks an extension of his/her work permit/residence document "in order to

49 Case C-98/96 *Kasim Ertanir v Land Hessen*, judgment of 30 September 1997, para. 43; *Günaydin*, para. 31.

50 *Tetik*, para. 41.

51 *Bozkurt*, paras. 38 and 39; *Tetik*, para. 45.

52 Such as eg Regulation 1251/70 or Directive 75/34 in relation to EC nationals.

53 Case C-386/95 *Süleyman Eker v Land Baden-Württemberg*, judgment of 29 May 1997.

continue working for the same employer after the initial period of one year's legal employment"[54]. It is therefore not possible under the first indent to change employers after the first year of legal employment and then seek an extension of the work permit in order to work for the first employer again. The ECJ has stated that this would allow the worker the benefits of the second indent without fulfilling the three year requirement and would deprive EC workers of the priority enjoyed by them under the second indent.

The second indent provides that the Turkish worker may, after three years legal employment (and subject to priority given to EC workers) change employers and respond to another offer of employment "for the same occupation".

The third indent provides that after *four years* legal employment, the worker "shall enjoy free access ... to any paid employment". This includes "the unconditional right to seek and take up any employment freely chosen by the person concerned"[55]. In so holding the ECJ made express reference to its decision in *Antonissen*[56]. This right to seek employment entails that the Turkish worker must be able:

> "... for a reasonable period, to seek effectively new employment in the host Member State and must have a corresponding right of residence during that period, notwithstanding the fact that he himself terminated his previous contract of employment without entering immediately into a new employment relationship."[57]

It is for the Member States to determine the length of a "reasonable period" though it must not be so short as to deprive the right accorded by the third indent of its substance by jeopardising, in fact, the worker's prospects of finding new employment[58]. The ECJ held that "a period of a few days ... is in any event inadequate to allow him effectively to seek new employment."[59]

Under Article 6(2), when calculating the periods of legal employment, absences by reason of:

1. Annual holidays;
2. Maternity;
3. Accidents at work; or
4. Short periods of sickness;

are to be treated as periods of legal employment. Though periods of "involuntary unemployment duly certified by the relevant authorities" and "long absences on account of sickness" do not count as periods of legal

54 Case C-355/93 *Hayriye Eroglu v Land Baden-Württemberg* [1994] ECR I-5113, para. 13.
55 Case C-355/93 *Hayriye Eroglu v Land Baden-Württemberg* [1994] ECR I-5113, para. 13.
56 Case C-292/89, [1991] ECR I-745.
57 *Tetik*, para. 30.
58 *ibid.* paras. 32 to 34.
59 *ibid.* para. 34.

employment, Article 6(2) requires that they "shall not affect rights acquired as a result of the preceding period of employment.". This means that a Turkish worker who returns to work after involuntary unemployment or long term illness does not have to "start again" in order to achieve the required periods of legal employment under Article 6(1)[60].

Where a worker is without a valid residence and/or work permit for no more than a few days and each time received a permit, the validity of which was (at least on some occasions) with retroactive effect to the expiry date of the previous permit, this does not affect the calculation of the period of legal employment under Article 6(1)[61].

Family members of a Turkish worker "duly registered as belonging to the labour force of a Member State, *who have been authorised to join him*" are entitled to:

- Respond to any offer of employment after they have been legally resident in that Member State for "at least three years" (subject to priority given to EU citizens);
- Free access to any paid employment of their choice provided they have been legally resident for at least five years.

The rights thereunder are therefore dependent solely on the length of residence and no other criterion. In calculating the period of residence: holidays or family visits in the country of origin as well as time (less than 6 months) spent in his/her country of origin for reasons beyond his/her control are to be taken into consideration.

This provision has been described as

> "... designed to create conditions conducive to family unity in the host Member State, first by enabling family members to be with a migrant worker and then by consolidating their position by granting them the right to obtain employment in that State.
>
> In view of its meaning and purpose, that provision cannot therefore be interpreted as merely requiring the host Member State to have authorised a family member to enter its territory to join a Turkish worker without at the same time requiring the person concerned to continue actually to reside there with the migrant worker until he or she becomes entitled to enter the labour market.
>
> Such an interpretation would not only seriously undermine the objective of family unity pursued by that provision but would also entail the risk that Turkish nationals might evade stricter requirements of Article 6 by abusing, in particular by entering into sham marriages, the favourable conditions contained in the first paragraph of Article 7"[62].

---

60 *Tetik*, para. 39.

61 *Ertanir*, paras. 67 to 68.

62 Case C-351/95 *Selma Kadiman v Freistaat Bayern* [1997] ECR I-2133, paras. 36 to 39.

Article 7 therefore requires that the family member must in principle reside with the Turkish worker "uninterruptedly" during those three years[63]. The requirement of cohabitation will only not apply where there are objective circumstances justifying the failure to cohabit; eg. excessive distance between worker's residence and place of employment/vocational training establishment attended by the family member.

Children of Turkish workers who have completed a course of vocational training in their host country may "respond to any offer of employment there"[64], irrespective of their length of residence. The only prerequisite for the enjoyment of this right is that one of their parents must have been legally employed in that Member State for at least three years. Again this right is independent of the purpose for which the right to enter was initially given. A Turkish graduate of a German university was therefore held to have been entitled to rely on Article 7(2) in order to respond to any offer of employment and to have her residence permit extended for that purpose[65]. The ECJ is currently seized of a case, in which the extent of this provision is at issue. In *Haydar Akman v Oberkreisdirektor des Rheinisch-Bergischen-Kreises*[66] the issue before the Court is whether a Turkish child who has completed a course of vocational training can benefit from this provision where the parent has already returned to Turkey.

Article 9 of Decision 1/80 further extends the right provided by Decision 2/76 that children residing legally with their parents, who have been legally employed in a Member State, are to be admitted to courses of general education. Unlike Decision 2/76, this right is, however, further extended to cover apprenticeships and vocational training. Access to these facilities must be given subject to the same educational entry requirements applicable to nationals of that Member State.

In Decision 3/80, the Association Council sought to make provision for the application of the social security schemes of EC Member States to Turkish workers and members of their family. This is done mainly by reference back to EC Regulation 1408/71. This Decision, which does not state its date of entry into force, entered into force on the day of its adoption, 19 September 1980[67].

The ECJ, in its judgment in *Taflan-Met*, has held that:

> "... even though some of its provisions are clear and precise, Decision No. 3/80 cannot be applied so long as supplementary implementing measures have not been adopted by the Council."[68]

---

63 See by contrast the ECJ's judgment in case 267/83 *Diatta v Land Berlin* [1985] ECR 567, where the Court held that there can be no requirement of permanent cohabitation between EC nationals exercising their right to freedom of movement and their spouses (with reference to Article 11 of Regulation 1612/68).

64 Article 7, second sentence.

65 *Eroglu*, para. 23.

66 Case C-210/97.

67 Case C-277/94 *Taflan-Met v Bestuur van de Social Verzekeringsbank* [1996] ECR I-4085, para. 21.

68 *ibid.* para. 37.

In coming to this conclusion the ECJ referred both to Regulation 574/72, implementing Regulation 1408/71 and a Commission proposal for the implementation of Decision 3/80 submitted to the Council on 8 February 1983 but not yet adopted[69]. For that reason, Articles 12 (invalidity benefit) and 13 (Old Age and death (pensions)) were held not to have direct effect.

RIGHT OF ESTABLISHMENT

In the context of the right of establishment and/or services, Article 41 of the Agreement provides that:

> "The Contracting Parties shall refrain from introducing between themselves any new restrictions on the freedom of establishment and the freedom to provide services." (and the progressive abolition of restrictions on those freedoms.)

Though there is no case law directly applicable to Article 41 and whether it has direct effect or not, the ECJ, in *Sevince v Staatssecretaris van Justitie*[70], held that similar standstill clauses in Association Council Decision 2/76 and 1/80 do have direct effect.

The English High Court (McCullough J) has just referred the question of whether Article 41 is directly effective to the ECJ[71]. In this reference the Court is seeking to establish whether the operation of Article 41 requires the UK to apply the Immigration Rules as at 1 January 1973[72] to an application made in 1994 and prevented it from imposing additional restrictions on Turkish nationals through subsequent amendments to the Immigration Rules.

THE MAGHREB CO-OPERATION AGREEMENTS[73]

These agreements, unlike the EEC-Turkey Association Agreement or the Europe Agreements, were never intended to prepare Algeria, Tunisia and/or Morocco for eventual membership of the EC. All three agreements have a small chapter headed "Co-operation in the Field of Labour" which is in virtually identical terms. This includes two important nondiscrimination provisions: in relation to working conditions and remuneration and in the field of social security.

---

69 OJ 1983 C 110/1.

70 Case C-192/89, [1990] ECR I-3461.

71 *R v Secretary of State for the Home Department ex parte Abdulnasir Savas*, CO/1753/96, Order of 27 August 1997.

72 Date of UK accession to the EC.

73 These Agreements have now been replaced by new agreements with Morocco and Tunisia which entered into force on 1.3.98. The provisions on non-discrimination remain in substance the same as the earlier agreements.

Article 40 of the EC-Morocco Co-operation Agreement provides

> "The treatment accorded by each Member State to workers of Moroccan nationality employed in its territory shall be free from any discrimination based on nationality, as regards working conditions or remuneration, in relation to its own nationals."

Article 41 of the Morocco Agreement provides for a prohibition of discrimination on grounds of nationality against Moroccan workers and their family *in the field of social security*. It is in this area that the ECJs case law is the most developed.

In the case of *Hallouzi-Choho* the ECJ stated that:

> "... the principle laid down in Article 41(1) of the Agreement, of freedom from any discrimination based on nationality in the field of social security against Moroccan and members of their family living with them in relation to nationals of the Member States in which they are employed means that the person referred to by that provision must be treated as if they were nationals of the Member State concerned.
>
> ... so that the national legislation at issue cannot impose upon those persons more or stricter conditions than those applicable to nationals of that Member State"[74].

It was therefore contrary to the principle of non-discrimination, not only to impose a nationality requirement but also to impose a requirement of residence longer than that applicable to nationals or a requirement of pursuit of a professional or trade activity which nationals did not have to fulfil. In its recent decision in *Babahenini v Belgium*[75] the ECJ further held that the application of a provision that the person applying for the social security benefit in question [here: the spouse of a retired Algerian national] must be engaged in a trade or profession where no such condition is imposed on nationals is incompatible with the prohibition of discrimination on grounds of nationality.

In *Kziber*[76] the ECJ, following its judgment in *Demirel*, states expressly that both the provision in relation to social security and those in relation to working conditions and remuneration (with which the Court was not directly concerned) are clear, precise and unconditional in its terms and therefore directly effective[77]. Furthermore, the Court held that in the field of social security the provision in the Co-operation Agreement "must be deemed to be analogous with the identical term"[78] used in the related EC provision and

---

74 Case C-126/95 *A. Hallouzi-Choho v Bestuur van de Sociale Verzekweingsbank*, judgment of 3 October 1996, paras. 35 and 36.

75 Judgment of 15 January 1998.

76 Case C-18/90 *Office national de l'emploi v Bahia Kziber* [1991] ECR I-199.

77 *ibid.* paras. 21 to 22; see also Case C-58/93 *Zoubir Yousfi v The Belgian State* [1994] ECR I-1353, para. 18 – where the ECJ confirmed its position despite an invitation by the German government to review its case-law; Case C-103/94 *Zoulika Krid v CNAVTS* [1995] ECR I-719, para. 21; Case C-126/95 *A Hallouzi-Choho v Bestuur van de Sociale Verzekeringsbank*, judgment of 3 October 1996, para. 19.

78 *Yousfi*, para. 24, Kziber, para. 25.

"cannot receive a definition different to that indicated in the context" of that provision, in that case in Regulation 1408/71[79]. In its judgment in *Babahenini* the ECJ confirmed that *ratione materiae* the provisions are identical to those of Regulation 1408/71. However, the Court also made clear that *ratione personae* these provisions are *not* the same as those of Regulation 1408/71, in that they apply irrespective of the distinction drawn under Regulation 1408/71 between the derived rights and the personal rights of members of the migrant worker's family[80].

The Court also defined "worker" in the social security provision as "both active workers and those who have left the labour market after reaching the age required for receipt of an old-age pension or after becoming the victims of the materialisation of one of the risks creating entitlement to allowances falling under other branches of social security"[81] and therefore includes those incapable of working following an industrial accident[82]. In *Krid*, the ECJ held that this provision also applied to those members of the family of a Moroccan worker who continue to live in the Member State in which he was employed after his death and could be invoked by them directly[83]. In *Hallouzi-Choho*, this Principle was also applied to those members of the family, living with the worker who now received an old-age pension after having pursued a professional or trade activity there.

In *Kziber* the above criteria led the Court to find that where a family member of a Moroccan worker, living with him, who fulfilled all the criteria for eligibility to *unemployment allowance*, may not be refused such allowance on the grounds of his nationality. In *Yousfi* the applicant, on the basis of this provision was held to be entitled to *disability benefit* [84]. In *Krid* the provision was held to cover a *supplementary allowance paid to recipients of survivor's pension* paid by the French State to its own nationals. In *Hallouzi-Choho* it applied to *transitional benefit under the Dutch old-age pension regime.*

Working Conditions: There is no ECJ case law (yet) addressing the effect of this provision for Maghreb workers. It seems clear, however, from the case law on the EEC-Turkey Association Agreement that Article 40 does not create either a right of entry to a Member State[85] nor a right of access to employment for a Moroccan national resident in a Member State.

---

79 In *Krid* the Court stated "must be deemed to bear the same meaning as the identical term used in Regulation No 1408/71.", para. 32; In *Hallouzi-Choho*, the Court stated "must have the same meaning as the identical term used in Regulation No 1408/71", para. 25.

80 *ibid.* para. 24 with reference to *Krid* at para. 39 and Case C-308/93 *Bestuur van de Sociale Verzekeringsbank v Cabanis-Issarte* [1996] ECR I-2097.

81 *Kziber*, para. 27.

82 Case C-58/93 *Yousfi*, para. 23.

83 *Krid*, paras. 30 and 39 (refusing to follow its jurisprudence under 1408/71 about the distinction between derived rights and personal rights).

84 See also *Babahenini* at para. 27.

85 See *R v Secretary of State for the Home Department, ex parte Benhade* (Auld J; 21 June 1994) and *Najia Bent Ahmed Abidi v Secretary of State for the Home Department* [1994] ImmAR 532, CA.

It is yet to be decided how far this provision provides a (continued) right of residence to those Moroccan workers who are both lawfully present in a Member State and who have a subsisting employment relationship. In December 1996, an Immigration Adjudicator referred a set of questions to the ECJ seeking to ascertain whether the *de facto* termination of such an employment relationship by virtue of a non-renewal of leave to remain constituted "discrimination ... as regards working conditions"[86]. Based on ECJ case law in relation to time limits on employment contracts with nationals of other EC Member States[87] the first question asks whether the term "working condition" includes "security of such employment for the duration of such employment as freely determined between the employer and the employee (ie. length of employment) and the benefits arising from such security, such as career structure providing the possibility of promotion, vocational training and pay and retirement pensions commensurate to the seniority of the Applicant."

Support for this approach was derived from *inter alia* Alcantara J in the Supreme Court of Gibraltar[88], who held that:

> "... a Moroccan worker in Gibraltar has the same rights as say a Spanish or Danish worker, but a Moroccan national has no equal rights to those of a Spanish or Danish national. The rights of Moroccan worker arise after he has been accepted as such ...."[89]

However, as the Adjudicator pointed out in his reference: what would be the advantage or benefit conferred upon Moroccan nationals in employment which they did not enjoy already under the law of all jurisdictions in the UK if a narrow construction was applied to the provision on working conditions.[89]

---

86 Case C-416/96 *Nour Eddline El Yassini v Secretary of State for the Home Department.*

87 eg Case C-272/92 *Spotti v Freistaat Bayern* [1994] ECR I-5185.

88 *R v Director of Labour and Social Security ex parte Amimi Mohammed* [1992] 3 CMLR 481.

89 The Hessischer Verwaltungsgerichtshof in a judgment of 14 August 1995, InfAuslR 1/96 at p. 11 held that the Co-operation Agreement does not contain any provisons affecting questions of right of entry, access to the labour market, extension of residence permits and/or other aspects of the residence status of Moroccan workers.

Chapter Eight

Citizenship Rights and Migration Policies: The Case of Maghrebi Migrants in Italy and Spain

Joanna Apap

Introduction

In recent years, there have been significant changes in policies at national level towards labour migrants from the Maghreb in two new receiving states – Italy and Spain. Until the late 1970s, both countries were significant countries of emigration, and although both served as passageways to Northern Europe for migrants coming from North and sub-Saharan Africa, the need for immigration, rather than emigration policy, was highly limited. From the early 1980s onwards, however, with the tightening of visa restrictions in Northern Europe, coupled with an increase in prosperity in Southern Europe, both Italy and Spain have become receiving countries for long-term migrants. In response, by 1985–86, both countries had begun to develop legislation with respect to immigration into their territories. This legislation was initially quite similar, and appeared to be driven by a desire to match evolving policy at an European level under the Schengen Agreement. More recently, though, legislation has evolved in different ways in the two countries, reflecting somewhat different patterns of immigration, and different local circumstances. In this sense, Spain and Italy provide an interesting case study, in which the relative strength of policy driven by European harmonisation on the one hand, and local and national factors on the other, can be compared.

The focus of this chapter is mainly centred upon policy as it concerns labour immigration from the Maghreb countries (Morocco, Algeria and Tunisia). Not only do Maghrebi migrants constitute a high absolute number and percentage of immigrants currently residing and working in the EU – about 2.5 million according to the European Commission[1] – but also migration from the Maghreb region has continued to increase in the 1990s. In part, this increase is due to an increase in poverty, unemployment and an uncurbed boom in population growth, which have increased the pressure to emigrate from the Maghreb region. In turn, although there has been an increase in female education and family planning, and the birth rate has already started to stall slightly, a significant fall in birth rates is still unlikely in the next few years, even if it will not increase at the high rate predicted

---

1 Commission for the European Communities (1994) Communication from the Commission to the Council and the European Parliament on "Strengthening the Mediterranean Policy of the European Union: Establishing a Euro-Mediterranean Partnership" in *COM (94) 427 final*, Brussels, p 28.

by some authors[2]. In contrast, it is certainly true that political, religious and ethnic conflicts have led to a worldwide increase in forced migration. This is particularly relevant in the case of Algeria, which has been a significant source of migrants to Spain and Italy. Nonetheless, forced migration does not account for the majority of migrants in either country [3] whilst there is little evidence that the proportion of forced migrants is increasing.

In this context, the main concern here is with policy towards legally resident migrant workers in the EU, and their families. This does not imply that the position of illegal immigrants, or of non-working migrants, is insignificant. Indeed, illegal immigrants, who enter receiving countries either clandestinely (on boats, through mountain pathways, etc.) or by overstaying their tourist or student visas, have had a significant impact on immigration policy development. However, whilst some attention has been paid in the academic literature to new arrivals of migrants[4], of whom clandestine migrants are clearly an important part, much less attention has focused on the position of those who have remained in southern European countries for a longer time period. And yet it is this move towards the establishment and settlement of immigrants that is perhaps most important in terms of a transition from 'country of emigration' status, to being a 'country of immigration'. In turn, it is the position of legally resident migrant workers that has perhaps been most significant in the development of European policy towards migrants, a policy based on principles of free movement of persons within the Community, equal treatment under the law and social justice – including combatting social exclusion.

DEFINING THE TERMS 'IMMIGRANT' AND 'IMMIGRATION'

The term immigrant is at times used in the very broad sense of its root-word – *migrant,* who is a person who moves from one country to another. However, a discussion of immigration policy development requires a more robust

---

2 Collinson, S (1993) – *Beyond Borders: West European Migration Policy Towards the 21st Century,* London, Royal Institute of International Affairs; Collinson, S. (1996) *Shore to Shore – The Policies of Migration in Euro-Maghreb Relations,* London, The Royal Institute of International affairs p 35; Lopez Garcia, B (1990) L'Espagne entre le Maghreb et l'Europe: imaginaire et interferces de l'opinion dans la politique Maghrebin de l'Espagne, *Annuaire de l'Afrique du Nord,* pp 23–37. Moisi D in Glen St J Barclay (1995) The European Union and the Maghreb: A Clash of Civilisations? In *Australia and World Affairs,* (25, winter issue, p 5 – 17).

3 Commission of the European Communities, (1991) Immigration of citizens from third countries into the southern Member States of the European Community in *Social Europe,* Brussels, Supplement 1/91, p 25 (Dr M Werth, project co-ordinator).

4 Tapinos, G (ed) *Immigracion e Integracion en Europe,* Barcelona: Fundacion Paulino Torres Domenech; Collinson, S (1996) *Shore to Shore – The Politics of Migration in Euro-Maghreb Relations,* London, The Royal Institute of International Affairs, p 35.

definition of the group this policy is aimed at, whilst at the same time, the nomenclature used is also quite revealing of the nature and purpose of policy development. For the purposes of this paper, an *'immigrant'* is therefore defined as someone who moves to another country and resides there for more than three months. In the case of non-EU nationals, this represents a cut-off point, beyond which a residence permit is required in most EU countries[5]. Within this group, it is also helpful to focus on long-term resident migrants, who have been in the EU legally for five years or more, since the development of regulations concerning these migrants is both more fundamental and potentially more problematic for receiving states. In turn, *immigration* can be seen as the actual entry into a country by a person or group of persons with the intention of staying there for more than three months. However, this does not imply that these persons may not decide to return to their country of origin after a period of time; nor does it mean that they will necessarily work. In other words, immigration can lead to, but does not necessarily lead to, the creation of long-term immigrants and migrant workers.

Whilst this might be seen as a somewhat pedantic discussion, the issue of terminology is not simply an academic issue. For example, the terms 'immigrant' and 'immigration' are applied in different ways in different EU Member States, and related policies are equally shaped by each country's experience and the particular national needs. As Hammar[6] argues: 'There is an obvious relation between a country's immigration policy and its terminology'. Thus in Germany and Switzerland immigrants are 'foreign workers' *(Ausländische Arbeitnehmer* in Germany and *Fremdarbeiter* in Switzerland and they are controlled by 'aliens bureaux' *(Ausländerbehörde* in Germany, *Fremdenpolizei in* Switzerland): the concept of 'immigrant', in the strict sense outlined above, is unknown. In contrast, France has always used the term *les immigrés* and *l'immigration,* whilst Sweden has also used similar terms – *invandrare and invandring* – since the 1960s when it launched its new immigration policy. Britain has used the term 'immigrant' especially for non-whites, but it defines its immigration policy as *race relations;* whilst in the Netherlands, the new policy for immigrants is called *minorities policy*[7]. Terminology tends to influence the way in which immigration policy is conceived and understood in each country and these terms, initially instruments of description, then became fixed concepts limiting flexibility and creativity.

One can also go further, to differentiate between perceptions of the host society with respect to different groups of migrants, perceptions which place some groups in a more precarious position than others. For example, if one considers the current situation in Europe, migration flows are coming from two main directions, Eastern Europe and North Africa. On the one hand,

5 The UK and Ireland are exceptions.

6 Hammar, T (1992) *European Policy, UK, Cambridge Policy*, UK, Cambridge University Press, p 12.

7 Hammar, T (1992) *European Immigration Policy, UK, Cambridge University Press,* p 12.

Eastern Europeans are often seen as related through blood to Western Europeans, and as such are seen as having always been 'in' Europe, albeit not in the EU. In this sense, they are often perceived as one of 'us', whereas North Africans are given a 'them' status. In contrast, suspicion of North Africans is such that they are often viewed more as a threat: an Algerian in France being seen by many simply as a potential terrorist.

Of course, the world of Islam is and always has been so lacking in monolithic qualities as to make the concept of an Islamic threat *per se* literally meaningless. But neither can there be any doubt that the Member States of the European Union are confronting problems in their relations with the predominantly Islamic states of North Africa which raise issues about the whole future development of the EU. Thus Moisi[8] describes the emerging situation in Europe as that of 'a white, wealthy and Christian 'Fortress Europe' pitted against a largely poor, Islamic world.' Such issues of terminology, and the way that the 'immigrant threat' is perceived in Italy and Spain, are returned to below.

IMMIGRATION AND CITIZENSHIP

In addition to the way in which immigrants are categorised and viewed by host country populations, the presence of immigrants in southern Europe also raise wider questions for government policy in the field of citizenship – as Zolberg[9] puts it, 'immigrants pose a challenge to traditional conceptions of states as self-contained population entities.' For example, with the arrival of immigrants, the traditional definition of membership in a community is no longer so self-evident, and one cannot directly relate such membership to formal citizenship. In an important sense, anybody inside a national territory, including illegal immigrants, is in some way a member of that particular community because he/she takes part in the life of the receiving society by, for instance, participating in the labour market (both formal and informal), sending children to school, being a neighbour and/or paying taxes.' [10]

Nonetheless, citizenship does mean more than simple presence in, or even membership of a community. Garcia[11] for example provides the following definition of citizenship:

---

8 Moisi, D in Glen St J Barclay (1995) The European Union and the Maghreb: A Clash of Civilisations? In *Australia and World Affairs*, (25), winter issue, p 5–17.

9 Zolberg, A. (1987) Keeping them out: ethical dilemmas of immigration policy in Robert J Myers, *International ethics in nuclear age,* Lanham, Maryland, University Press of America, pp 261–297.

10 Levelt, U.(1995) The European Union as a Political Community Through the Lens of Immigration Policy in Marco Martiniello (ed) *Migration, Citizenship and Ethno-National Identities in the European Union,* UK, Avebury, Ashgate Publishing Limited, p 199.

11 Garcia, S (1993) Europe's Fragmented Identities and the Frontiers of Citizenship in RIIA *Discussion Papers* (45, London, The Royal Institute of International Affairs, p 19.

> "Citizenship in the modern world constitutes legal, economic, political and social practices which define social membership and which counteract social cleavages. In this sense the practice of citizenship becomes a method of social inclusion which gives people who differ in age, sex, beliefs or colour of skin the same basic entitlements. It is this aspect of citizenship that has contributed to the legitimacy of the modern state. Citizenship has become also an element of legitimisation for the new Europe. To what extent is citizenship going to be universalised in Europe, and to what extent are people going to be excluded?"

There are various issues which arise in the European context with respect to the boundaries of citizenship. However. as Antje Wiener correctly states: "Union citizenship needs to be distinguished from national citizenship".[12] She goes on to argue that 'every citizen of the Union enjoys a first circle of nationality rights within a Member State and a second circle of new rights enjoyed in any Member State of the EU'. One of the main questions which arises in this regard is the extent to which the division between European Union citizens and third country nationals will increase, especially if further entrenchment of the idea of 'Fortress Europe' occurs due to 'deepening' of the Community.

ITALY AND SPAIN AS NEW RECEIVING STATES

As noted above, during the late 1980s the southern European states – Spain, Italy, Greece and Portugal – were transformed from being countries of emigration to countries of immigration. The main reason for this transformation can be attributed principally to three processes, namely economic growth in southern Europe; the 'stop' on immigration to northern Europe; and a marked increase in push factors throughout the less developed world, but especially in North Africa. Thus for example, the control measures taken by the traditional receiving countries of north-west Europe led to an increase of immigration into southern European countries, "either because these were the traditional staging-posts for clandestine migrants routing to the north, or because Southern Europe was seen as a straightforward alternative to direct entry to Northern Europe". [13]

At the same time, migration studies and policy in Italy and Spain had, until the late eighties, focused on emigration from as opposed to immigration to southern Europe and both research and policy have been confronted with problems in the face of this transformation. For example, legislative procedures

12 Wiener, A (1996) Rethinking Citizenship: The Quest for Place-Oriented Participation in the EU in *The Oxford International Review*, VII (3), pp 44–51.

13 King, R and Konjhodzic, I (1995) Labour, Employment and Migration in Southern Europe. Paper prepared for a conference on *Problems of Labour and Employment in Southern Europe and the Maghreb: European and US Policy Options,* in J Van Oudenaren (ed) – *Employment. Economic Development and Migration in South Europe and the* Maghreb, Sta Monica, California, p 57.

in the two countries tended to refer to the foreign tourist rather than the immigrant worker, whilst statistics were generally either absent altogether, or unreliable. It is also difficult to establish the exact number of immigrants over the last twenty years in Italy and Spain, due to initial lack of legislation.

Nonetheless, in the recent years, a great effort has been made to gather statistics appropriate to the new situation and hence analyse more precisely and in greater detail immigration and its implications as well as furnish appropriate legislation which could cope better with the new problems involved. Thus recent estimates put immigration from outside the EU at around a million in Italy, with the number of illegal immigrants estimated at about half a million[14]. For example, an official estimate made in 1989 by the Italian National Statistics Institute (ISTAT 1990) put the figure at 963,000, although this may have been an overestimate due to an apparent failure to subtract the number of return migrants who were no longer on Italian soil.

In turn, in Spain estimates vary between 450,000 and 657,000 with respect to numbers of third country immigrants known to be residing on Spanish territory, whilst the number of illegal immigrants in Spain is said to be about another 450,000.[15]

The predominance of push over pull factors, the limited capacity of the labour markets of the receiving countries and increased migration for political reasons are all elements which, interacting with the migration dynamics, have led to significant changes in migration policy, and in attitudes towards migrants, in Italy and Spain in recent years. New immigration flows are only partly absorbed in the hidden economy of the receiving countries and in sectors and jobs where the distinction between legal and illegal is minimal. This encourages the social exclusion of the immigrants as well as compromising their integration within the receiving society, not to mention the ethnic, cultural and religious divide which often separates the immigrant from the local population. In effect, the list of potential areas for policy development is vast.

SIMILARITIES BETWEEN ITALY AND SPAIN

An initial point to make concerns the similarities between the way in which Spain and Italy have reacted to changes that have affected them. As stated earlier, both Spain and Italy have had past histories as sending countries and both countries in the early 1980s started experiencing the transformation from 'sending' country to becoming a 'receiving' country. Both countries were used as a passage-way to the North of Europe; later on, after tightening of visa restrictions in northern Europe and an increase in the prosperity of the tertiary sector in Italy and Spain, both countries have now started experiencing the settlement of migrants on their territory. The differential of economic growth

14 *il Manifesto* 12 October 1996.

15 *Migration News Sheet*, September 1996, pp 6–7.

between the countries of southern and north west Europe has also narrowed considerably as EC membership has brought Italian and Spanish (and to a lesser extent, Greek and Portuguese) wages closer to average EU levels.

In the midst of these dramatic changes, an initial lack of demographic analysis of the situation, coupled with the lack of initial concrete migration policy in Italy and to a lesser extent in Spain, have led to over-reactions by the media and exaggerations in the numbers thought to be present. Earlier surveys in Italy dealt with communities of immigrants coming from the Philippines, Cape Verde, Somalia, Eritrea, Morocco, Tunisia, Egypt, Iran, and recently the list has expanded to include immigrants from Algeria and other African and Asian countries such as Senegal, Ghana, Sri Lanka, Pakistan, China. In the absence of a clear direction from researchers or policy-makers, this apparently unending immigration has led to sporadic acts of xenophobia being carried out against individuals and immigrant communities.

However, in both countries a distinction is nonetheless drawn between 'elite' immigrants, and other, more marginalised groups. In both countries, the 'elite' (such as Americans and Japanese) are viewed as 'investors'; whereas the term 'immigrant' is attributed to the poorer groups of migrants. In Spain, the 'elite' includes northern Europeans who retire to Spain for its climate and lower cost of living, as well as migrants from Spain's former colonies, who are usually very well qualified and manage to secure a standard of living similar to that of the Spaniards, if not better. These groups have a substantially different experience in Spain to the 'marginalised' group, composed of North and sub-Saharan Africans, and to a certain extent poorer Portuguese and Filipino immigrants. Meanwhile, the most marginalised of all in both countries are the illegal immigrants.

The different demographic regimes between the two sides of the Mediterranean basin act as a strong push factor for immigration which is common to both Italy and Spain. Equally, an important and common pull factor is the large informal sector of the economy and labour market which is also significant in both Italy and Spain. Rapidly rising official wage rates, a squeeze on productivity and, until recently, devaluation of the lira in Italy (and to a lesser extent the peseta in Spain) have led firms to recoup their competitiveness by tax evasion, reduced labour costs and more flexible use of labour. In this context, informal and irregular demand for migrant labour in certain sectors such as agriculture, construction, the tourist industry and domestic services is very high. In fact, both Spain and Italy have a problem of expanding informal labour markets which assimilate undocumented migrants.

In both countries the predominant group of labour migrants from the Maghreb are from Morocco, and in both cases the distribution of migrants on the territory of the receiving states is not homogeneous. Reasons for the increase in the number of immigrants from North Africa entering Italy and Spain are various, but a principal one is geographical. The geographical proximity and 'openness' of both Italy and Spain, including their reliance on tourism, and their long coastlines, both make control of migrant inflows very difficult.

In terms of immigration policy development, meanwhile, both countries have had amnesty laws for illegal immigrants[16]: in Spain, in 1985–86, 1991 and 1996; and in Italy, in 1982, 1987–89, 1990–92 and 1996. In all of these regularisations, a lower than expected number of undocumented workers actually regularised their position in the host country, probably out of fear of being repatriated. In Spain, for example, the first legalisation process in 1985–86 resulted in 34,832 residence permits being issued (Ministerio del Interior 1989[17]), whilst as a result of the 1991 process, a further 109,135 work and residence permits were issued, well below the estimated number of undocumented workers.

DIFFERENCES BETWEEN ITALY AND SPAIN

Albeit there are similarities in the position of Italy and Spain with respect to their experience of immigration, differences prevail too. Differences are particularly evident in terms of the types of migrants that are present in Italy and Spain; the interpretation given to the word 'integration'; and the extent to which there is integration of the immigrants within the host societies. There have been important implications for changing attitudes towards migrants and hence the evolution of immigration and citizenship policies in Italy and Spain, issues dealt with in the next section.

One reason for this difference might be the variations in the spatial distribution of immigrants in the two countries. In Italy, immigrants are spread throughout the country, although they are found particularly in the Centre-North and certain areas of the South (Sicily and Campania) which are easy landing places for migrants coming by sea from the Maghreb. In contrast, in Spain, the majority of the immigrants are in either Madrid or Catalunya, where most job opportunities can be found. Southern regions such as Andalucia have also received a number of seasonal workers, who look for jobs in the tourist sector or on the agricultural harvest, although this conflicts with the interests of the locals who themselves look to the tourist and harvest seasons for extra income from part-time work. As a result of the spatial concentration of immigrants in Spain, one does not find such well-pronounced regional policies as one does in Italy, since the numbers of immigrants are not very high in most regions, and where numbers do increase dramatically, this usually occurs during the summer period, for a short time, after which the immigrants return back to their country of origin.

CHANGING ATTITUDES TOWARDS MIGRATION IN ITALY AND SPAIN

The Italian public has grown increasingly interested in the question of migration, both because of greater numbers involved and due to episodes, often quite serious, of intolerance which have caught the attention of the mass media

---

16 Collinson, S (1996) *Shore to Shore – The Politics of Migration in Euro-Maghreb Relations,* London, The Royal Institute of International Affairs, p 35.

17 Quoted in Izquierdo, 1992.

and the general public. Nonetheless, with some local exceptions, the impact of migration on Italy is still quite modest in comparison with other European countries, in particular because migrants' access to social and welfare services remains limited – particularly if they are illegals. This, however, has not prevented the outbreak of various forms of racism.[18]

Meanwhile, a number of opposing reactions to immigration have emerged from Italian society. On the one hand, one can find 'solidarity' towards migrants as expressed by various Catholic voluntary organisations, such as Caritas, by some political parties, and by trade unions. On the other hand, in Italian, as in other European cultures, a form of ethnocentrism does exist which, under certain conditions, could give rise to xenophobic or racist behaviour, although to date, for various historic reasons, this has had less occasion for expression than elsewhere. In a survey carried out by Bonifazi[19], it was interesting to note the overestimations given by respondents of the number of immigrants present in Italy, and that these overestimations grew between 1987/88 and 1991 (Table 1). It is perhaps this, as much as actual growth in the number of immigrants, that has led to the feeling that there are too many immigrants in the country (Table 2).

TABLE 1 EVALUATION OF THE NUMBER OF FOREIGNERS LIVING IN ITALY (PERCENTAGES).

	Evaluation	**Survey**
	1987-1988	1991
		18-65
Low (a)	13.60	9.8
Medium (b)	18.8	15.3
High (c)	17.6	19.7
Very high (d)	13.7	20.9
Don't know	36.2	34.3
Total	100.0	100.0

Note: (a) 1987–88: under 750,000; 1991: under 700,000;
(b) 1987–88: 750,000–1,500,000; 1991: 700,000–1,500,000;
(c) 1,500,000–3,000,000'
(d) over 3,000,000.

Source: (Bonifazi, see footnote 19, P.40).

18 Treves, C, Di Gioacchino, R, Masoubi, M Toaff, E Spini, V Pascucci, G, Mussi, F and Trentin, B (1989) *Sindacato dei diritti e società multietnica,* Rome, Ediesse, pp 47–49, Vicarelli, G (1994) – *Le Mani Invisibibili,* Roma: Ediesse.

19 Bonifazi, C (1992) Italian Attitudes and Opinions Towards Foreign Migrants and Migration Policies in *Studi Emigrazione,* 105 pp 21–42.

	Opinion	Survey
	1987-1988	1991
Too many	49.7	74.5
Neither too many nor few	35.7	19.1
Not many	1.7	1.1
Don't know	12.8	5.4
Total	100.0	100.0

Source: (Bonifazi, see footnote 19, p 40)

Spain's immigrant population accounts for less than two per cent of the country's total population and the immigrant proportion of the official labour force is even smaller (about 0.7 per cent)[20]. Nonetheless, especially in the period from 1988–92, the press and government encouraged the belief that immigration is one of Spain's most serious political and social problems by exaggerating numbers and pointing to its negative effects on the labour market and its implications for petty crime, terrorism and drug trafficking. As in Italy, the sensationalism of the press concerning increases in the number of migrants caused people to panic about the numbers actually present. In response, in 1992 the government modified the *Ley Corcuera, a* piece of public order legislation, granting wider powers to the police to crack down on the supposed link between immigrants and crime.

However, following the murder of a Dominican woman in 1992 and statistical results showing a lower level of immigration than previously thought[21], the government accepted that they had overstated the situation, and in 1994 a social policy was established with respect to migrants working and residing on Spanish territory which sought to soften some of the stricter regulations of the foreigners law *(Ley Extranjeria)* and to avoid further demonstrations of xenophobia. In turn, the press practically stopped writing about the issue and the situation calmed down considerably.

As in Italy, there have been surveys of public opinion about immigration in Spain, with a survey by Collective IOE[22], although now rather dated, showing quite a differentiated pattern of opinions depending on social class. From their survey, five distinct attitudes emerged:

---

20 Collectivo IOE (1990) – "Spain's Illegal Immigrants" in *Contemporary European Affairs*, no 3, pp. 117–137.

21 Cornelius, W A (1994) – "Spain: A Country in Transition", in Cornelius, W A, Martin P L and Hollifield, J F (eds) (1994) *Controlling Immigration – A Global Perspective,* California, Stanford University Press, pp 322–335.

22 Collectivo IOE (1986) – "Los immigrantes".

- *Nationalism:* a view which supports the rights of Spanish citizens and can be found across the entire spectrum of Spanish society; however, this is most prevalent, unsurprisingly, in right wing press, amongst many employees, and the unemployed, but least strong amongst middle class women and civil servants. As in Italy, those holding a nationalist view tended to overestimate the numbers of third country nationals present on Spanish territory, and this view was particularly dominant in the poorer southern regions of Spain, where Spaniards feel more in competition with immigrants for work in the tourist industry and in manual labour, due to higher levels of unemployment.
- In contrast, company directors tended to put *economic* considerations first and foremost, in keeping with Spain's constitutional commitment to the market economy. They tend to accept the presence of foreign workers on the grounds that Spanish workers increasingly reject certain forms of employment, or impose demands on their employers that are simply too costly to fulfil.
- *A Christian universalist* view defends the concepts of equality and fraternity and supports the weak and needy – in this case, immigrants. Middle class women were found to be the most staunch defenders of this view, although they accepted elements of the nationalist, view, notably in believing that Spanish people should be given first preference for employment
- *A workers' universalist* viewpoint which opposes exploitation of foreign workers, but also arguably has more to do with nostalgia for the past than with concrete alternatives for the present.
- *A practical* view which stresses the need for better border controls, but also accepts the need to move towards legalising the status of most of the country's foreigners. This view is dominant in government departments and NGOs, although the former places more emphasis on immigration controls to control illegal immigration, whilst the latter stress improvement in legal and social conditions for immigrants already in the country.

These variations in public perception of immigrants, and what should be done by the government in response, help to explain why in both countries, although there has been legislation with respect to immigrants, there is little, as yet, in the way of wider-ranging policy. This distinction between legislation and policy reflects Roger Scruton's distinction, in *the Dictionary of Political Thought,* between legislation as the 'making' of law ... (which) will always stand in need of subsequent interpretation by the judiciary, and policy, which encompasses the general principles which guide the making of laws, administration, and executive acts of government in domestic and international affairs[23]. Indeed, policy implies consistency over time which is not necessarily the case for legislative measures: and certainly inconsistency could be seen to characterise Italian and Spanish policy, as is discussed in the next section.

---

23 Scruton, R (1991) Dictionary of Political Thought, London, Penguin Book Publishers.

IMMIGRATION, POLICY DEVELOPMENT AND CITIZENSHIP

The above sections have discussed a number of important similarities between the situation of immigration in Italy and Spain, in terms of their numbers, patterns of arrival and public perceptions, although there are also certain differences, notably concerning their geographical distribution. However, when one turns to the development of legislation and policy, differences between the two countries become more evident; indeed, it can be argued that although policy development is at a very early stage, the two countries are progressively moving towards quite different models with regard to long-term resident migrants.

In Italy, the most significant legal norms to date referring to immigrants in Italy from outside the EU are represented by two laws, the first passed in 1986 (Law no 943: *Norms on the employment and treatment of immigrant workers from outside of the EC and the prevention of undocumented migration)* and the second in 1990, the so-called 'Martelli Law' (Law no 39: *Special measures on political asylum, entry and residence for non-EU national and stateless citizens already present in the country).* Both laws stipulate criteria, procedures and time limits for regularisation of the status of those immigrants who were in an irregular or illegal position, and it is this aspect of the laws that have perhaps received most attention. Law 943 upholds the principle that non-EU workers already present in the country should enjoy the same treatment and rights as Italian workers. The law is divided into separate administrative provisions, such as the granting of an entry visa being dependent on the existence of an authorisation to work (Article 8). Work and residence permits normally last two years and may be extended. Meanwhile, the law envisages three categories for entry: asylum seekers, family reunification for immigrants legally resident and fully employed, and labourers called individually by employers who guarantee both employment and adequate housing.

However, in addition, both laws go further. For example, Law 943/86 also provided for the setting up of regional immigrant advisory councils, new representative bodies of immigrants, and task forces at the Ministries of Labour and Foreign Affairs to foster immigration policy for employees, while Law 39/90 stipulated new norms for entry, sojourn and expulsion and approved funds to the Italian regions for the creation of primary reception centres for immigrants. Meanwhile, since the publication of the Martelli Law, the Italian government has issued a number of decrees and amendments to the law, which further regulate flows of new immigrants and conditions for those already in the country. This system is seen as a pliable instrument, able to meet labour market demands although some have described the changes as xenophobic.[24]

Across these various decrees, a pattern is clear, of the development of a preventative policy with regard to new immigration, and attempts to assimilate immigrants already in the country. Thus, for example, in Italy measures taken include the allocation of immigrants' children in a dispersed fashion to Italian

24 *Migration News Sheet,* December 1995, p 3.

schools, partly in order to maintain a majority of Italian children per classroom and hence prevent the development of 'immigrant ghettos' in certain neighbourhoods. In this sense, Italy can be seen as moving towards the French model of 'assimilation', which Solé describes as the melting pot idea[25]. It implies the cultural, social and political subordination of one group to the other, and the partial or total loss of immigrants' identity as they merge with the majority group; it can be contrasted with 'integration', in which the indigenous population and a minority group gradually move towards equality on the socioeconomic, cultural and political levels, becoming a single population unit.[26]

With regard to citizenship, there has also been some legislative development. Italian citizenship is now based on a new law, approved in 1992, which abolished the previous law that dated back to 1912. In essence, the old law favoured return migrants of Italian origin, but made the achievement of citizenship difficult for third country nationals. Thus Italian citizenship can now be obtained:

- *ius sanguinis,* ie by having an Italian parent, including by adoption;
- *ius soli,* but only where the parents of a child found in Italy are unknown;
- *by decree,* to a foreigner whose father or mother was an Italian citizen by birth; to an adult foreigner adopted by an Italian citizen; to a foreigner who has served for at least five years as an employee of the Italian state, or to a foreigner who engages in military service in Italy;
- *By marriage* to an Italian citizen, after residing legally in Italy for at least 6 months, or after three years of marriage; and,
- *by naturalisation:* on some conditions, as service rendered to the Italian state for a period of five years, even if abroad, or through residence in Italy for ten years.

However, naturalisation, by decree of the President of the Republic, only comes into effect when loyalty has been sworn to the Republic of Italy and to its President, and is not easy to *obtain* [27]. In turn, citizenship can be refused in the case of a prison sentence of more than one year and for attempts to undermine the security of the Italian Republic. Italian citizenship may also be lost if a new citizenship is acquired.

In Spain, the basis for migrants to obtain citizenship is very similar to Italy. For example, in both cases, preference is given to descendants of emigrants; in the Spanish case, these are mainly Ibero-Americans, who are citizens of Spain's former colonies in Latin America, whilst in the case of Italy, which had few such colonial ties, the main target group is descendants of former Italian

---

25 Sole C, (1981) La integración sociocultural de los Immigrantes en Catalunya, Madrid CIS.

26 Sole C, (1988) Catalunya: societat receptora d'immigrantes, Barcelona: Institute d'Estudis Catalans.

27 *Migration News Sheet,* December 1995, p 3.

emigrants or to those married to Italians in the United States, northern Europe and Australia. However, differences do begin to open up when one considers the broader spread of immigration policy, rather than the detail of citizenship law. Thus to a certain extent, the emerging situation in Spain with respect to longer-term resident migrants can be described more akin to the German model, whereby immigrants are viewed as temporary guests. For example, the Foreigners' Law *(Ley Extranjeria)* of 1985, which was the first Spanish law ever to regulate directly the rights and responsibilities of foreigners in Spain[28], was very much based on the German legislation for migrants, reflecting Spain's active participation in the Schengen Agreement, for which Germany was the driving force[29].

The need for such a law, as noted earlier, arose from continuing migrant pressure, and the pressure of public opinion within Spain. The main objectives of the law were fourfold and can be summarised as:

1. to systematise entry and residence procedures for foreigners in Spain;
2. to protect the national job market;
3. to guarantee acceptable working conditions for foreigners, as well as to assist them to integrate, avoiding illegality and marginalisation;
4. to harmonise Spanish legislation with that of other EU Member States, working within the framework of the European unification process and especially the Schengen agreement.

However, three articles of this law were found unconstitutional in July 1987 and in itself the law was very difficult to implement in many cases, because of its technical complexity and the deficient infrastructure of a country unfamiliar with the administrative actions of immigration[30]. Most of the criticisms of the law were centred upon its discriminatory character, although in reality, Spain was only following European immigration policies which facilitate freedom of movement *within* EC Member States, but *restrict* the entry of third country nationals, especially those from the Third World. Within Spain, meanwhile, although discrimination is directed towards various ethnic minorities, some groups, notably Ibero Americans, Portuguese, Filipinos, Andorrans, Equatorial-Guineans and the original inhabitants of Gibraltar are given preferential treatment. This is not simply a question of former colonial and other historical ties – for example, no such treatment exists for Moroccans coming from the region which was a Spanish protectorate until 1956.

---

28 Bodega, I, Cebrian, J A Franchini T, Lora-Tamayo, G, Martin-Lou, A (1995) Recent Migrations from Morocco to Spain in *International Migration Review, 29 (3), pp 800–819.*

29 Santos, L (1993) Elementos juridicos de la integración de los extranjeros in Tapinos, G (ed) *Inmigracion e Integracion en Europe,* Barcelona: Fundacion Paulino Torres Domenech, pp 91–125. Cornelius, W A (1994) – "Spain: A Country in Transition", in Cornelius, W A, Martin, P L and Hollifield, LF (eds) (1994) *Controlling Immigration – A Global Perspective,* California, Stanford University Press, pp. 322–335.

30 OECD report cited in Bodega et al 1995 see footnote 28, p 308.

With respect to immigration policy, Spain has tightened its borders in full compliance with Schengen, and has moved towards the regularisation of foreigners already living in Spain. Thus 1996 saw the onset of two very important processes for immigrants in Spain: first, a new regularisation process aimed at some 50,000 foreigners without residence permits; and secondly, a modification of the regulations of the *Ley Extranjeria,* making it slightly less strict. For example, one of the amendments of the *Ley Extranjeria* allows immigrants to obtain visa extensions of two years after their first year of residence and then of longer duration until they are considered permanent residents, where previously they had to renew their visas each year. However, even though it initially was the only country in the southern European region which can claim to have moved a step further towards an immigration policy in its broader sense, rather than just passing legislation on an *ad hoc* basis, the social and judicial dimensions of this policy are still not so well established. Of course, it could be argued that having no defined policy is also a policy, since it gives the State the flexibility to respond to arising needs.[31]

One important development in Spain has been the establishment of a quota system for those who apply for work and residence visas. This system allowed 20,600 migrant workers to obtain visas in 1993, 29,349 in 1995, and 20,600 in 1995, and included the possibility for workers who were already residing in Spain illegally to regularise their situation.

In both Spain and Italy, autonomy of the regions is evident, but one further difference is that in Spain, the region of Catalunya is working on its own policy of integration of immigrants, independent of the rest of the country. In Italy, some regions have taken more initiative than others to demonstrate their support towards the immigrants, as is discussed in the following section. However, there is no region with such a developed policy of integration of immigrants as in Catalunya. Here, the regional government – *the Generalitat de Catalunya* has enacted a plan of integration for migrants *(Pla Interdepartmental d'immigració),* in collaboration with the trade union CITE and other local organisations based in Barcelona and neighbouring towns, in which theoretically, it implements the politics of *ius soli.* According to this principle, the children of immigrants are considered as Catalans, and receive compulsory schooling in Catalan, and measures to promote their integration (a principle that also applies to other Spaniards). This reflects the fact that the Catalan government is working towards asserting Catalunya as an autonomous entity with its own language, as well as perhaps a greater degree of open-mindedness to diversity, and tolerance of immigration, in a relatively rich part of Spain that has long been a recipient region of migrants – especially other Spaniards. Of course, the development of this policy has its limits: for example, the application of the politics of *ius sanguinis v ius soli* is ultimately left to the jurisdiction of the central state in Madrid, and Catalunya at the moment has

---

31 Cornelius, W A (1994) – "Spain: A Country in Transition", in Cornelius, W A, Martin, P L and Hollifield, J F (eds) (1994) *Controlling Immigration – A Global Perspective,* California, Stanford University Press, pp 322–335.

no power to apply the principle of *ius soli* to third country nationals residing upon its territory. Notwithstanding Catalan calls for more autonomy, at present, it can only decide how to integrate immigrants, rather than give them legal status.

REGIONAL, LOCAL AND PRIVATE INITIATIVES

In Italy, regional initiative is more extensive and relevant than Spain, not least because immigrants are much more widely dispersed around the country. Nonetheless, a study by CENSIS (1990) which examined regional measures on immigration and the extent to which these measures were actually put into practice, revealed a significant gap between the planned norm and the concrete initiatives undertaken. In practice, Italian regions are highly differentiated in the extent to which they have managed to activate concrete policies on immigration. The first initiatives regarding immigrants were launched in the early 1980s in some of the larger cities of central and northern Italian regions. In Lombardy, Umbria, Piedmont, Liguria, Emilia Romagna and Tuscany, there is arguably a high degree of sensitivity as far as planned norms and concrete initiatives are concerned. For example, in Brescia, the city authorities have not only organised their own structures, but have also coordinated the activities of other bodies. In 1989 an *ad hoc* local service was created in Brescia: the Reception and Orientation Office for non-EU foreigners, and it at once assumed an important role in orientating immigrants in the use of public services. The Office keeps a register of users, as well as helping them find work and accommodation. Initiatives in this field have included the restoration of old buildings, an agreement with hotels, and the formation of housing co-operatives. There has also been an increase in the number of immigrants' associations, for which the local authorities act as co-ordinators. The industrial sector has organised an occupational training course for metal-workers[32]. Meanwhile in Turin, unions and businesses have both been active in promoting occupational training for immigrants. Local authorities have played an important part in job finding, placing immigrants in public building projects or in other areas of public interest. There have been some interesting initiatives in the area of education: apart from literacy courses and school integration and middle school certificate projects, there is also a multicultural training course for teachers on the agenda. Nonetheless, the meeting of social needs, and especially accommodation needs, has arguably been less successful.

Elsewhere in Italy, however, the situation of immigrants is not as good. Apart from a general lack of preparedness, delays in dealing with immigrants have been attributed to the slowness of administrative procedures. A regional Council for Immigration Problems (with the participation of some co-opted

---

32 Treves, C Di Gioacchino, R Masoubi, M Toaff, E, Spini, V Pascucci, G, Mussi, F and Trentin, B (1989) *Sindacato dei diritti e società multietnica,* Rome, Ediese, pp 47–49. Vicarelli, G (1994) – *Le Mani Invisibili,* Roma: Ediesse.

or elected immigrant representatives) has been set up in almost all regions, but this body only appears to work in a third of these regions. In principle, its responsibilities cover cultural and educational initiatives, social welfare, economic assistance, reception centres, domestic help, accommodation, health care, and initiatives encouraging the formation of associations 'for' and 'of' non-EU immigrants, although these are not always acted upon, or necessarily successful. In particular, in the south of Italy, public measures have not been so successful and social forces and the voluntary sector have acted in a climate of general indifference. Meanwhile, there has also been an absence of any real commitment on the part of the public institutions.

In Spain, the number of immigrants is lower and there is a quota system which to some extent controls entry, such that the number and variety of regional initiatives for immigrant integration is much lower. Beyond the example of initiatives of the Catalan government mentioned above, however, there are some well-known organisations which are involved in voluntary work with immigrants across the whole of Spain, and especially in Barcelona, Baleares, Canahas, Malaga, Andalucia and Madrid, where the majority of the migrants reside. These organisations include the *Comissiones Obreras,* a trade union which helps migrants through its specialized information centre (CITE), as well as SOS Racisme, *the Centro d'informacio e Documentacio de Barcelona* (CIDOB), the *Association de Solidaridad con los Trabajadores Immigrantes* (ASTI), CARITAS, Jaina Kafo, and the *Colectivo IOE.* These organisations organise tours of Barcelona and neighbouring localities, hold classes in vocational training to help immigrants achieve qualifications which are recognised by Spanish employers, and help with finding jobs.

Most of the organisations mentioned above support the maintenance of migrants' own cultural identity, as a better way to allow integration in Spanish society in the short term, and allow the possibility of return migration in the longer term. This is based on the premise that expecting an immigrant to renounce almost completely to his or her previous identity could cause serious conflicts and a sense of insecurity within the individual, especially if they find it difficult to achieve citizenship rights in the host country. Such organisations are trying to help the migrants to integrate in Spain but are also holding evening classes of Arabic and Arabic culture, for example for North Africans, so that the children of Maghrebi migrants will always feel they have the choice of returning to their country of origin if they choose to.

CONCLUSION

Individual European countries' migratory policies have featured restrictive and coercive elements in recent years. In the light of this, a basic need for co-ordination above all has often been felt. Yet, neither the EU nor any other international organisation has so far managed to make effective progress in this direction. The attempt to standardise the practices of some European countries (eg in Schengen) does not seem to have overcome problems caused by viewing the issue of immigration in purely conjectural or local terms. In fact, in spite of the same economic crisis, the same social problems and – what seems to be the most important the same targets (more or less agreed upon) – each country still seems to be reacting in its own way: even when a comparison of the solutions adopted (especially restrictive ones) could lead one to think that there might be room for an European agreement on migratory policies.

What can be seen quite clearly from the situation in Southern Europe is the extent to which immigration of workers from poor countries can be described as "a direct response to specific demands for cheap labour articulated by employers and their representatives in the political and administrative process; or whether the migration process is essentially supply-driven by factors of poverty and demography".[33] It is still unclear to what extent competition exists between immigrants and national workers. Initiatives to integrate legalised immigrants and decisions with respect to the extent that migrants can achieve citizens' rights are still at very early stages. Even in the areas where migrants have secured certain rights, the gap is still very wide between these rights and what is truly done to help them benefit from these rights.

One thing is more certain however: there are various disequilibria prevailing between the northern and southern banks of the Mediterranean which will continue to persist for some time. Too strict immigration policies will only help fuel an increase in clandestine entries. In this sense, as Collinson states, "the central issue ... is development, not migration. Migration is likely to continue in some form or another, and may even increase, whatever the outcome of future economic co-operation between the EU and the Maghreb."[34] EU Member States, including Italy and Spain, have placed much reliance on traditional forms of immigration regulation, as reflected recently in the Barcelona declaration of November 1995. So far, migration has been treated as "a problem with straightforward solutions, rather than as a continuous structural component of international interaction and integration, to which there may be no solution as such, but which continues to pose a challenge throughout all levels of domestic and international policy-making"[35]. Rather than preventing and regulating migration, which may represent a short-term solution, states such as Spain and Italy may need instead to co-operate, to study what kinds of interventions would tackle the root causes of the new immigration flows.

---

33 King, R and Konjhodzic, I (1995) Labour, Employment and Migration in Southern Europe. Paper prepared for a conference on *Problems of Labour and Employment in Southern Europe and the Maghreb: European and US Policy Options,* in J Van Oudenaren (ed) – *Employment. Economic Development and Migration in South Europe and the* Maghreb, Sta Monica, California, pp 74.

34 Collinson, S (1996) *Shore to Shore – The Politics of Migration in Euro-Maghreb Relations,* London, The Royal Institute of International Affairs, p 98.

35 Collinson S (1996) *Shore to Shore – The Politics of Migration in Euro-Maghreb Relations,* London, The Royal Institute of International Affairs, P 95.

Notes

Re methodology carried out for the purpose of this paper involved mainly two approaches:

1. The first part was literature based and involved a close study of legislative measures and the use of papers and articles which so far have dominated relevant schools of thought over the years.
2. The second part involved collecting and analysing quantitative data resulting from population census surveys. Following on from this, I then carried out qualitative interviews with national ministry civil servants, academics, migrants' representatives and NG0s in the two receiving countries. Interviews were also carried out with EU Commission officials in DG1, DG1A, DG V, DGX/A, and DG XV/A and members of the relevant committees in the European Parliament. The "snow-ball method" was used to widen the network of contacts.

This does not apply to EU nationals moving within the EU, even though some EU States still require their own nationals and other EU citizens to be registered at the town hall.

ISTAT is the National Statistics Institute which is an annex to the Ministry of the Interior.

Ley Corcuera, named after its convenor – the Minister Corcuera, who until 1992 was Minister of Interior Affairs, was a law establishing the powers the police had on Spanish territory in order to cut down on drugs, criminal offenses and terrorism.

At this point, one should distinguish between legislation and policy. These two terms are not mutually exclusive, in fact prevailing legislation is usually the basis for a policy. According to Roger Scruton's, *Dictionary of Political Thought,* legislation is "the 'making' of law (inverted commas needed as some believe that law is not made but discovered). It involves the express decree by the legislature, which decree may be oral or written, and will always stand in need of subsequent interpretation by the judiciary. It also involves the establishment of a legal custom, with no express enactment of the legislature, but with an entrenched obedience to precedent. It is a decision taken by the highest court." On the other hand, policy encompasses "the general principles which guide the making of laws, administration, and executive acts of government in domestic and international affairs. Policy has to be distinguished from doctrine – the system of beliefs and values which generate policy, and which purport to describe the ends to which policy is the means". Policy implies consistency over time which is not necessarily the case for legislative measures which tend to be more malleable according to arising needs of the country.

When one states the term "integration" one assumes that it is meant to be a process through which the indigenous population and the minority settled in the same place gradually intermingling and moving towards equality on the socioeconomic, cultural and political levels, becoming a single population unit (with its own cultural traits, of which language is a fundamental component) that shares the same identity but differs from other population units or groups. See Solé C (1981) *La integración sociocultural de los immigrantes en Catalunya*, Madrid: CIS and Solé, C (188) *Catalunya: societat receptora d'immigrantes,* Barcelona: Institut d'Estudis Catalans. This concept of integration, then differs from that of assimilation, which implies the cultural, social and political subordination of one group to the other – which Solé (1988) describes as "the melting pot idea". This implies the partial or total loss of immigrants' identity as they merge with the majority group. A receiving society can, however, develop selective mechanisms *vis-a-vis* the immigrants, foreigners or otherwise, who settle there. Potential intra- and inter- class conflicts are aggravated by the introduction of ethnic discrimination which limits the opportunities open to certain immigrants, regardless of how well their education and experience compare with those of the local population.

Nowadays, the average wage of a Spaniard worker is round about 150,000 Pesetas a month, whereas migrants are said to earn an average of 60,000 pesetas a month. Bank of Spain statistics show that on average, a Moroccan migrant sends back home 60,000 pesetas a year, which is quite low to justify their stay in Spain. This could mean that 60,000 pesetas is sufficient due to exchange rate and cost of living in their home country, or otherwise that they spend their money on rent and living expenses and cannot afford to save a lot. Another possibility could be that they transfer other non-declared money earned from the informal sector by other means.

In Catalunya, as in other migration-receiving societies, certain occupational segments or categories are unofficially reserved for different ethnic groups.

Spain had been used in previous years as a "corridor" or "waiting room" for migrants who wanted move up to northern Europe. Thus, the immigrant was not viewed, until recently, as a possible settler, but only as a transient person who would carry out seasonal work on a temporary contract and who would leave the country within a short period of time. This led the authorities to base the "Foreigners' Law" of 1985 on the German *"Gastarbeiter policy".* Moreover, Germany has so far, been the country on the forefront of the implementation of Schengen in the EU (France has not yet implemented Schengen fully) especially in southern Europe and due to Germany's driving force, Spain's immigration policy design was designed on the German model.

CUPO means number limit, ie, quota.

See the *"Pla Interdepartmental d'immigracio"* a publication by the Generalitat de Catalunya, Department of Social Welfare.

With respect to iberoamericans, the problem of recognition of qualifications does not exist because due to bilateral agreements existing between Spain and the Latin-American countries about education standards, even though some employers did claim that but for these bilateral agreements, the iberoamericans' would also have been rated as of a lower standard to the Spanish ones.

REFERENCES

Bodega, L, Cebrian, L A, Franchini, T, Lora-Tamayo, G, Martin-Lou, A (1995) Recent Migrations from Morocco to Spain *in International Migration Review,* 29 (3), pp. 800–819

Bonifazi, C (1992) Italian Attitudes and Opinions Towards Foreign Migrants and Migration Policies in *Studi Emigrazione,* 105, pp 21–42.

Bonifazi, C (1992) *ibid.,* pp. 21–42.

Bonifazi, C and Gesano, G (1994) – "L'immigrazione straniera tra regolazione dei flussi e politiche d'accogliemento in *Tendenze Demografiche e Politiche per la Popolazione,* in Golini, (ed), Roma, IRP.

Collectivo IOE (1986) – "Los immigrantes en España in *La Documentation social,* no 66, Madrid, 1987, pp 22–40.

Collectivo IOE (1990) – "Spain's Illegal Immigrants" in *Contemporary European Affairs,* no 3, pp 117–137.

Collinson, S (1993) – *Beyond Borders: West European Migration Policy Towards the 21st Century,* London, Royal Institute of International Affairs.

Collinson, S (1996) *Shore to Shore – The Politics of Migration in Euro-Maghreb Relations,* London, The Royal Institute of International Affairs, p 35.

Commission of the European Communities, (1991) Immigration of citizens from third countries into the southern Member States of the European Community in *Social Europe,* Brussels, Supplement 1/91, p 25 (Dr M Werth, project co-ordinator).

Commission for the European Communities (1994) Communication from the Commission to the Council and the European Parliament on "Strengthening the Mediterranean Policy of the European Union: Establishing a Euro-Mediterranean Partnership" in *COM (94) 427 final,* Brussels, p 28.

Cornelius W A (1994) – "Spain: A Country in Transition", in Cornelius, W A, Martin, P L and Hollifield, J F (eds) (1994) *Controlling Immigration – A Global Perspective,* California, Stanford University Press, pp 322–335.

Garcia, S (1993) Europe's Fragmented Identities and the Frontiers of Citizenship in *RHA Discussion Papers* (45), London, The Royal Institute of International Affairs, p 19.

Hammar, T (1992) *European Immigration Policy,* UK, Cambridge University Press, p 12.

King, R and Konjhodzic, I (1995) Labour, Employment and Migration in Southern Europe. Paper prepared for a conference *on Problems of Labour and Employment in Southern Europe and the Maghreb: European and US Policy Options,* in J Van Oudenaren (ed) – *Employment, E* California, pp 7–106.

King, R and Konjhodzic, I (1995) *ibid.,* p 74.

Levelt, U (1995) The European Union as a Political Community Through the Lens of Immigration Policy in Marco Martiniello (ed.) *Migration, Citizenship and Ethno-National Identities in the European Union,* UK, Avebury, Ashgate Publishing Limited, p 199.

Lopez Garcia, B (1990) L'Espagne entre le Maghreb et l'Europe: imaginaire et interfereces de l'opinion dans la politique Maghrebin de l'Espagne, *Annuaire de l'Afrique du Nord,* pp 23–37.

Moisi, D in Glen St l Barclay (1995) The European Union and the Maghreb: A Clash of Civilisations? in *Australia and World Affairs,* (25), winter issue, p 5–17.

OECD in Bodega, I et al (1995) *ibid,* p 308.

Santos, L (1993) Elementos juridicos de la integración de los extranieros in Tapinos, G (ed) *Inmigracion e Integracion en Europe,* Barcelona: Fundacion Paulino Torres Domenech, pp 91–125.

Scruton, R, (1991) *Dictionary of Political Thought,* London, Penguin Book Publishers.

Sole, C, (1981) *La integración sociocultural de los immigrantes en Catalunya,* Madrid: CIS.

Sole, C, (1988) *Catalunya: societat receptora d'immigrantes,* Barcelona: Institut d'Estudis Catalans.

Treves, C, Di Gioacchino, R, Masoubil M Toaff, E, Spini, V Pascucci, G, Mussi, Fand Trentin, B (1989) *Sindacato dei dirittie societtià multietnica,* Rome, Ediesse, pp 47–49.

Tapinos, G (ed) *Inmigracion e Integracion en Europe,* Barcelona: Fundacion Paulino Torres Domenech.

Vicarelli, G. (1994) – *Le Mani Invisibili,* Roma: Ediesse.

Wiener, A (1996) Rethinking Citizenship: The Quest for Place-Oriented Participation in the EU *in The Oxford International Review,* VII(3),pp 44–51.

Zolberg, A (1987) Keeping them out: ethical dilemmas of immigration policy in Robert J. *Myers, International ethics in the nuclear age,* Lanham, Maryland, University Press of America, pp 261–297.

Chapter Nine

The Europe Agreements: The Right to Establishment in the Central and Eastern European Agreements

Elspeth Guild

The Political Context

Between 1991 and 1996 the European Community concluded Association Agreements with ten Central and Eastern countries formerly within the sphere of influence of the USSR which Agreements are unique in providing a right to natural persons to come to the Member States to exercise economic activities[1]. Negotiating mandates towards the first of these Agreements were issued late in 1989, in other words, at a time when revellers were still taking down pieces of the Berlin wall. The speed with which the Agreements were concluded evidences the political will within the European Union to embrace these countries in Central and Eastern Europe and to participate in the process of reconstruction.

The ten countries in respect of which Europe Agreements provide a right of establishment (which includes self-employment for natural persons) to nationals of those states within the Member States of the European Union are Bulgaria, the Czech Republic, Estonia, Hungary, Latvia, Lithuania, Poland, Romania, Slovenia and Slovakia. At the time when the Agreements were entered into it was by no means clear that these states would, in the short or even medium term, be acceding to the European Union.

The Agreements cover a wide variety of economic areas in which co-operation is to be pursued. Economic integration of the Central and Eastern European countries into the Community is the clearly stated objective. There are provisions on approximation of laws, agricultural and industrial standards, technical regulations etc. However, here, I am only concerned with the inclusion in these Agreements of provisions relating to the movement of natural persons. Specific reference will be made to the EC/Poland Agreement which constituted the blueprint upon which the other Agreements were based. There are variations between the Agreements but the fundamental provisions of interest here, specifically the right of establishment are, in substance, consistent. The Agreements make provision for workers, the self employed and service providers. In this respect they are modelled on the EC Treaty, dividing into the same categories types of economic activity carried out inter alia by natural persons. However, the free movement of persons is not an object in itself of the Europe Agreements.

The Europe Agreements form part of Community law having been concluded under Article 238 EC in conformity with the procedure set out in

---

1 This is loose designation as one of those countries is Slovenia.

Article 228 EC. As such they form an integral part of the Community legal order and within that framework the European Court of Justice has jurisdiction to give preliminary rulings concerning their interpretation[2].

It does not necessarily follow though that a provision of an Agreement must carry the same interpretation as a similar or indeed identical provision in the EC Treaty[3]. The extension of the interpretation of a Treaty provision to a provision worded in comparable, similar or even identical terms in an Agreement concluded by the Community with a non-Member country depends in particular on the aim of each provision in its own framework. A comparison of the objects and the context of the Agreement on the one hand and those of the Treaty on the other are very important in this connection[4].

The aims of the Agreements are:-

1. to provide a framework for political dialogue;
2. to promote expansion of trade and harmonious economic relations in order to foster dynamic economic development and prosperity;
3. to provide a basis for financial and technical assistance;
4. to provide a framework for integration into the community;
5. to promote cooperation in cultural matters[5].

The aims of the EC Treaty are much wider. They are contained in Part 1 of the Treaty and after the Maastricht amendments included 20 specific areas in which the general objective of a harmonious balanced development of economic activities, sustainable and non-inflationary growth respecting the environment, a high degree of convergence of economic performance, a high level of employment and of social protection, the raising of the standard of living and quality of life and the economic and social cohesion and solidarity among the Member States would be achieved (Article 2 EC – the Amsterdam Treaty has added one more specific area to the list in Article 3 – the promotion of co-ordination between employment policies of the Member States). This includes, however, the entry and movement of persons.

I will be arguing in this chapter for a uniform and consistent interpretation of the Europe Agreements with the EC Treaty. The lack of an identical or similar principle or aims provision in the Europe Agreements should not justify differential interpretation.

In light of the objective of the Europe Agreements to facilitate the economic integration of these countries into the Community a uniform interpretation is not only justified but highly desirable. There are already indications from courts in some Member States that such a uniform interpretation is being applied[6].

---

2 12/86 *Demirel* [1987] ECR 3719.

3 270/80 *Polydor* [1982] ECR 329.

4 C-312/91 *Metalsa* [1993] ECR I-3751.

5 Article 1(2) EEC – Poland Agreement.

6 The Belgian Raad Van State – No 52.631–10th Chamber, Decision of 3.4.95.

FREE MOVEMENT OF WORKERS

Each of the Agreements contains a title "movement of workers, establishment and supply of services". As regards movement of workers, this is something of a misnomer as there is no right for workers to move either between the Central and Eastern European countries and the Member States nor within the Community. For example, Article 37 of the Poland Agreement requires that equal treatment of Polish workers legally employed in the territory of a Member State shall be free of any discrimination based on nationality as regards working conditions, remuneration or dismissal as compared to own nationals. However, the opening words of the Article state "subject to the conditions and modalities applicable in each Member State". What does this proviso mean?

In terms of the Community legal order, a conflict is hereby created as to whether the general principle of equal treatment as applicable in Community law applies directly to workers nationals of these countries or whether national discretion still has primacy. Could a Polish worker experiencing discrimination on the basis of nationality, for instance, in dismissal, rely on Article 37 of the Agreement to seek redress? This will depend very much on the interpretation to be given to "the conditions and modalities applicable in each Member State". It is by no means clear that a right can be founded on this basis.

The scope of such a non-discrimination provision without the limitation of national discretion contained in an Agreement with a third country, specifically Morocco, was held to be directly effective in the legal order of the Member States. This means that a protected worker may rely directly on the Community law provision (in the EEC-Morocco Agreement) to defeat a national provision to the contrary. The context of that decision of the European Court of Justice was equal treatment in access to social security benefits. In a recent opinion, Mr Advocate General Jacobs has helpfully itemised the principal elements of the non-discrimination provision of the Maghreb Agreements as:-

1. The term "worker" encompasses former workers (ie. inclusive in a wide Community context).
2. The term "social security" must be interpreted in accordance with the Community definition contained in Regulation 1408/71.
3. The non-discrimination provision has direct effect so that persons to whom it applies are entitled to rely on it in proceedings before national Courts (*Babahenini* C-113/97, Opinion 13.11.97).

Another case on the EEC-Morocco Agreement's non-discrimination provisions relates to security of residence to enjoy employment. This is currently before the Court of Justice in the matter of *El Yassini* C-416/96. In that case, it is argued that the non-discrimination provision relating to working conditions must extend also to permission to continue to work in respect of a Moroccan worker who has been lawfully employed in a Member State and whose employment is continuing but in respect of whom the Member State has sought to withdraw his permission to reside and work otherwise than on grounds of public policy.

In the Europe Agreements, the addition of the "conditions and modalities" proviso relating to national law raises serious questions as to whether the non-discrimination right can be directly effective. Until the meaning of the proviso is clarified by the Court of Justice it may be premature to suggest a *mutatis mutandis* application of the jurisprudence relating to the Maghreb Agreements.

In view of the sensitivities of the Member States in respect of protection of the labour markets, it is not surprising that no right of free movement of workers was included in any of the Agreements with Central and Eastern European countries. What is perhaps more surprising is that these Agreements do not expressly include protection of residence for workers of those states already present and working in the Member States. Such a right of continuing access to the labour market and residence is a hallmark of the subsidiary legislation under the EEC-Turkey Association Agreement. Therefore as regards security of continued residence, the Europe Agreements are less favourable than the corresponding provisions of the EEC Turkey Agreement. If workers from Europe Agreement countries enjoy any protection of continuing residence and work such a right could only be found in the non-discrimination provision on working conditions.

THE RIGHT OF ESTABLISHMENT

All of the CEEC Agreements include provisions in virtually identical terms to the Poland Agreement relating to the right to exercise self-employment. In the Poland Agreement Article 44 states:

> "Each Member State shall grant from entry into force of this Agreement, a treatment no less favourable than that accorded to its own companies and nationals as defined in Article 48 and shall grant in the operation of Polish companies and nationals established in the territory a treatment no less favourable than that accorded to its own companies and nationals."

Article 44(4) of the Agreement provides:

> "For the purposes of this Agreement, "establishment" shall mean as regards nationals, the right to take up and pursue economic activities as self-employed persons and to set up and manage undertakings, in particular, companies, which they effectively control."

The equivalent provision in the EC Treaty is Article 52, which states:-

> "Within the framework of the provisions set out below, restrictions on the freedom of establishment of nationals of a Member State in the territory of another Member State shall be abolished by progressive stages in the course of the transitional period. Such progressive abolition shall also apply to restrictions on the setting up of agencies, branches or subsidiaries by nationals of any Member State established in the territory of any Member State.
>
> Freedom of establishment shall include the right to take up and pursue activities as self-employed persons and to set up and manage undertakings, in particular, companies or firms under the conditions laid down for its own nationals, by the law of the country where such establishment is effected....".

The right of establishment as interpreted in Community law[7] includes a right of access to the territory of the Member States in order to carry out the economic activity in addition to a right to remain on the territory for that purpose. I will briefly look at this aspect of the right which is perhaps the most important in terms of development of the Community immigration policy.

A RIGHT OF ACCESS TO THE TERRITORY

Only once before in Community law has a personal right of access to the territory of the Member States been extended to natural persons nationals of a non-Member State. This previous example, in the European Economic Area Agreement 1992 concluded with five of the EFTA states (Finland, Iceland, Liechtenstein, Norway and Sweden) provided for the full extension of all free movement rights to nationals of those states. This example is perhaps not so exceptional in view of the level of economic development of these states and the similarity of their employment markets with those of the European Union. Further, by the time the Agreement came into force on 1.1.94, it was clear that most of these states would accede to the Community in the near future.

By contrast, the countries of Central and Eastern Europe, even at the time when these Agreements were entered into, were still substantial sending countries for asylum seekers. In particular, Romanian and Bulgarian asylum seekers in the Member States in 1991 formed a substantial proportion of the overall numbers. Out of a total of 392,329 applications for asylum in the EC 12 in 1991, 59,265 were from nationals of Central and Eastern European States (the figure includes a very small number from the former USSR) (Migration Statistics 1994, Eurostat). In view of the tendency of the Member States to see numbers of asylum applicants as an indicator of the pressure to emigrate, particularly when paired with high rates of refusal of those asylum applications the decision to give a right of access to the territory to nationals of these states is noteworthy. However, two provisions of the Agreements seek to restrict the right, I shall return to these shortly.

THIRD COUNTRY NATIONALS AND THE EUROPEAN COMMUNITY

In terms of the context of the creation of a right for third country nationals to enter the territory of the Community it may be useful briefly to review the position of third country nationals in Community law. By 1991, natural persons fell into four main categories vis a vis Community law:

1. Community nationals with full free movement rights and in the process of getting a generalised right of residence;

---

7 2/74 *Reyners* [1974] ECR 631.

2. Third country nationals with a derived right of entry and residence including: family members of Community nationals who, irrespective of their own nationality enjoyed derived rights equivalent to their Community national principals; third country national employees of a Community based company who are sent to another Member State to provide services for their employer[8]. The right to enter the territory of another Member State for these persons is strictly limited to a derived right.
3. Third country nationals whose residence right is protected by an Agreement between the European Community and their state of nationality (specifically Turkey) and the exceptional category of the nationals of European Economic Area Agreement states. No third country agreement except the EEA Agreement gave a right of access to the territory of the Member States to third country nationals.
4. Others with no claim to residence or movement under Community law unless such a claim could be founded on Article 7A EC, the Single Market provision. "The internal market shall comprise an area without internal frontiers in which the free movement of goods, persons, services and capital is ensured....." (Article 7A EC).

In respect of those third country nationals in categories 2 and 3 whose rights derive from Community law, Member State discretion as regards the recognition of their rights is extremely limited. It is a feature of Community provisions on movement and residence of persons that once a category comes within the competence of the Community national discretion is in effect excluded.

At the same time as the negotiation of the Europe Agreements the Member States among themselves were engaged in a major reconsideration of their treatment of third country nationals. Specifically, in the context of the re-negotiation of the Treaties which lead to the Treaty on European Union the Member States agreed that migration policy and measures in respect of third country nationals in general should fall outside the scope of the European Community and be dealt with fundamentally intergovernmentally, within the so-called Third Pillar created by the Treaty on European Union. Within that intergovernmental forum, the primary preoccupation of the Member States in their deliberations and in the measures adopted was the retention of national discretion on admission and residence of third country nationals. Further, the measures adopted in the Third Pillar were characterised by an unvarying diet of restrictive measures designed to limit access to the territory of the Member States.

Within this political context, the creation within the First Pillar, the Community, of a right of access to the territory for nationals of countries whence there was a perceived pressure to emigrate is exceptional. It exemplifies a difference of perspective between interior ministries charged with a control function which effectively dominated the Third Pillar and wider Community economic policy.

---

8 C-43/93 *Vander Elst* [1994] ECR I-3803.

In 1991 the European Commission issued a Communication on immigration[9] which perhaps is revealing. In that Communication the Commission not only drew attention to the positive aspects and consequences of immigration but also warned the Member States that excessively restrictive policies which provide no flexibility can lead to greater problems particularly in respect of illegal migration. Such a result, particularly holds true in respect of policies towards nationals of countries in close physical proximity to the Union. Unless mechanisms are developed to relieve migratory pressure in a consistent and regulated fashion Member States run the risk of losing control over the process. Within this context, the extension of the right of establishment to nationals of Central and Eastern European countries is an extremely important development in the Community's immigration policy.

THE ESTABLISHMENT PROVISION

The right of establishment covers two types of activity:

1. The right of the individuals nationals of the Europe Agreement states to establish themselves personally in self-employment in the Member States. This is the right to take up employment and pursue economic activities as self-employed persons and to set up and manage undertakings, in particular companies, which they effectively control[10].
2. As regards companies, the right to take up and pursue economic activities by means of setting up and managing subsidiaries, branches and agencies and in order to do this to send key personnel, as defined in the Agreements[11].

The right is subject to a limitation on grounds of public policy, public security or public health.

As regards the definition of self-employment, Community law relating to free movement does not permit the Member States to insert their own national definitions. As with employment, self-employment is a Community concept the defining feature of which is whether or not the individual carries out work within a relationship of subordination[12]. So long as a person is not subordinated to another person or an organisation but is performing services for remuneration then he or she is self-employed for the purposes of Community law. There are of course factual problems related to self-employment which do not arise in respect of employment. For instance, establishing the date on which the right is exercised is more difficult in respect of self-employment where there may be a lapse of time between the decision

9 SEC (91) 1857 final.

10 For instance, Article 44(4)(a)(i) of the Poland Agreement.

11 For instance, Article 44(9)(a)(ii) of the Poland Agreement.

12 C-107/94 *Asscher* [1996] All ER (EC) 757.

to become self-employed and the point at which the self-employed activity becomes economically viable. There is no clear guidance from the European Court of Justice on this issue. Guidance may however be taken from the Court's pronouncements as regards employment in that so long as the activity is genuine and effective, and irrespective of the intention of the individual, it comes within the Community concept of employment[13].

An exception to the Community definition of employment and self-employment exists as regards these concepts for the purposes of Article 51 EC and its implementing Regulation 1408/71, co-ordination of social security systems. Because Article 51 EC and Regulation 1408/71 do no more than co-ordinate between national social security systems, national definitions of these terms apply. To find otherwise would throw into disarray the Member States social security systems, which are outside Community law except for the purposes of co-ordination.

DISCRIMINATION AND OBSTACLES

The right of establishment for nationals of the Central and Eastern European countries is constructed in terms of non-discrimination. In the EC Treaty where such a right of movement for the purpose of self-employment is created, obstacles to the exercise of the right are prohibited[14]. This means that measures which are likely to hinder or inhibit the exercise of the right by an individual entitled to take advantage of it may be contrary to the right itself even where indistinctly applicable to own nationals[15]. The jurisprudence of the Court of Justice as regards obstacles to free movement extends more widely than the concept of non-discrimination. This is not least because of the purpose which is to give effect to the exercise of the rights. For example, the right to family reunion in Community law derives not from a non-discrimination right which would result in the application of national family reunion provisions to Community nationals exercising their free movement rights but rather from the right to the abolition of obstacles which could hinder the exercise of the right[16].

The development of the rights of Community nationals moving within the Member States has been formulated by reference to two principles, non-discrimination and obstacles in respect of which the second has allowed the development of Community rules considered necessary by the legislator irrespective of any national provisions at Member State level to enable the right to be exercised, in the words of Regulation 1612/68 "in freedom and dignity". A right to equal treatment prohibits both direct and indirect discrimination, which the Court of Justice has defined as the application of criteria of

---

13 53/81 *Levin* [1982] ECR 1035.

14 C-415/93 *Bosman* [1996] ECR I-4921.

15 C-4-5/95 *Stöber* [1997] 2 CMLR 213.

16 Pre-amble, Regulation 1612/68.

differentiation other than nationality which lead in fact to the same result (of discrimination)[17] .

The dividing line between obstacles and discrimination is evolving in the case law of the Court (see in particular the recent decision in *Stöber*; [1997] 2 CMLR 213). It will be important to determine whether both or only one concept applies to those seeking to exercise self employment in the Member States under the CEEC Agreements. Clearly such nationals on the wording of the provision are entitled to non discrimination. However it is also arguable that on the basis of the creation of a right to movement, for that right of access to the territory to be effective obstacles to its exercise are also unlawful.

In the opinion of the Court of Justice as regards the exercise of the right of establishment in the EEC Treaty any obstacles or measures liable to hinder or make less attractive the exercise of the right must fulfil four conditions:

1. They must be applied in a non-discriminatory manner.
2. They must be justified by imperative requirements in the general interest.
3. They must be suitable for securing the attainment of the objective they pursue.
4. They must not go beyond what is necessary to obtain it[18].

It is the introduction of the free movement right which may render these principles applicable for nationals of the Central and Eastern European countries. If so, then the rights of CEEC nationals are much enhanced – for example, a Polish national who is self-employed in the UK may have overstayed or been classified as an illegal entrant. If the *Gebhard* principles apply to his or her situation, then any measure by the Home Office to penalise the individual on the basis of his or her unlawfulness must meet the criteria not least that the measures must be suitable to secure the attainment of the objective pursued and must not go beyond what is necessary to attain it. The object is the maintenance of firm immigration controls. However, the Court of Justice has consistently held that a measure amounting to expulsion is not proportional to the offence of failure to comply with immigration requirements as regards the exercise of free movement rights by Community nationals[19]. Therefore any measure by the Home Office designed to require the individual to return to Warsaw to make an entry clearance application in order to return to resume self-employment would be disproportionate. Just such a situation is currently being referred to the Court of Justice from the High Court in London. The clarification of the law in this case will be very important to understanding the scope of the rights of CEEC nationals in the exercise of self-employment.

---

17 152/73 *Sotgiu* [1974] ECR 153.

18 C-55/94 *Gebhard* [1995] ECR I-4165.

19 48/75 *Royer* [1976] ECR 497; 118/75 *Watson & Belman* [1976] ECR 1185.

CLAWING BACK NATIONAL DISCRETION

Two aspects of the Agreements indicate a contrary tendency to one of convergence. In the Poland Agreement, and reflected in all other Agreements, Article 58 provides that as regards the right of establishment "nothing in the Agreement shall prevent the parties from applying their laws and regulations relating to entry and stay, work, labour conditions and establishment of natural persons, and supply of services provided that, in so doing they do not apply them in such a manner as to nullify or to impair the benefits accruing to any party".

This provision has not been overlooked by the Home Office and DSS. In a recent letter to the AIRE Centre regarding the issue of national insurance numbers to self-employed CEEC nationals the DSS advised on the basis of information from the Home Office that the Agreements "All contain an Article which enables the parties to apply their laws and conditions regarding entry and stay, work, labour conditions and establishment of natural persons and supply of services, provided that they do not nullify or impair the benefits accruing under the terms of a specific provision of the Agreement". Clearly at least one Member State is seeking to justify differential treatment of CEEC nationals on the basis of proviso.

Secondly, each Agreement has annexed to it the joint declaration providing that "the sole fact of requiring a visa for natural persons of certain parties and not for those others shall not be regarded as nullifying or impairing benefits under a specific commitment".

Both of these provisions clearly run contrary to the intention to create a right of establishment. Both seek to insert into the right a role for national discretion to be used in such a way as to circumscribe the individual's right to choose whether to move or not for the purpose of self-employment. To this extent both measures negate the right granted in the Agreement. On the other hand, both may give comfort to nervous national administrations concerned about influx. It will be a matter, ultimately, for the European Court of Justice to determine the full extent of "nullify or impair". As any restrictive measure is likely to impair the exercise of a right it is not entirely clear what content this phrase can have.

From the wider perspective, it is difficult to reconcile the individual's right which in Community law includes a right to the abolition of obstacles, with the possibility of a fetter of national discretion which by its very nature will, where exercised, result in variations in the exercise of the right in different Member States.

GOOD FAITH AND MEMBER STATES EXECUTION

In each of the Agreements a provision equivalent to Article 115 of the Poland Agreement provides that "the parties shall take any general or specific measures required to fulfil their obligations under the Agreement". Accordingly, between the European Community and each of the Central and Eastern European countries there is a duty of good faith. This duty applies also to each of the Member States individually. However, as regards each individual state's duty to the Central or Eastern European country implementation and enforcement are issues. In view of the current state of international law on enforcement of treaties and the eagerness of the Central and Eastern European countries to join the Union, inter-state action to enforce the right of establishment for CEEC nationals is highly unlikely.

In respect of the duty of the Community to ensure the fulfilment of its obligations under the Agreement the situation is different. Assuming, as I have done here, that the right of establishment has direct effect in the territory of the Member States it is therefore a commitment of the Community to the Central and Eastern European countries as well as a commitment of the Member States. This means that the duty of good faith of each of the Member States to the Community is engaged to ensure that the Community itself can fulfil its obligations under the Agreements. It is important to note that as regards the right of establishment, the Europe Agreements are not "mixed" unless such quality is acquired by virtue of Article 58 of the Poland Agreement and as reproduced in the other Agreements. A mixed agreement is one where the competence exercised is joint between the Member States and the Community, for example in environment or development co-operation. A mixed competence in a third country Agreement can also arise where the Community has potentially exclusive competence but this has not been exercised. In the field of establishment the Community competence has been fully exercised within the Union (implementation of Article 52 EC) therefore its external competence must be exclusive within the terms of the Agreement[20].

Article 5 EC requires Member States to take "all appropriate measures, whether general or particular, to ensure the fulfilment of obligations arising out of the Treaty or resulting from action taken by the institutions of the Community".

So, on the one hand, the Member States, under the terms of the Agreement itself, must act in good faith to fulfil their obligations. As regards a mixed Agreement, this would certainly be relevant to those obligations which are within the competence of the Member States to carry out. On the other hand the duty of good faith to the Community is also engaged. It is through the actions of the Member States, the issue of visas, residence and self-employment permits that the Community is able to fulfil its obligations to the countries of Central and Eastern Europe as regards the right of establishment for their nationals. Therefore, any failure on the part of the Member States to give full effect to the establishment right of nationals of Central and Eastern Europe may be a breach of Article 5 EC.

It is within this capacity that the fulfilment of the objective of the Community must be viewed. Where there is a conflict between the preference of, for instance, the Home Office to maintain its discretionary power to admit

---

20 D McGoldrick, International Relations of the European Union, Longman 1997 p.78 et seq.

or refuse admission to an individual to the territory and the duty of that same ministry to fulfil the commitment of the Community to a third country to provide free access to the territory for the purposes of self-employment the latter duty must prevail.

Chapter Ten

The Social and Political Context of Migration Between Central Europe and the European Union

Dariusz Stola

Since the fall of the Iron Curtain at the eastern border of European Union there has emerged a new migration space. Under the communist regimes international population mobility was strictly controlled and in most cases severely restricted. The Soviet Block acted as a negative determinant of the world migratory configuration[1]. This resulted in highly consequential developments that seemed natural but were a byproduct of Cold War history. For example the fact that Germany and France since the 1960s massively imported labor from Turkey and North Africa instead of Central Europe, as they had done during more than half a century before 1945, had obvious consequences for what makes a large part of the "immigration question" of today's Europe. Among human rights that inhabitants of Central and Eastern Europe regained after 1989 was the right to leave one's own country. As a part of general liberalization new democratic regimes opened wider their borders to foreign visitors. Different paths of economic reforms and their outcomes have generated new factors that push and pull people to move. Since that time international migrations in the region have been a phenomenon of greater complexity and variety than expected.

Various similarities between four Central European countries – the Czech Republic, Hungary, Poland and Slovakia — and the region geographic, socioeconomic and political position between the EU and the former Soviet Union make it distinct as a migratory Middle Zone or Buffer Zone[2]. This chapter will present briefly migrations from the so defined Central Europe to Western Europe in the 1990s, as well as major movements to and across Central Europe, with emphasis on their social and political conditions.

Presenting the movement from Central Europe to the West one should stress the difference between long-term and short-term flows, and different migration propensities in the countries of the region. Poland was, has been and very probably will be the by far largest source of migrants to the West, therefore it must be given particular attention. Similarly Germany was, and has been the major recipient of Central European migrants both before and after 1989. The 1989 change was more than a series of political revolutions,

---

1 Zolberg, A., Migration theory for a changing world, *International Migration Review* vol. 23 no 3 (Fall 1989), p. 412.

2 Stola, D., "Migrations in Poland: transition and transit, *EpiCenter,* Vol. 1, No 2 (Fall 1995); Wallace C., Chmouliar O. and E. Sidorenko, "The Eastern Frontier of Western Europe: mobility in the buffer zone, *New Community* 22 (April 1996), and "The Central European Buffer Zone", Institute for Advanced Studies 1997. Slovenia political and economic recovery and its direct border to the EU make it probably the fifth country of the region.

velvet or bloody. It was the beginning (or turning point) of a set of political and socioeconomic processes, such as the collapse of communist parties' monopoly of power, introduction of rule of law and democratic procedures, economic transformation, the Soviet military withdrawal from the region and the end of the Cold War, disintegration of the Soviet Block and ensuing disintegration of the Soviet Union itself. To these developments Western countries reacted with new policies, including migration policies. Each of these factors and their respective consequences have influenced international migrations in the region.

Return to Diversity and New Migratory Developments

A common feature of international migrations before 1989 in the countries under consideration and all Soviet satellites was the undiversified character of flows. In the whole Soviet Block they consisted predominantly of permanent emigrants to the West. Moreover, this category consisted of a few sub-categories according to eligibility, first and foremost of "patrials" having their external homelands sufficiently influential in international relations: Germans and Jews. Another sub-category was asylum-seekers. Both streams of permanent emigrants were strikingly unstable which reflected the political nature of factors that ruled their flow, namely relaxing the "grip" of restrictions on emigration[3].

Since 1989 new categories of migrants have come to the fore and dominated the former. International migrations in the region differ from the pre-1989 period in terms of scale and variety. Moreover, new forms of large-scale international population mobility have been noted, previously marginal or unknown. One should note in particular the explosion of cross-border mobility including quasi-migratory circular movements, the emergence of transit migration, and the development of labor migration to the countries of Central Europe. New, sometimes unprecedented migratory phenomena reflect the radical change that the countries have gone through. Mass migrations are reactions to social change. Analysis of international migrations brings us knowledge about migrations themselves but also about the changes behind them.

The Decline of Permanent/long-term Emigration

There was substantial difference in scale of emigration from Central European countries before 1989. Since late 1970s Polish communists had gradually opened the gate and in late 1980s practically ceased to control exit. In its last decade People's Poland experienced a true exodus of some 1.3 million people,

---

3 Okolski M., 'New migration trends in Central and Eastern Europe in the 1990s *ISS Working Papers,* Warsaw University 1997.

mostly in 1987–1989. Other countries had much smaller outflows because of more restrictive exit policies (Czechoslovakia) or lower migration propensity (Hungary) than in Poland. These two factors (restrictions on exit to the West and readiness to go) refer to two internal actors in migration process: the home country government and the migrants. While most theories of migration focus on explaining the behaviour of the latter, the history of migrations in the Soviet Block stresses the role of the former.

The 1990s did not bring mass outflow from Central Europe, as was the case with such post-communist countries like Albania, Romania, former Yugoslavia and Soviet Union[4]. Contrary to the fears expressed in the West in the early transition period, after an initial growth the 1990s brought a decline of long-term emigration from the region. This unexpected development resulted from a combination of factors, in particular the relative stability of the countries of the region resulting from the peaceful nature of their 1989 revolutions, successful economic reforms and Western support. But at least equally important were the new Western policies towards migrants from Central Europe, in particular the German *Aussiedler policy.*

With the introduction of a democratic regime in the countries under consideration, the end of the Cold War era and the refugee crisis in the West caused by much larger South-North flows, there was no longer justification nor willingness to extend political asylum to Poles, Czechs or Hungarians. New German policy towards the *Aussiedlers* (ethnic German immigrants) had greater impact on statistics than new asylum policies, as until 1990 they had been the largest group of emigrants from Central Europe. In the summer of 1990, after the massive arrival of *Aussiedlers* from Poland in 1989 and their growing movement from the Soviet Union, Germany altered its policy towards the Central European applicants for the status. The requirement to apply in the home country and more rigorous examination of credentials resulted in a dramatic decline in statistics: the figures for the stream from Poland fell from 250,000 in 1989 to 18,000 in 1992 and just 2,400 in 1994[5].

Two comments of general character are in order here. First, the history of Central European migrations at the end of Cold War and the beginning of the post-Cold War era introduce to us the third key actor of East-West migrations: the receiving country government. Since the former Soviet Block countries ceased to restrict exit, the burden of regulating East-West flows moved to the receiving countries. But before Western leaders realized what the collapse of communism was bringing in terms of migration, Central Europeans willing to emigrate had a unique window of opportunity: when the government of the sending country had ceased to restrict their emigration and the government of receiving country did not yet restrict their immigration. Second, despite the often-heard assertions that liberal democracies cannot effectively

4 Frejka T. (ed.), *International migration in Central and Eastern Europe and the Commonwealth of Independent States,* United Nations, New York and Geneva 1996.

5 German Interior Ministry data.

control immigration, new policies for East-West migration were quite effective, as the above figures show[6].

DEVELOPMENT OF SHORT-TERM MOVEMENTS

In the 1990s temporary, mostly short-term migrations replaced long-term/ permanent migration as the main type of flow from Central Europe[7]. These new movements are the way Central Europe reintegrates into the European migration system after several decades of isolation. The restrictions on permanent immigration to Western countries were not the only cause of the change. While restricting settlement, West European countries allowed for Central Europeans' visa-free entry thus greatly facilitating their travel and temporary stay abroad. For example, between 1989 and 1995 the number of the Poles' trips abroad (i.e. exits registered by the Border Guard) rose from 10 million to 36 million, most of them westward. Simultaneous development of bus transportation to major destinations in Western Europe had similar results, that is it made travel cheaper and more convenient. Since the end of restrictions on exit, not only going abroad but also coming back has been easier. The fear that one may be refused his/her passport next time, which pushed many not to come back from abroad, is no longer there. At the same time migration propensity, that is the readiness to go among many Central Europeans, did not disappear. There were winners and losers of the economic transformation; in the first years of restructuring there were more of the latter than the former. In reaction to changing conditions certain groups became particularly prone for seeking income abroad.

Thanks to recent research we can see how these factors influenced migrants' decisions, for example in the evolution of migrations from long-term, long-distance movement to the United States to short-term, short distance migrations in Europe. Peasants' sons from Monki in northeastern Poland or highlanders from Podhale used to go to Chicago, where they worked hard several years and returned home. In the 1990s they have increasingly gone to Brussels or to Vienna respectively, and for much shorter stays. The migrations have new forms and directions but fulfill the same economic function while being much cheaper in terms of transportation and communication costs, bureaucratic burden (a trip to the United States requires a visa), as well as psychological and social costs of long separation from the family[8].

The movements are indeed short or very short-term. Migrants stay abroad

---

6 Freeman G.P., "Can Liberal States Control Unwanted Immigration?" *Annals of the American Academy of Political and Social Science* vol. 534 (July 1994).

7 Organization for Economic Cooperation and Development, *Trends in international migrations,* Paris 1996 (and other years) – SOPEMI report.

8 Jazwinska E. and Okolski M. (eds.), *Causes and consequences of migration in Central and Eastern Europe. Podlasie and Śląsk Opolski: basic trends in 1975–1994,* Warsaw 1996; Mydel R., Fassman H., *Nielegalni robotnicy cudzoziemscy i czarny rynek pracy: polscy nielegalni pracownicy w Wiedniu,* Kraków 1997.

for a couple of months, a few weeks or just several days, but many do it repeatedly. In regions bordering with Germany and Austria there are also commuters crossing the border daily or people who have an extra job abroad on weekends. Experts in Central European migration point at the development of new, mass population movements, which they call "pendular", "circular" or "incomplete" migration, as the most distinct migratory phenomenon in the region[9].

The migrations are undoubtedly of economic character. Sharp wage disparities between EU and Central Europe provide a strong pull factor. Looking for a job in a neighbouring country where wages are several times higher than at home is a rational choice. The folk wisdom of Polish labor migrants says "Earn there [in the West] - spend here". They have tested empirically that short-term migration enables one to maximize the benefits of the combination of higher wages "there" and lower prices "here". Earnings abroad also diversify household sources of income, which is important under conditions of fast changes and economic instability. Observers noted two different approaches to migration earnings, which seem highly significant as reactions to the transformation. The first approach treats earnings abroad as a way for accumulation of capital necessary to start up or expand a business and exploit new opportunities opened by the market economy. The second approach is defensive: remittances are to protect the household against relative degradation in consumption and social hierarchy[10].

The flows are selective in terms of destination. Most of the Central European migrants go to Germany and (obviously on a much lesser scale) to Austria. Germany, as immigration statistics show, is the European country most attractive for all kinds of migrants from various countries. For Central Europeans Germany is a big neighbour of high wages. Moreover, under a series of bilateral agreements Germany offers legal employment for temporary workers from the countries of the region. The agreements pertain to seasonal work, project-tied employment (subcontract employment), on-the-job training programmes and cross-border commuters. The total number of Central European employees varied between 151,000 and 324,000 annually, depending on demand and quotas set in relation to situation in German labour market. Most of the migrants are seasonal workers (for example 203,000 out of 260,000 in 1996). Since the seasonal workers can work in Germany for up to three months, their actual yearly employment is much less. Altogether Central European programme workers make about 10% of foreign employees and 1% of total employment in Germany[11].

---

9 Morokvasic M., "Entre l'est et 'Ouest, des migrations pendulaires", in Morokvasic M., Rudolph H. (eds.), *Migrants. Les nouvelles mobilites en Europe,* Paris 1996; Okolski M., "New migration trends..."; Biffl, G. *(ed.) Migration, Free Trade and Regional Integration in Central and Eastern Europe,* Wien 1997; Jazwinska E. and Okolski M. (eds) *op.cit.*

10 Jazwinska E. and Okolski M. (eds.), *op.cit.;* Morokvasic M., *op.cit.*

11 Hoenekopp E., *Labour Migration to Germany from Central and Eastern Europe – Old and New Trends,* Institute for Employment Research, Nuremberg 1997.

Although they concentrate mainly in Germany, Central European migrants reach all countries of Europe. Besides countries with established Polish or Hungarian diasporas such as France, UK or Austria, they work – legally or not – in places as distant as Greece, Portugal and Norway[12].

While all countries of the region send migrants to the West, the large majority of them comes from Poland. For example in Germany, the figures for legal immigration from Poland (both stock and flow) are at least five times higher than respective figures for Hungary or the Czech and Slovak Republics. Between 80% and 90% of the seasonal workers are Poles. This obviously results from the relative size of each country's population but also from a greater propensity for migration among the Poles. According to Polish Ministry of Labour more than 300,000 Poles work temporarily in the West every year, but the phenomenon is certainly much larger in scale. Official data on labour migration of Poles only partially reflect the scale of the flow, which has a substantial stream of migrants in irregular situations. The number of unregistered Polish labour migrants to EU is difficult to estimate but research on migration in Poland as well as among Polish groups in the West shows that most of the identified new migrants take unregistered jobs. Therefore the total figure of labour migrants from Poland very probably exceeds half a million annually.

The substantial illegal component of Polish labour migration (in the case of other countries of the region the ratio of irregular to regular migration is probably lower) is not incidental. This is a result of a combination of 1) restrictions on the migrants' access to labour markets of EU countries; 2) their visa-free (i.e. unrestricted) entry to these countries; 3) the obviously existing demand for their wage-competitive and highly flexible labour; and 4) last but not least their large migrant networks. Thanks to the rich old and recent history of emigration, Polish diaspora can be found in most European countries. Networks of friends, relatives and friends' relatives provide practical information, advice and assistance in seeking a job, finding accommodation, etc.

MOVEMENTS TO CENTRAL EUROPE

Migrations to Central Europe deserve our attention not just because of the expected integration of the region to the EU. They also reflect Central Europe's position as a Middle Zone between Western Europe and former USSR (and the rest of Eurasia). The emergence of migration to countries of Central Europe was a historical novelty. The region experienced in the 20th century large population transfers resulting from wars and changing borders but voluntary immigration was an unusual occurrence. Except for the Czech Republic which historically imported labour and belonged rather to the European industrial core than its periphery, countries like Poland and Hungary have been for more than a century classic emigration countries with very small immigration. In addition, main flows into Central Europe are new also at their origins – in

---

12 Organization for Economic Cooperation and Development, *Trends in international migrations,* Paris 1996 (and other years); Jazwinska E. and Okolski M. (eds), *op.cit.*

countries which had emigration severely restricted before 1990, in particular the Soviet successor states. The flows occur between countries undergoing radical socioeconomic change. The phenomenon is therefore new, dynamic, largely unregistered and only partially explored.

Most of migrants to Central Europe come from Eastern Europe, that is former socialist countries further East, the post-Soviet republics in particular. Among the main factors that contributed to the development of movements between the former USSR and Central Europe were: a) divergent paths and outcomes of socioeconomic transformation in Central and Eastern Europe, which generate strong push and pull factors; b) favourable entry policy (no visa requirement) inherited from the COMECON period; c) large and easily accessible informal markets/economies; d) geographic and cultural (linguistic) proximity. Restrictions on entry of East Europeans to Western Europe and on their access to its labour markets make Central Europe their second best option: less attractive but more accessible than the West[13].

BETWEEN FOR-PROFIT MOBILITY AND LABOUR MIGRATION

The first notable development in international population movement was the explosion of cross-border mobility. In particular the Czech Republic and Poland have each in recent years registered more than a quarter of a billion border crossings annually, mostly by their non-nationals. Large majority of the entrants, especially at the western border of Central Europe, is one-day shoppers attracted by significantly lower prices on various products and services, from food, fuel and cigarettes to hairdressing, car repairs and prostitution. Mobility across Central Europe's eastern borders is more complex. Opening of the Soviet Union brought to the region millions of Ukrainian, Belorussian, Russian, Armenian, etc. 'false tourists' whose trips abroad were clearly for-profit undertakings, mostly in petty trade. The international petty trade in Central Europe underwent significant evolution, including a) the process of specialization, institutionalization and expansion of trade networks; and b) the reverse of trade trends (from dominant import to Central Europe to dominant export to ex-USSR) resulting mostly from changing price relations between the countries[14]. Poland seems most attractive for petty traders from the former USSR who come from regions as distant as Siberia and Caucasus. Petty traders visit Hungary also from former Yugoslavia, Romania and Bulgaria.

A part of commerce-oriented mobility evolved increasingly into labour migration. The boundary between the two is not clear and migrants often

---

13 Iglicka K., "The economics of petty trade on the eastern Polish border", in Iglicka K. and K. Sword (eds.), *Stemming the flood? Challenges of East-West migration for Poland,* forthcoming; Wallace C., Bedzir V., Chmouliar O., "Spending, saving or investing social capital: the case of shuttle traders in post-communist Central Europe", Institute for Advanced Studies, Vienna 1997.

14 Stola, D, Mechanizmy i uwarunkowania migracji zarobkowych do Polski w Swietle wywiadow z przybyszami z b ZSRR, ISS Working Papers Warsaw 1997.

combine earnings from trade and (self) employment. The for-profit nature of international mobility between Central Europe and former Soviet Union (and other post-communist countries outside the Middle Zone) that involves millions of people seeking income from suitcase trade, irregular employment or any economic activity makes it functionally similar to migration[15]. The quasi-migratory (pendular, incomplete) movements make a significant part of flows into Central Europe across its eastern border, certainly a larger part than the above mentioned quasi-migrations make in the westward flows from the region.

Besides significant quasi-migratory, irregular flows Central Europe receives a number of regular labour migrants. The Czech Republic, which has imported labour for many decades, seems the most attractive for this flow and has the largest (and growing) group of more than about 100,000 foreigners allowed to work: holders of work permit or "business authorization". The figures for Hungary, Poland and Slovakia are much smaller (19,200, 13,500 and 2,800 respectively in 1996) but their ratio of irregular to regular migrants is probably higher. Foreign labour tends to concentrate in big cities, in particular Prague, Budapest and Warsaw. Ukraine is the main country sending labour migrants to the region. Migrants from this 50 million nation lead among registered as well as unregistered foreign workers, especially in construction[16]. Among economic migrants to Central Europe there is also a non-negligible group of Westerners. This group includes employees of corporations operating on a global scale, foreign investors' managers, consultants, trainers, language teachers and businesspeople who found new opportunities in Central European emerging markets, and *leisure migrants* who come to spend not to earn. Again Czech Republic, Prague in particular, seems the most attractive destination for Western expatriates.

With the war in former Yugoslavia and political instability in former Soviet Union, Central Europeans were well afraid of the possibility of a large influx of refugees. The fears materialized only partially. In the tensest years of 1989– 1993 Hungary received more than 100,000 asylum-seekers while other countries of the region less than 6,000 each. Besides former Yugoslavia, refugees come from such distant countries as Sri Lanka, Afghanistan, Somalia, Armenia, Iraq etc. Many of them make part of the stream of transit migrants heading towards more affluent countries of Western Europe (see below). Much larger influx to Hungary is explained by its geographic proximity to former Yugoslavia but also by the ethnic structure of asylum-seekers most of whom were members of Hungarian minorities in Yugoslavia and Romania[17].

---

15 Okolski M., "New migration trends..."; Morokvasic M. and Rudolph H. Heds.), op.cit.7. Maresova L, "SOPEMI report for the Czech Republic", paper presented to the meeting of the SOPEMI correspondents, Paris 1996; Juhasz J., "SOPEMI report for Hungary", paper presented to the meeting of the SOPEMI correspondents, Paris 1996; Okólski M., "SOPEMI report for Poland", paper presented to the meeting of the SOPEMI correspondents, Paris 1996.

16 In Czech Republic 67,000 foreigners hold work permits and 39,000 are registered as entrepreneurs (data for mid-1996).

17 Sik E., *et al. (eds.), Refugees and migrants: Hungary at a crossroads,* Budapest 1995.

Hungary and Poland (the Czech Republic and Slovakia in a smaller scale) have large groups of their respective coethnics living abroad. These diasporas are a product of border changes and forced population displacements that affected heavily Central Europe in this century, as well as old voluntary migration outflows[18]. At least a part of the diasporas is a pool of potential migrants. Their members have an emotional, and to some extent a legal, basis for a privileged immigrant status (Law of Return) similar to German Aussiedlers. When they are perceived as victims of ethnic discrimination calls for their "return" intensify, although they are not returning migrants but mythical returnees, i.e. who move from their homeland to their "titular fatherland". Hungary has already become destination of many ethnic Hungarians from Romania and former Yugoslavia. Poland receives ethnic Poles from places as distant as Kazakhstan, where some 100,000 children and grandchildren of Stalin's deportees live. Many more ethnic Poles, probably more than two million live in the western part of former USSR. There are also migrants actually returning to Central Europe after having spent sometimes many years in the West.

TRANSIT MIGRATION AND ITS CONSEQUENCES: CENTRAL EUROPE AS A BUFFER ZONE

The Soviet Block acted as a negative determinant of the world migratory configuration not only in terms of outmigration but also in terms of transit. Before 1990 the Soviet transcontinental empire separated Europe from Asia, now it is a huge but relatively easy to cross bridge between the poles of global inequality. A large part of illegal transit migrants apprehended in Central Europe come from southeastern Asia. According to International Organization for Migration estimates as many as 100,000 – 140,000 migrants may transit annually through the Czech Republic and 100,000 through Poland, the two preferred countries for illegal entry into Germany[19]. The transit migration in Central Europe emerged because of a coincidental disintegration of the transcontinental USSR and increasing demand for illegal entry to Western Europe resulting from increasing immigration restrictions there. Principally, this transit migration would not have been very consequential for Central Europe but for its side effects: growing groups of unsuccessful transit-seekers who extend their stay in the region and new policies of final destination countries, in particular the introduction of the readmission principle. A group that mirrors the effects is illegal migrants who unsuccessfully sought asylum in Germany and were returned to a "safe third country" in Central Europe

18 Stola D., "Forced Migrations in Central European History", *International Migrations Review,* 26/2, 1992.

19 18. International Organization for Migration, *Transit migration in Poland, Transit migration in the Czech Republic* (and similar volumes for Bulgaria, Russia and Ukraine), Budapest 1995.

under the readmission agreements, where they immediately apply there for refugee status and then disappear from refugee reception centres evidently to try a second time.

Central Europe As A Semi-periphery, Interface, Buffer, Secondary Migration Pole

Various terms have been used above to define key features of Central European migration space. Sending temporary migrants to the West, Central Europe (primarily Poland) has become a source of highly flexible, rotating, "extra-territorial" labour. A similar relationship existed between economically backward Central and Eastern Europe and the West European industrial core before World War II. In terms of East-West migrations the concept of core-(semi)periphery relations seems well applicable. Was therefore the communist period just a long and costly detour from periphery to periphery?[20]

Located between Western Europe and its further peripheries, the region both sends migrants to the West and receives migrants from the East. Moreover, migrants going to the West and those coming from the East often have similar qualifications and perform similar types of work. In terms of labour migrations, having both migrant labour input and output, the region may thus be called a Middle Zone and compared to a migratory interface.

Countries of the region receive refugees but do not generate them. In particular, as safe third countries they readmit unsuccessful asylum-seekers returned from the West. For the movements of asylum-seekers and other third country nationals seeking transit to the West, Central Europe acts as a buffer or a sieve. Through the logic of readmission agreements it has been made a buffer to absorb possible larger flows in case of a refugee crisis further east. For the time being it acts as a sieve which fragments and absorbs a part of the flows. Being the sieve for less successful transit-seekers and second best option for labour migrants from the East, Central Europe has become a regional migration pole. The pole's magnetism is to some extent secondary to the attractiveness of the less accessible Western Europe.

---

20 On economic and social misdevelopment under communist regimes see Berend I.T., *Central and Eastern Europe 1944–1993.. Detour from the periphery to the periphery,* Cambridge 1996.

CHAPTER ELEVEN

RAISING MINIMUM STANDARDS, OR RACING FOR THE BOTTOM? THE COMMISSION'S PROPOSED MIGRATION CONVENTION[1]

Steve Peers

INTRODUCTION

Previous chapters in this book have examined the current status of third-country nationals of various nationalities and the continuing restrictions on Community nationals, thirty years after the free movement of persons was agreed. Both issues would be affected by the Commission's formal proposal July 30 1997 for a Convention on Member States' migration policies[2]. This ambitious proposal would, if adopted, remove some of the distinctions between third-country nationals based on nationality, and would also abolish elements of the 'reverse discrimination' rule affecting many third-country national family members of EU citizens. These aspects of the Convention are welcome, as are the important rights that it would grant to long-term resident third-country nationals (LTRs). However, certain provisions would either compel Member States to reduce rights available to third-country citizens or create a risk of competitive lowering of standards among Member States: a 'race to the bottom'.

BACKGROUND

The proposed Convention did not spring full-blown from the brows of Commission staff, but rather is strongly influenced by five resolutions adopted by the Council within the framework of the 'Third Pillar' of the European Union, as well as a sixth proposal that was never adopted[3]. This harmonisation process has been intergovernmental, occurring outside the framework of Community law. The Commission was invited to observe; the European Parliament and Court were excluded entirely; and the process was vastly more secretive than the Community legislative process, itself suffering from a serious openness deficit. Measures resulting from this process conferred the legal effect

---

1 Portions of this chapter draw upon documents obtained by the author under the EC rules on access to documents. My thanks to Nick Bernard, Dr. Gillian Mulder and Professor Janet Dine of the Dept. of Law, University of Essex, for their assistance; and especially to Tony Bunyan, *Statewatch* editor, for his invaluable ongoing advice and assistance.

2 COM (97) 387, 30 Jul. 1997; OJ 1997, C 337/9.

3 Technically the first of these resolutions, on family reunion, was adopted by Member States' Immigration Ministers, rather than the EU Council comprising those Ministers, because the Maastricht Treaty formally establishing the 'third pillar' was not in force yet.

of public international law, rather than directly effective rights for individuals under Community law.

After earlier negotiations had resulted in the Dublin Convention, determining the Member States who would be responsible for an asylum application, and the External Frontiers Convention (EFC), blocked by UK and Spanish disagreement over the status of Gibraltar, the Member States' immigration specialists addressed themselves to the possibility of substantive legal harmonisation[4]. The result was a detailed report on the future agenda for immigration and asylum law, submitted by the Immigration Ministers to the same European Council that reached agreement on the Maastricht Treaty in December 1991[5].

This agenda led to a series of 'soft law' resolutions[6]. First of all, negotiations on family reunion policies resulted in an agreed resolution of Immigration Ministers in June 1993[7]. In the meantime, the UK Presidency of 1992 had submitted the text of a proposed Resolution on admission for employment, with agreement reached nearly two years later in June 1994[8]. The Belgian Presidency of 1993 submitted texts on admission of the self-employed and students, which led to agreed resolutions in December 1994[9]. Shortly afterward, the incoming French Presidency proposed a 'Joint Action' on integration of existing legal residents, which was watered down into a weak resolution and formally adopted in March 1996[10]. In the meantime, the Spanish Presidency in 1995 attempted to reach agreement on a Joint Position governing admission of persons entering on 'other' grounds, but negotiations were suspended without agreement in January 1996, in light of the implacable opposition of the German, Danish, Dutch and Austrian representatives[11]. Finally, subsequent to the Commission's proposal for a Convention, the Council agreed a Resolution on marriages of convenience in December 1997, based on a proposal from the Luxembourg Presidency in July[12].

---

4 Dublin Convention, in force Sept. 1 1997 (OJ 1997, C 254); after initial near-approval in 1991, the EFC was later the subject of a revised proposal from the Commission, blocked for the same reasons (COM (93) 684, 10 Dec. 1993; OJ 1994, C 11).

5 Document SN 4038/91, 3 Dec. 1991, published in E. Guild and J. Niessen, *The Emerging Immigration and Asylum Law of the European Union*, (1996) 449–491.

6 For a detailed analysis of the negotiation of the resolutions and their effects in practice, see S. Peers, 'Building Fortress Europe: the Development of EU Migration Law' (forthcoming).

7 Document SN 2828/1/93, 1 June 1993, not published in the Official Journal: see Guild and Niessen, note 299 above, 251; T. Bunyan, ed., *Key Texts on Justice and Home Affairs in the European Union, Volume 1* (1997), 98.

8 OJ 1996, C 274/3.

9 OJ 1996, respectively C 274/7 and C 274/10.

10 OJ 1996, C 80/2.

11 Initial draft of proposed Joint Position, document 8630/95, 30 Jun. 1995; Outcome of Proceedings of Steering Group I of 9 Jan. 1996 (document 4233/96, 18 Jan. 1996).

12 OJ 1997, C 382/1; initial draft of proposal in document 9392/97, 2 July 1997.

These measures have been subject to considerable criticism on a number of grounds. First, in many cases, they fail to achieve the goal of harmonisation, with a variety of options still left to Member States. Secondly, they have ambiguous legal status as non-binding and unenforceable soft law instruments, which nonetheless often use imperative language and provide for deadlines for compliance. Indeed, the Third Pillar provisions in the Treaty on European Union do not even provide for resolutions[13]. Thirdly, they require or encourage reductions of standards for treatment of third-country nationals below that required by international law or the existing standards of Member States. Finally, they confirm or even widen the gap between the treatment accorded to EC nationals and the treatment accorded third-country nationals, resulting in indirect racial and ethnic discrimination[14].

The Commission had long desired the replacement of the non-binding measures by a binding instrument. Since the most binding instrument available in the Third Pillar is an international convention, the Commission expressed its support for the idea of a convention on family reunion in a 1994 discussion paper. In the following autumn, Commissioner Gradin stated the Commission's intention to draft and propose itself a Convention on all aspects of admission and integration policies, during a speech to the European Parliament's plenary debate on migration policy[15]. There are anecdotal reports that there were internal disputes within the Commission on the wisdom of proposing a Convention when Member States did not appear very interested in further harmonisation of migration policy. Nonetheless, the Commission made its proposal just before its summer break in 1997, reportedly some time after the draft was actually completed.

By the time the Commission made its proposal, the Amsterdam Treaty had been agreed, resulting in a complete transfer of asylum and immigration competences now in the Third Pillar of the European Union to the 'First Pillar', Community law[16]. The Commission addresses the change in circumstances

13 For an assessment of the legal status of third pillar resolutions, see B. Meyrins, 'Intergovernmentalism and Supranationality: Two Stereotypes for a Complex Reality' (1997) 22 ELRev. 221, especially 234–35.

14 See criticisms of the family reunion resolution and the proposed employment resolution in P. Boeles, et. al., *A New Immigration Law for Europe: the 1992 London and 1993 Copenhagen Rules on Immigration* (Standing Committee of Experts on Immigration, 1994); of the first four resolutions in Guild and Neissen, above; of the integration resolution and measures combatting illegal immigration in S. Peers, 'Undercutting Integration: Developments in EU Policy on Third-Country Nationals' (1997) 22 ELRev. 76; and of the integration resolution and the third pillar treatment of third country nationals generally in M. Hedemann-Robinson, 'Third-Country Nationals, European Union Citizenship and Free Movement of Persons: A Time For Bridges Rather than Divisions', (1996) 16 YEL 321.

15 Respectively, Communication on Immigration and asylum policies, COM (94) 23, 23 Feb. 1994, 21 and 41; EP Debates, 4–467/93, 20 Sept. 1995.

16 See future Part 3, Title IV (Articles 61–69) of EC Treaty, OJ 1997, C 340. Certain immigration issues already form part of Community law and so will not fall within the new Title IV.

in the explanatory memorandum to the Convention, asserting that it will make a fresh proposal for a Community directive once the new Treaty enters into force, taking account of the state of negotiations up to that point. Thus the final clauses of the proposed Convention, and one clause in the preamble, are in brackets, since they will not be relevant to the future proposal for a directive but are necessary provisions in any proposed Convention. Therefore we will have to await the future proposed directive for the Commission's final view as to when the proposal should enter into force and for the proposed method of implementing several important provisions.

There is no formal indication as to the likelihood of adoption of the Convention or any future proposed directive. In early 1998, the UK Presidency convened discussions in the Council's migration working group on aspects of the Convention, and also indicated that, pending agreement on the Convention, it might prepare a measure to harmonise family reunion rules further[17]. At the moment, the environment for the adoption of binding immigration rules does not seem propitious; if there were strong interest among the Member States, one of them would probably have proposed a Convention by now. But even if the Convention is not agreed in the next several years, revised versions may be presented in the future if the climate for harmonisation improves. In any event, the proposal tells us much about the attitude to immigration and integration in the European Union today.

ANALYSIS OF THE CONVENTION

The Convention is clearly based upon the five resolutions agreed by 1996 and the proposed Joint Position which Member States could not agree. However, the Commission has taken the opportunity to propose revised or more detailed rules governing certain issues, or less detailed rules governing others. Even where the proposal is substantively the same as the resolutions, the Commission has usually reworded much of the text. It must be said that the Commission proposal is vastly better drafted than the resolutions, whose provisions are often unclear and whose scope appears either to overlap or to leave ambiguous gaps.

The Convention has been organised into Chapters, with the first (Articles 1 and 2) comprising the definitions and scope; the second (Articles 3–6) setting out general rules; the third (Articles 7–10) covering employment; the fourth (Articles 11–14) covering self-employment; the fifth (Articles 15–21) covering students; the sixth (Articles 22–23) covering 'other' categories; the seventh (Articles 24–31) covering family reunion; the eighth (Articles 32–35) covering long-term residents; and the ninth (Articles 36–44) including the (vestigial)

17 Presidency work programme, document 13292/97, 15 Dec. 1997, 11. This resulted in a questionnaire on family reunion (document 13552/97, 15 Dec. 1997). Later, the Austrian Presidency announced that it would propose new family reunion provisions, including rules on 'marriages of convenience' (work programme, document 9375/98,9 Jun. 1998).

final provisions. It is immediately obvious that the Chapters follow the subject-matter of the resolutions, although there are some important changes. The scope, definitions and general rules have been placed in two chapters of their own rather than at the start of each chapter; several family reunion rules that existed in resolutions other than that on family reunion have been incorporated into the family reunion chapter; artists have apparently been moved from 'self-employed' to 'other'; and trainees have been moved from the 'employed' into 'students'.

What is not clear is the extent to which the Commission wishes the Convention to replace national law, rather than integrate with existing national rules. For instance, would third country nationals in the UK still be eligible to obtain "indefinite leave to remain" status after four years under UK law, and then obtain LTR status under EC law after five? Or would the UK and other Member States have to replace national forms of permanent or long-term residence status with the EC version? Neither the Convention nor the explanatory memorandum clarify the relationship, but it is crucial: in the former case the Convention *might* result in a "race to the bottom", but in the latter case, the rights of third country nationals in the UK and other Member States would definitely be reduced.

DEFINITIONS AND SCOPE

The definitions clause of the Convention makes it clear that it would only relate to stays longer than three months[18]. This draws a distinction between migration policy and visa and border policy, as the latter relates to stays under three months. However, the distinction does not occur in any of the previous resolutions, only one of which specifies any minimum time limit for its application[19]. The distinction would lead to some awkwardness, given that the Commission made few changes to the personal scope of the various resolutions when drafting the Convention. The three month rule may explain the disappearance from the Convention of business visitors and of potential students apprising themselves of conditions at institutions in Member States[20]. However, seasonal workers would still be included in the Convention, and they would likely be entering for periods of under three months, since they would be restricted to work in sectors 'dependent on the passing of the seasons'[21]. Similarly, service providers, students and trainees would in some cases be entering for less than three months. It would be anomalous if slightly longer contracts, courses or periods of work experience led to an important difference of legal status under Community law.

---

18 Art. 1.

19 The integration resolution, for obvious reasons.

20 See respectively point C (vi), employment resolution, although a visit might extend to six months; point C (2), students' resolution, although a would-be student liking an institution can then make a residence application without departing.

21 Art. 9(1), although a stay might be as long as six months in a year (Art. 9(2)).

As for the scope of the Convention, the exclusions from its scope are based on the exclusions from the existing resolutions and proposed Joint Position, but with some important variations[22]. First, the Convention would not *reduce* rights under agreements between the Community and/or the Member States with third states[23]. This would represent no change from the *status quo* in the resolutions. Secondly, it would exclude entirely *applicants* for refugee status under the UN Convention relating to the status of refugees 1951 and its 1967 Protocol (the Geneva Convention), persons granted temporary protection and persons granted humanitarian leave to remain. This would be an important change in the personal scope of European migration law, as the existing resolutions also exclude those who have been *granted* Geneva Convention refugee status, and although only three of them exclude persons granted temporary or humanitarian residence permits[24], it is unlikely that the other resolutions were intended to include such persons[25]. The Commission's explanatory memorandum states that Geneva Convention refugees were included in order to give them rights if they qualify for LTR status[26], but the text of the Convention does not exclude them from the scope of any provision. Therefore they must be covered by all its chapters, and the Convention provides only in its recitals that the Geneva Convention prevails where its standards are higher.

Including Geneva Convention refugees within the scope of the LTR provisions would indeed prove a genuine enhancement of their rights, but would constitute a further widening of the gap between Convention refugees and persons with humanitarian permits. The Commission defends exclusion of the latter on the grounds that 'their admission is limited to a territory of a single Member State on the basis of a decision taken by that Member State alone'[27]. This reasoning is unconvincing: the same could be said of *any* third-country national resident of a Member State at present, except those providing services[28], and in any event it cannot explain why persons with humanitarian permit status could not be granted the rights available to LTRs within a single state.

---

22 Recitals 7–9, family reunion resolution; section B of each of the employment, self-employment and students' resolutions; point II, integration resolution; point 2(2), proposed Joint Position.

23 On the rights in these agreements compared with the third pillar position, see S. Peers, 'Towards Equality: Actual and Potential Rights of Third-Country Nationals in the European Union', (1996) 33 CMLRev. 7; or M. Cremona, 'Citizens of Third Countries: Movement and Employment of Migrant Workers Within the European Union', (1995) 2 LIEI 87.

24 The employment, self-employment and students' resolutions.

25 They do not contain any reference to any third pillar 'legal bases' except immigration law. In any event, persons granted temporary protection could not logically qualify as LTRs or fall under the family reunion resolution (since it only covers persons joining LTRs) unless a Member State has altered their initial temporary status.

26 Explanatory memorandum, 9.

27 Explanatory memorandum, 9.

28 See Case C-43/93, *Vander Elst*, [1994] ECR I-3803.

The final exclusions from the scope of the Convention are EC nationals and those third-country nationals 'enjoying a right of residence in a Member State by virtue of Community law'[29]. The explanatory memorandum defines the latter as all those enjoying rights as family members of migrant EC citizens or those with identical rights under agreements ratified by the Community (presently only Norway, Iceland and Liechtenstein under the European Economic Area (EEA) treaty, although the Swiss might eventually enjoy the same status)[30]. But the actual text of the Convention itself could also be interpreted as excluding many Turkish nationals entirely from its scope. The Convention's wording should be clarified on this point.

In addition, the explanatory memorandum makes clear that persons providing services and resident in another Member State are not covered by the Convention, since their position is covered by Article 59 EC[31]. This conclusion is quite correct but again it would be better to state it expressly in the text.

GENERAL RULES

Chapter II of the Convention pulls together a number of rules repeated earlier in the various resolutions. First, it would be generally necessary to apply for admission from outside the Member States first[32]. Incoming residents would have to hold appropriate documents, including entry permits and visas specified by national law[33]. Member States would be entitled to check potential entrants for their public policy or health threats[34]. Renewals of permits could not be granted unless the conditions for the initial grant of the permit still applied, a principle later elaborated upon in greater detail in the specific chapters of the Convention[35]. Indeed, it would still be impossible to switch from one category of migrant to another before classification as a Long-Term Resident, with a limited provision for exceptional switching between

29 For a discussion of these categories, see Peers or Cremona, above.

30 Page 9, explanatory memorandum. OJ 1994, L 1/1 (EEA); on negotiations with the Swiss see most recently (at time of writing) Transport Ministers' Council of 17 March 1998 (Council Press Release PRES/98/70, document 6886/98).

31 Page 9, explanatory memorandum; see *Vander Elst*, above.

32 Art. 3(1); compare family reunion resolution, principle 14; employment resolution, point C(ii); self-employed resolution, point C(3)(1); students' resolution, point C(2).

33 Art. 4; compare family reunion resolution, principle 15; employment resolution, point C(ii); self-employed resolution, point C(4)(1); students' resolution, point C(2); proposed Joint Position, point 3(1), first indent.

34 Family reunion resolution, principle 17; self-employed resolution, point A(11); students' resolution, point A(9); proposed Joint Position, recital 6.

35 Employment resolution, point C(v); self-employed resolution, points C(4)(2) and C(5); students' resolution, point C(3); proposed Joint Position, point 4.

employment and self-employment[36]. One welcome provision in this chapter is the clause on permitted absences, clarifying that third-country nationals could leave the Member State for thirteen weeks/year in total before losing residence rights, and extending this to twenty-six weeks for LTRs.

EMPLOYMENT

The resolution established three general principles governing admission for employment, without making clear the hierarchy between them. Member States should refuse admission; they should admit only for vacancies that could not be filled by EC nationals or third-country nationals with permanent residence in that state; and without prejudice to the first two principles, they could admit a worker temporarily for a specific period if the worker fit into a specified category. These categories were: specialists; persons filling a vital post which would not otherwise be filled; seasonal workers; trainees; frontier workers; and intra-corporate transferees[37].

The Convention would replace this awkwardly drafted list with one general rule: third-country nationals could only be admitted for employment if a vacancy could not be filled by EC nationals, third-country nationals already in the labour market (as distinct from permanent residents) in that Member State or persons qualified as LTRs, presumably in any Member State[38]. So there would be no general rule of non-admission; the priority granted to EC nationals would be weakened; and in place of the list of specified exceptions in the resolution are scattered clauses on seasonal workers, frontier workers and trainees (but none on specialists or intra-corporate transferees)[39]. The Convention would keep the rule that an initial residence permit could only be granted for a maximum of four years, and it would add a new rule that a person could not enter initially unless he or she had a contract for at least one year[40]. This latter rule creates a problem: it would seem to remove *employed*

---

36 Point C(v), employment resolution bars switches into regular employment by students, trainees or service providers. Point C(7), self-employed resolution bars switches to self-employment from the foregoing groups or contract workers; however, point C(8) allows that the self-employed might request employment access after being granted LTR or permanent status. Point C(4), students' resolution, reiterates the bar on switching from student status to employment or self-employment, while point C(2) bars switches the other way around. However, point 5 of the proposed Joint Position envisaged possible future authorisation for gainful activity. On switching after gaining LTR status, see Point VII, integration resolution.

37 Point C(i).

38 Art. 7(1).

39 The seasonal worker clause is similar to that in the resolution (Compare Art. 9 to Annex and points C(iv) and C(v)). It is still not clear what rule governs third-country nationals in a Member State who wish to be frontier workers in another Member State, as Art. 10 only governs those not resident in the Community.

40 Compare Art. 8 to point C(iv).

service providers entirely from the scope of the Convention, unless they are admitted for over one year, as the subsequent reference to service providers is in the self-employment chapter.

SELF-EMPLOYMENT

Chapter IV on the self-employed fundamentally differs little from the rules agreed in the resolution. Both the definition of self-employment and the conditions for taking up self-employment have been reworded, but the principles remain the same: an independent person can enter where he or she has sufficient resources and will provide economic benefits for the host state[41]. However, this apparently has the effect of removing artists from the scope of the self-employment rules. A minimum residence authorisation of two years would be provided for in the Convention, as opposed to the unspecified potential limitations under the resolution. The Commission convincingly argues that such a period is necessary to allow the entrepreneur to develop the business, but it inaccurately asserts that the two-year period aligns periods of residence for self-employment and employment[42]. Finally, the Convention mentions service providers, only to leave their status to future implementing measures; as noted above, because of its place in the Convention this clause can govern only *self-employed* service providers[43].

STUDENTS

Chapter V on students has copied the scope of the existing resolution, excluding school pupils and apprentices but including all involved in higher education, whether for study, research or preparatory work beforehand[44]. However, as noted above, trainees have been moved here, away from workers, albeit with the same definition[45]. This change at least makes clear that apprentices are excluded from harmonisation altogether: the current separate resolutions exclude apprentices from the students' resolution but leave open the possibility that some of them might be classified as 'trainees' under the workers' resolution. The conditions for admitting trainees are slightly more restrictive, with new insistence that trainees have a training agreement and social security to be admitted; and the renewable annual permit for trainees remains the same, although the possibility of an initial permit lasting longer

41 Compare Arts. 11 and 12 to points C(1)(2) and C(2)(1). The details on how to assess benefit to the host state (point C(3)) have been lost, but could resurface in provisions to implement the Convention.

42 Compare Art. 13(1) to point C(4)(2); and see explanatory memorandum, 14.

43 Art. 14.

44 Compare Arts. 15 and 21 to point C(1), students' resolution.

45 Compare Art. 19 with Annex to employment resolution.

than a year has been removed and an absolute ban on remaining for employment has been added[46]. The revised provisions governing trainees likely reflect existing national practice.

As for students, the conditions for admitting them are very similar to those in the students' resolution, although certain details from the resolution are omitted, perhaps with a view to adopting them as implementing measures[47]. However, under the Convention students would be definitely allowed to take up work in every Member State (albeit subsidiary or seasonal work only), rather than leaving this as an option[48]. The provisions on the requirement to leave after the end of studies are very similar, except that the Convention would allow students to remain in the country if applying for a follow-on course of studies[49]. Finally, the possibility of EC funding for trainees, researchers and students, merely an exhortation under the students' resolution, would be the subject of detailed implementing measures under the Convention[50]. Such measures can surely only address the admission and residence rules for such persons, rather than the funding details, for the appropriate legal bases for the latter are the education and vocational training provisions of the EC Treaty[51]. Also, although national measures for facilitating entry of such persons are no longer mentioned, the Convention could not have the effect of transferring exclusive competence over such schemes to the Community, since education and vocational training are explicitly areas of shared competence.

'OTHER' MIGRANTS

Chapter VI on admission of 'other' classes of persons follows the core provisions of the first draft of the abortive Joint Position[52]. However, as noted above, it would seem that artists have been added to the personal scope of the rules on 'others' in light of the changes to the self-employment rules. Since there was a lengthy debate among Member States over whether to include artists within the latter rules, some Member States may welcome this transfer[53].

---

46 On admission, there are no particular rules for trainees in the employment resolution, but compare Art. 19(2) to the general rules in point C(ii) of the resolution. On renewal, compare Art. 19(3) to point C(iv), indent 2, employment resolution.

47 Compare Art. 16 to point C(3), students' resolution. Point C(2) contains the omitted details.

48 Compare Art. 17 to point C(4), students' resolution.

49 Compare Art. 18 to point C(3), indent 5, students' resolution.

50 Compare Art. 20 to point A(8), students' resolution.

51 Arts. 126–127, EC Treaty.

52 Agendas of the migration working group and Steering Group I indicate that three subsequent drafts were produced during the Spanish Presidency, but the Council has refused to disclose these drafts to the author under its rules on access to documents.

53 For details of the earlier debate, see S. Peers, 'Building Fortress Europe', above.

The main conditions for entry are a little different from those contained in the draft Joint Position, with a requirement for health insurance expanded into a requirement of social security cover, and a requirement for sufficient support expanded into an obligation to show the lawful origin of that support[54]. As for the length and renewal of the residence permit, again the rules are quite similar. The draft Joint Position provided that the original permit might be restricted to one year, while the Convention would provide for initial permits of at least one year; and while the draft Joint Position provided that renewals would take place on the same basis as the original issue of the permit, the Convention would require renewals for at least one year, again with a check on fulfilment of the original conditions[55]. As a final point, it should be emphasised that this chapter, like its counterpart EC legislation, would not simply cover the 'rich'. Apart from artists, the Commission points out that the provisions would cover pensioners, writers living on royalties and *au pairs*[56].

FAMILY REUNION

Family reunion, the subject of Chapter VII, is presently covered by a somewhat perplexing set of rules in the various resolutions. The main family reunion resolution from 1993 only covers those with 'an expectation of permanent or long-term residence', the definition of which 'is for determination by reference to national laws and policies'[57]. Thus any persons whose residence status is deemed limited or uncertain might face different (presumably less favourable) family reunion policies. The resolution also excludes not only the 'standard' groups, as discussed above – refugees and the third-country national family members of EC or EEA nationals in another Member State, or returning to their home Member States but also the third-country national family members of an EC national in his/her own Member State[58]. The latter exclusion leaves intact the 'reverse discrimination' problem of Community law, in which EC nationals who have never their own states cannot utilise the free movement provisions – whether to take advantage of the more liberal rules on family reunion or family members' access to employment and equal working conditions; to contest Member States' internal exclusion orders restricting them

54 Compare Art. 22 with draft Joint Position, point 3. The accommodation requirement remains and the requirement to follow entry rules and obtain visas in the draft Joint Position is now covered by the general rule in Art. 4 of the Convention.

55 Compare Art. 23 with draft Joint Position, point 4.

56 See Explanatory memorandum, page 17. Compare with EC legislation on pensioners (Dir. 90/365, OJ 1990, L 180/28) and 'others' (Dir. 90/364, OJ 1990, L 180/26). *Au pairs* are specifically excluded from the current employment resolution (point B, fourth indent).

57 Principle 1 and recitals 6 and 9, family reunion resolution.

58 Recitals 7–9 of Resolution.

to one part of the national territory; or to rely upon the recognition of their qualifications[59].

In perhaps its most radical provision, the proposed Convention would sweep away the 'reverse discrimination' rule in Community law as it affects third-country national family members. Article 25 specifies simply that Articles 10-12 of Regulation 1612/68 (on family reunion, access to employment and childrens' education benefits) and 'all other relevant provisions of Community law' would apply to such persons. In its explanatory memorandum, the Commission justifies this proposal by a remarkable extension of the concept of Union citizenship: as this status is 'a single citizenship, the gaps in the current situation should be filled in by a provision for equal treatment of all Union citizens'[60]. Not long before, in its second report on EU citizenship, the Commission had taken a conservative view of the personal scope of the rights that come with citizenship, analysing only the formal rights set out in Articles 8a to 8d of the EC Treaty[61].

The Court of Justice has also passed up several opportunities to expand upon the scope of Community citizenship, holding to date that the formal concept in the Treaty is both narrow and subsidiary[62]. Space does not permit a detailed discussion of the scope and potential of EU citizenship, a subject which has been thoroughly analysed by legal, political and sociological commentators[63]. However, it is interesting to note the Commission's stress on citizenship as an equality right, a concept similar to that prevailing in France (and expressed in part by Advocate-Generals Léger, La Pergola and

59 See *Morson & Jhanjan*, Joined Cases 35-36/82, [1982] ECR 3723 (family reunion); *Uecker & Jacquet*, Joined Cases C-64 and 65/96, [1997] ECR I-3171 (family members' equal working conditions); *Saunders*, Case 175/78, [1979] ECR 1129 (exclusion orders); *Aubertin and others*, Joined Cases C-29 to 35/94, [1995] ECR I-301 (recognition of qualifications). For analysis of the problem, see D. Pickup, 'Reverse Discrimination and Freedom of Movement for Workers' (1986) 23 CMLRev. 135. However, if a Member State wishes to give its own nationals the same rights as migrant EC nationals, the Court of Justice will accept references from national courts and interpret those rules (*Dzozdi*, Joined Cases 297/88 and C-197/89, [1990] ECR I-3763). Recital 7 of the resolution preserves Member States' right to establish such equality rules if they wish (and see point II(3), first indent, of the integration resolution).

60 Page 18, explanatory memorandum.

61 COM (97) 230, 27 May 1997.

62 See respectively *Uecker and Jacquet*, note 59 above; *Skanavi*, Case C-193/94, [1996] ECR I-929. But see now the important judgment of the Court of 12 May 1998 in Case C-85/96, *Martinez Sala*.

63 From a vast literature, see J. Shaw, 'Citizenship of the Union: Toward Post-National Membership', *Harvard Jean Monnet Chair Working Paper* 6/97, and citations therein.

Jacobs)[64]. The last draft of the Convention before its official publication as a proposal suggests that this particular provision was inserted at a very late stage, so it may well be a response to the conservative *Uecker and Jacquet* judgement of June 1997[65]. Of course, it should be noted that the reference to citizenship comes in the explanatory memorandum only; a reference in the main text would run the risk that the relevant provision would be deemed a proposal to expand on the citizenship provisions in the EC Treaty, and thus subject to approval under national constitutional procedures under the provisions of Article 8e EC.

Important aspects of the clause are unclear. Regulation 1612/68 governs only *workers'* family members, with family members of other categories of migrant Community nationals dealt with differently depending on the primary right-holders' exact status. Is the Commission proposing that any third-country national family members joining an 'unmoving' Community national family member will be governed by the rules on migrant EC workers, or does its reference to 'all other relevant provisions of Community law' mean that the incoming family members will derive rights equivalent to those enjoyed by each corresponding category of EC migrant? It is possible that the reference to 'all other relevant provisions of Community law' alternatively or additionally refers to the rules on such matters as expulsion or refusal of entry, mutual recognition of qualifications and rights after death, retirement or injury of the primary right-holder. The Commission's explanatory memorandum gives no indication of its intended meaning.

As noted above, the provisions on other aspects of family reunion in the various resolutions are scattered. The rights of refugees and other persons in need of protection are beyond the scope of this paper, but it is worth noting that Member States did not begin negotiations on the French Presidency's proposed Joint Action on the legal status of Geneva Convention refugees and had not (by April 1998) reached agreement on the Commission's proposed Joint Action on temporary protection. Both proposals incorporated family reunion rights[66]. As for immigrants, during negotiations on the employment resolution, Member States considered extending the principles of the family reunion resolution to certain classes of workers other than those admitted for long-term or permanent residence, while confirming that other classes of worker were not entitled to family reunion at all, but the final resolution

---

64 See respectively Opinions in *Boukhalfa* (Case C-214/94, [1996] ECR I-2253, para. 63) and *Stöber and Pereira* (Joined Cases C-4 and 5/95, [1997] ECR I-511, paras. 50 and 51) and *Bickel and Franz* (Case C-274/96, pending, Opinion of 19 March 1998, paras 23 and 24). For Advocate-General Ruiz-Jarabo Colomer's comments on citizenship, see Opinions in Joined Cases C-65/95 and 111/95, *Shingara & Radiom,* [1997] ECR I-3343, para 33 and 34, and Case C-171/96, *Roque,* para. 32 (judgment of 16 July 1998, not yet reported).

65 See draft rev4.en.doc of 29 July 1997, in which the provision was Article 23a.

66 Respectively document 6784/95, 28 April 1995, Art. 3; COM (97) 93, 5 Mar. 1997, Art. 7.

ultimately makes no mention of the subject[67]. The self-employment resolution provides that the family reunion resolution applies to all self-employed persons, while the students' resolution leaves the admission and employment of family members up to national law[68]. The draft Joint Position on admission of 'other' persons also contained a *renvoi* to the 1993 family reunion resolution[69]. The integration resolution grants rights to the family members of an LTR, and it is left ambiguous whether the family members of an LTR might themselves qualify as LTRs by their relationship[70]. Finally, the resolutions on employment, self-employment and students each provide conversely that persons admitted for family reunion are beyond their scope, so family members' rights of residence and access to employment are governed entirely by the family reunion resolution, not the subsequent measures[71]. The Convention thus represents an opportunity to weave together much of this unconnected tapestry of rights.

The Convention begins by providing that family members would have to wait at least one year to join the primary right holder. In contrast, the family reunion resolution only provides for the possibility for Member States to allow for a delay[72]. The proposed rule in the Convention would impose a minimum waiting requirement without a maximum requirement, or even a standstill, and so by definition would both worsen the position of family members in the most liberal Member States and fail to improve the position in the states which give the least regard to family reunion rights.

However, the Convention would result in a modest widening in the personal scope of those entitled to join a primary right-holder. The joining persons would include a spouse, children born to or adopted by the couple (if unmarried and under the host state's age of majority) or step-children over which the couple had legal authority. In contrast, the resolution only allows the admission of step-children, and of children adopted from a third state after entry into the host state, as an option; and children must be excluded if they have formed an 'independent family unit' or 'independent life', as well as if they are married[73]. The Convention does not repeat the resolution's proviso that the spouse and children must live with the primary right-holder[74]. Family members other than spouses and children would also receive better treatment: rather than being allowed in only for 'compelling reasons which justify the presence of the person concerned', the Convention would require Member

67 See S. Peers, 'Building Fortress Europe', above.

68 Self-employed resolution, point C(9); students' resolution, point C(5).

69 Draft Joint Position, point 5.

70 See integration resolution, points V and III(1), second indent, respectively.

71 Point B, second indent, of each Resolution. However, the students' resolution in part governs the status of family members admitted *with the student* (see above) as distinct from persons admitted as family members of other classes of migrant. The draft Joint Position on 'others' contained no exclusion for persons admitted for family reunion.

72 Compare Art. 24(1) to principle 3, family reunion resolution.

73 Compare Art. 27(1) and (2) to principles 7–9, family reunion resolution.

74 Principle 2, family reunion resolution.

States to give 'favourable consideration' to admitting dependents in the ascending and descending lines[75]. However, Member States would have to subject entry of all family members to accommodation and means tests; this is only an option under the current resolution[76]. Finally, the present resolution leaves entry of students' family members up to national law, but under the Convention they would only have rights to family reunion if they had spent two years in a Member State and had at least one more year to go[77]. This proposal would dramatically curtail students' rights to be with their families in Member States which presently have more generous provisions.

The Convention provision on fraud necessarily does not reflect the 1997 resolution on marriages of convenience, which was agreed months after the Commission formally made its proposal for the Convention. The relevant clause in the 1993 resolution, upon which the recent resolution has expanded, has been subject to criticism on the grounds that it goes beyond preventing entirely false marriages and in fact permits Member States to impose variants of the UK's 'primary purpose' rule (since substantially amended)[78]. This rule prevents entirely legitimate spouses from moving into a state, on the grounds that the partner already resident in a Member State *could* have exercised the option to leave and live with the non-resident spouse. The 1993 resolution also applies the same principle to children adopted after entry into a Member State. The Convention would widen the material scope of the relevant rule, allowing Member States to refuse residence permits on such grounds, as well as withdraw them. But a suspect marriage or adoption would have to have been contracted 'solely' for the purpose of avoiding national law, not 'solely or principally', as in the 1993 resolution[79]. The Convention's clause on fraud would permit Member States to revoke residence rights or refuse entry where it is 'found' that fraud or forgery were used – an improvement from the 1993 resolution's highly questionable proviso that permits could be revoked merely if there were 'grounds for presuming' such practice[80].

The final two family reunion provisions are of particular importance to women: the ability to take up independent employment and the acquisition of separate residence status. Here the Convention is a great disappointment. The 1993 resolution provides that '[w]ithin a reasonable period of time' after entry, family members may be authorised to stay on a separate basis and may, 'if appropriate, be authorised to work'. In contrast, the Convention would impose a six-month minimum waiting period on employment rights with no maximum period, and it would allow family members to *request* independent residence status upon divorce, adulthood or death of the primary right-

75 Compare Art. 27(3) to principle 10, family reunion resolution.

76 Compare Art. 28(1) to principle 16, family reunion resolution.

77 Compare Art. 24(2) to point C(5), students' resolution.

78 See Guild and Niessen, above; principles 4 and 9, family reunion resolution.

79 Art. 27(1). The 1997 resolution refers to marriages 'with the sole aim' of circumventing national law (point 1).

80 Compare Art. 27(2) to principle 13, family reunion resolution.

holder[81]. Like the rules on waiting periods before initial entry, the former rule would reduce the rights of family members in some Member States without improving their rights in any. The latter rule would restrict applications for separate residence status to specified grounds and would still leave Member States full discretion to refuse the separate permits.

LONG TERM RESIDENTS

A bolder approach is entertained in Chapter VIII's provisions on long-term residents. First, acquisition of LTR status would be easier, as the integration resolution's unspecified waiting period (with a ten-year maximum) would be reduced to five years in all Member States – as long as the applicant was authorised to remain for another five years. The ensuing residence authorisation would have to be for ten years at least, a welcome clarification of the resolution; and an entirely new provision in the Convention would require a specific marker on the LTR's residence permit[82]. There is no mention of Member States' ability to double-check whether the applicant is a potential security threat and upon his or her means of support; and the definition of 'uninterrupted residence' earlier in the Convention will provide appropriate security for those who have left the relevant Member State for relatively brief periods during their qualifying stay[83].

The rights available to the LTRs would be wider than those provided for in the resolution. Within their Member State of residence, LTRs would enjoy five separate rights: free movement; access to employment, self-employment and education; residence rights for family reunion or 'other' purposes; increased protection against expulsion; and equal treatment[84]. However, the Convention would include less detail on the greater rights which an LTR enjoys on expulsion and it would no longer provide any rights for family members of the LTR.

A further substantial increase in the rights available to LTRs would be the right to reside in other Member States. This had initially formed part of the French Presidency's proposed Joint Action on integration[85]. Member States would have had to 'facilitate settlement' of a long-term resident who wished to move to another Member State, by recognising a long-stay visa already issued by another Member State. Also, Member States would have had the option of allowing an LTR from another Member State equal priority to apply for vacant positions. The later proposed Joint Action on the status of refugees contained a weaker clause, calling on Member States to 'facilitate the settling of genuine refugees' without providing for equality in employment applications[86].

---

81 Compare Arts. 30 and 31 to principle 12, family reunion resolution.
82 Compare Arts. 32 and 33 to point III, integration resolution.
83 See respectively point IV, integration resolution, and Art. 5(1).
84 Compare Art. 34 to points V to VII, integration resolution.
85 Document 12338/94, 22 Dec. 1994, Arts. 7 and 8.
86 Proposed Joint Action, note 66 above, Art. 7.

The Convention would go further than either French proposal. Both migrants and refugees with LTR status could apply for a vacant position or study in another Member State, and as noted above the employment rules would give them equal priority with EC nationals and other favoured groups[87]. For the first two years of residence in the second host State, the migrant would still retain LTR status with the first host State; then that status would cease and they would automatically enjoy LTR status in the second one. This provision does not make certain points clear. What rights, other than access to employment, would the LTR enjoy in the second host State during the initial two years? If LTRs in the second host State faced expulsion proceedings, where would they be expelled to – the first host State or their state of citizenship[88]? The Commission's proposal is clearly influenced by a study it commissioned in 1995 from experts in Dutch universities[89]. Yet it does not contain several elements of the experts' proposal, including the detailed incorporation of provisions of EC free movement legislation and provision for mutual recognition of qualifications. Nor does the Convention provide for implementing rules to be adopted on this point.

CONCLUSIONS

The Commission could not draft its Convention proposal in a political vacuum. It inevitably had to take account of existing rules when drafting the measure. However, the existing resolutions, including their negotiating history, show clearly that Member States were not yet ready in the mid-1990s to consider measures with formally binding legal effect; which significantly reduced the number of exceptions open to them; or which expanded or even confirmed the existing rights of third-country nationals. In that context, the Commission's proposal is quite bold.

Substantively the text has significant benefits as well as drawbacks. In particular, the 'reverse discrimination' rule should long ago have been consigned to the dustbin of history and the formal and guaranteed recognition of 'denizens' as long-term residents and the grant of additional rights to them would be highly valuable. But the drawbacks include a weakening of several family reunification rights by the imposition of minimum waiting periods with no corresponding maximum, and a failure to improve the position after death, divorce or other mishap. These drawbacks would be exacerbated if the Convention replaces national laws which allow early grants of national LTR

---

87 Arts. 35(1) and 7(1).

88 In the case of refugees, the latter would often constitute a refoulement barred by Article 3 of the European Convention on Human Rights: see *Chahal*, [1997] 27 EHRR 413.

89 D. Curtin, et. al., 'Draft Regulation on Freedom of Movement for Workers Within the European Community for Third-Country Nationals with Long-Term Residence in One Member State', in *Free Movement for non-EC Workers Within the European Community* (Standing Committee of Experts on Immigration, 1997).

or permanent residence status, or early grants of independent residence status for family members.

The Convention could be considerably improved, although based on past evidence Member States may be inclined to weaken its positive elements and strengthen its negative ones. It may be that the prospect of its adoption as a directive after entry into force of the Amsterdam Treaty is the most important feature of the proposal – and a factor which further discourages Member States from adopting the measure. The fear of direct effect may deter adoption of Community legislation in this area for some time to come.

Notes on Contributors

Robin Allen QC specialises in discrimination, European, employment and administrative law and human rights law. He is chair of the Employment Law Bar Association and practises at 1 Pump Court, Temple, London.

Joanna Apap is the research co-ordinator for ECAS (European Citizen Action Service) in Brussels. Her main research interests are issues dealing with European citizenship; welfare and social inclusion; the rights of European citizens and to what extent can citizenship rights be extended to third country nationals in the E.U.

Hans van Amersfoort is professor of cultural and population geography at the University of Amsterdam. His main research interest is international migration and the social position of migrant groups.

Nicholas Blake QC is co-author of the leading textbook on UK immigration law and former chair of the Immigration Law Practitioners Association. He practises in immigration and human rights law at 2 Garden Court, Temple, London.

Tim Eicke is a practising barrister specialising in European Community law and international human rights law. He is a member of the Chambers of Andrew Thompson and David Guy, Francis Taylor Building, Temple, London.

Elspeth Guild is a partner at Kingsley Napley and specialist in European Union migration law. She is also currently academic co-ordinator of the Centre for Migration Law at the University of Nijmegen. She is the UK expert to the European Commission's network on free movement of persons.

Linda Hantrais is the director of the European Research Centre and holds a chair in the Department of European Studies at Loughborough University. She is also convenor of its Cross-National Research Group. She has published widely on social policy in the European Union and the relationship between family and employment.

Advocate General Francis Jacobs is an Advocate General at the Court of Justice of the European Communities.

Zig Layton-Henry is the director of the Centre for Research in Ethnic Relations and Professor of Politics at the University of Warwick. He has written widely on race and immigration, and is currently researching citizenship and ethnic minorities in Britain, Germany and Canada.

Julia Onslow-Cole is a partner at Cameron McKenna and head of the UK Immigration and Nationality Law Group. She is chair of the Immigration Committee of the International Bar Association and secretary of the Immigration Law Practitioners' Association.

Steve Peers is a senior lecturer in law at the University of Essex, connected to the Human Rights Centre and Director of the Centre for European Commercial Law. He has written extensively on the rights of third country nationals in the European Union and the external relations law of the European Union. He is the author of 'Justice and Home Affairs in the European Union', forthcoming from Longmans.

Professor C S R Russell is a Professor of British History at Kings College London and Liberal Democrat Spokesperson on Social Security in the House of Lords.

Dariusz Stola is a member of the Institute for Political Studies, Polish Academy of Sciences and also at the Institute for Social Studies at Warsaw University. He has published widely on international migration and ethnic relations. His work on contemporary migration to and from Poland is trend-setting.

INDEX

Studies in Law

1. R. Müllerson, M. Fitzmaurice and M. Andenas: *Constitutional Reform and International Law in Central and Eastern Europe*. 1997 ISBN 90-411-0526-3
2. A.J. Cygan: *The United Kingdom Parliament and European Union Legislation*. 1998 ISBN 90-411-9650-1
3. E. Guild (ed.): *The Legal Framework and Social Consequences of Free Movement of Persons in the European Union*. 1998 ISBN 90-411-1073-9; Pb 90-411-1090-9

KLUWER LAW INTERNATIONAL – THE HAGUE / LONDON / BOSTON